LAND AND SOCIETY
IN ENGLAND 1750–1980

THEMES IN BRITISH SOCIAL HISTORY

edited by Dr J. Stevenson

This series covers the most important aspects of British social history from the Renaissance to the present day. Topics include education, poverty, health, religion, leisure, crime and popular protest, some of which are treated in more than one volume. The books are written for undergraduates, postgraduates and the general reader, and each volume combines a general approach to the subject with the primary research of the author.

LAND AND SOCIETY
IN ENGLAND
1750–1980

G. E. Mingay

Longman
London and New York

Longman Group Limited,
Longman House, Burnt Mill,
Harlow, Essex CM20 2JE, England
and Associated Companies throughout the world.

Published in the United States of America
by Longman Publishing, New York

© Longman Group Limited 1994

First published 1994

ISBN 0 582 49132 0

British Library Cataloguing-in-Publication Data

A catalogue record for this book is
available from the British Library

Library of Congress Cataloging-in-Publication Data

Mingay, G. E.
    Land and society in England 1750–1980/G. E. Mingay.
        p.   cm. — (Themes in British social history)
    Includes index.
    ISBN 0-582-49132-0 (pbk.)
    1. England—Social conditions.   2. Land tenure—England—History.
I. Title.   II. Series.
HN398.E5M55   1995
306'.0942—dc20
                                                                    94-1130
                                                                    CIP

Set 5B in 10 on 12pt Bembo
Printed in Malaysia

Contents

Introduction

This book is concerned with land and the society it supported in the England of the past three hundred years. At the beginning of that period, according to informed estimates, the land supported, directly and indirectly, perhaps as many as six or seven persons out of every ten. Those actually engaged in working the land formed a smaller proportion, possibly not greatly in excess of a half of the population; but to this nucleus have to be added the landlords, the country professional men, clergy, lawyers and doctors, and many of the very numerous tradesmen and craftsmen and workers in rural domestic industries – those whose livelihoods depended entirely or in large part on the needs of the farmers and their workpeople. And one must not overlook the families of all these people, and the many servants whom large numbers of them could afford to employ.

As time went by, industry and trade, based mainly in towns but also in industrialised villages, grew in size and became more important; and the pre-eminence of agriculture in the national economy was gradually reduced. By the middle of the nineteenth century it could be said that the rural and urban populations were roughly equal in size, though it has to be remembered that while by this date few townspeople had any close interest in agricultural land, considerable numbers of the residents in the countryside equally had little or no interest in farming.

The previous hegemony of land, therefore, greatly declined in the course of the 150 years after 1700, and was destined to decline much further in the next 150 years. Currently, near the end of the twentieth century, the agricultural land of Britain employs only about one in fifty of the population, though a greater proportion is involved in the making and supply of farm inputs such as machinery and fertilisers, in the transport, processing and marketing of farm products, and in the administration of the now highly regulated industry. In consequence, the importance of rural land in the national life has much diminished over the centuries, although it is interesting that the countryside has maintained a quite disproportionate influence in our culture, in literature and the media – witness the market for books about the countryside, for such journals as *The Field* and *Country Life*, and for the long-lived radio serial *The Archers*; and not least, in the desire of substantial numbers of townspeople to quit the towns and live in villages.

The story of the role of land in our national life is thus one of change, of gradual loss of power in government and political influence, accompanied by, and springing from, a prior decline in economic importance. Politically, the great turning point was the reform of Parliament in 1832, even though land remained over-represented for decades afterwards – basically, indeed, until 1918. In government the role of the great aristocrats and country gentry continued to be prominent, if diminishing, until well into the present century. As late as Asquith's first Liberal cabinet of 1908 the landed aristocracy still loomed large, accounting for six of the twenty members; even Winston Churchill's war cabinet of 1940 had seven of its twenty-seven members in the House of Lords. In local government the major turning point came as late as 1888, with the institution of County Councils and then the Rural District Councils, although the role of the squirearchy as magistrates had been shrinking from 1834 onwards.

In the economic sphere the age-old role of home farming in supplying the nation had begun to be undermined when significant imports of grain appeared near the end of the eighteenth century – even if the rising necessity of permitting the free entry of foreign foodstuffs for the swelling urban masses was not recognised politically until Repeal of the Corn Laws in 1846–49. Subsequently, the effects of free trade were much intensified by the remarkable fall in the costs of long-distance transport as railways and steamships brought in cheap food and raw materials from all over the world. By the beginning of the twentieth century an increasingly varied range of cheap imported food had forced British farming into accepting a much reduced (and depressed) place in the supply of home markets.

In providing employment on the land, home farming reached its peak about 1850 and then declined gradually down to the present, although its *share* of the country's total employment had been falling for a very long period before the mid-nineteenth century. As agricultural productivity rose, and as imports of food increased, so it was possible for home farm output to be maintained, or even increased, with first a fall in the share of the national labour force, and subsequently a fall in the numbers actually employed on the land. In this way agriculture helped to provide the rising numbers needed to man expanding industries and to service the rapidly growing towns; it also contributed to those many people who chose to emigrate.

The decline in the economic role of land slowly but inevitably weakened the old pre-eminence of landowners in society. Some landowners made up for the late nineteenth-century fall in their rent rolls by investing in industry and railways, or by exploiting any urban land they owned, or by a variety of other means. But generally the decline of agriculture was mirrored in the reduced circumstances of landowners, and ultimately in a decline in their political weight and command of social respect. Political and social decline, however, was protracted for long after English farming lost its paramount position as the major source of farm produce and the largest source of employment. Even in the socially egalitarian era of the close of the present century the current representatives of old landed families still receive some modicum of deference, if sometimes of a begrudging kind.

For farmers and their men and women the story is rather different. As more of the expanding home market for food was supplied from abroad, and with the shift to free trade, they found themselves in an era of increased instability and difficulty, an era which lasted until the return to protection and the initiation of a new, subsidised farming environment. Between the 1870s and the 1930s farming became largely unprofitable, although there were wide regional variations in the nature and extent of the problem. However, farmworkers, and to a lesser extent perhaps their employers, found living standards favourably influenced by the same fall in food prices which brought a degree of depression to the countryside. Other consumer goods fell in price also as the result of free trade and the development of modern industry. The farmworkers, indeed, gained in two ways in the hundred years after the 1870s: first, from rising real incomes as food, clothing and household necessities became cheaper; and second, from the flow of workers leaving the land, a movement which gradually made farmworkers less easy to find and slowly levered their pay upwards. At the same time the growing scarcity and rising cost of farm labour had the effect of gradually encouraging farmers to rely more heavily on their own family labour and helped reinforce the attractions of machinery, which farmers had begun to appreciate as far back as the end of the eighteenth century. Farmers, experiencing a welcome but brief relief of depression conditions during the acute shortages of the First World War, relapsed again into hard times in the 1920s and 1930s, despite some small-scale post-war government intervention. They were rescued again by the Second World War, and then much more permanently by the highly protective, comprehensive and profitable cocoon woven for them by government in the second half of the twentieth century.

With the spread of industry, the expansion of commerce and rise of urban occupations, the former kind of English society, living mainly in small towns and villages, and heavily dependent on the land for a livelihood, has largely passed away. Of course, the disappearance of the old England, while regrettable in certain respects, was in other important ways advantageous, and indeed welcome. The change was inevitable if the living standards of a rapidly rising population were to be maintained and improved. There was simply no way in which the limited supply of agricultural land in this country could have supported and employed a population which sprang up from 10.5m people in 1801 to nearly 49m in 1951 – not far from a five-fold increase in 150 years. If there had not been the rapid advance of industry and trade, living standards would have had to fall – as a distinguished economic historian once remarked, to Asiatic levels. As we know, industrialisation brought with it slums, poverty and suffering – but these were always present in the countryside, if on a reduced scale. In the longer run, industrialisation has made possible for the great majority living standards which would have been inconceivable a century ago.

Agriculture played its part in this transformation. Farming released men and women (and limited supplies of capital) from what were then low-productivity occupations to move into other occupations of higher productivity. This was a major key to the eventual achievement of markedly better national living standards despite the rapid growth in population. And, in turn, the changing nature of the markets and the competition of imported food forced British farming into structural changes and into raising its own productivity, and hence surviving.

Poverty and suffering have not disappeared, we know. The rise in living standards, in social security and welfare, has not succeeded in reaching everyone or meeting every need. And there is also a very obvious negative side to progress. We have a country in which the great majority are well fed (perhaps over-fed), are generally well-housed, have access to advanced medical care, have more leisure, and entertainment brought into their own homes. Large numbers have their own private transport – the equivalent of the former horse and carriage of the well-to-do – and can travel the world over, something which only a tiny minority was able to afford in the past. Yet there are also congestion, pollution, unemployment, uncertainty and stress, and crime and immorality – on a perhaps larger scale, in relative terms, than ever before. The change from the old society was inevitable, and in many ways beneficial. But perhaps we have lost a great deal by it, too.

CHAPTER ONE
Landed Society in the Eighteenth Century

A MOBILE SOCIETY

In the eighteenth century English society was marked by enormous distinctions – those between rich and poor, between the powerful and the powerless, and between the cultured and the illiterate. In the countryside especially, the gulf in incomes was tremendously wide, stretching as it did from the wealthiest landowners, some of whom disposed annually of incomes in excess of £20,000 or £30,000 or even more, to the poor husbandmen, country labourers and cottagers who, according to Joseph Massie's contemporary estimates, eked out an existence on some 5s or 7s a week.[1] The more prominent of the landowning class were also those who governed. Dominant in Parliament and in local government, they both passed the laws and executed them; and as magistrates they punished those who dared to transgress them. The culture of the wealthy, embracing art, literature, architecture, music and drama, and not least manners and the arts of polite conversation and correspondence, contrasted sharply with the unsophisticated country lore and confined horizons of the labouring folk, whose leisure hours were mainly devoted to rustic sports, often brutal and violent, and to the vulgar pleasures of the alehouse.

Such extremes were of course not new; nor were they confined to England; nor were they soon to diminish; although an emphasis on extreme contrasts ignores the complexity of the ordered society. Politically and socially the owners of land were supreme, but the gradations of society stretched down in relatively shallow steps from the exalted dukes and earls at the top, through the gentry, merchants and professional class, down to the petty farmers, tradesmen, artisans, servants and labourers at the bottom. Moreover, differences in station were at least partially effaced by the overlapping of incomes and living standards. The respectable country gentleman and parish priest often lived quite modestly on an income of a few hundred pounds, and in many cases less than a hundred, while many merchants, and even some lawyers, tradesmen and innkeepers, were able to support their lowly status in much greater affluence, if Joseph Massie's figures are to be accepted.[2]

Furthermore, there were common objectives and shared experiences which served as links between social groups which otherwise appeared as widely divided. The most significant of these, perhaps, was a common concern with the possession of property, and the enforcement of laws to secure its protection. Even the various kinds of property at issue were in some degree similar. True, there were of course fundamental differences between the country houses, farmlands, woods, quarries, mines and brickworks of landowners, and the town residences, counting-houses, works, warehouses, yards, wagons and sailing vessels of merchants, tradesmen and industrialists. But country gentry often owned some urban property (frequently inherited, but perhaps acquired for political purposes), and numbers of them dabbled in trading and industrial ventures. Further, many merchants, tradesmen and operators of industrial concerns required some land to fuel their work and transport animals, and for other purposes. Both groups, moreover, had an interest in financial institutions and the capital market, in government stocks and the stocks of the great trading companies, in mortgages, annuities, private loans and the developing banking system. Possession of capital, in both fixed and liquid forms, linked moneyed people in a community of interests regardless of the origin of their wealth, and gave rise to a common support for the constitution and existing form of government, on which the security of their capital was based.

Of hardly less importance were family connections existing between the different social groups. While, clearly, it was entirely natural for landed families to inter-marry (and especially where their estates were adjacent or complementary in some way), so also alliances between families of merchants and industrialists were an obvious means of acquiring new capital resources and of extending business empires. Yet there was indeed many a landlord who looked to marriage with a mercantile heiress possessing an attractively large dowry as the means of repairing a dissipated fortune or of advancing an old family in new wealth; and equally there were wealthy merchants, successful lawyers, contractors, industrialists and others who saw a marriage connection with the landed aristocracy as marking their ultimate arrival into the upper echelons of society. The landed classes were not a closed group, and in addition to marriage, there was always the possibility for an outsider of obtaining an *entrée* by acquiring a modest estate not too far from his place of business, and in time adding to it, erecting a larger house, and thus eventually becoming accepted in the ranks of the county gentry. There were, indeed, many examples of this process. Daniel Defoe, writing early in the eighteenth century, noted how successful London men of business had acquired country seats in the more westerly districts of Essex and other convenient parts of the Home Counties, where the pleasures and prestige of a country residence could be combined with regular attendance at their place in the City. It was even the practice for such people to take their families away to enjoy the attractions of a not too distant spa, such as Epsom, while they commuted daily the 17 miles to the capital.[3] Later, in the era of regular stage-coach services, it was even possible for London businessmen to travel daily the 50-odd miles from newly fashionable Brighton.

Among the successful men of business and the professions there were many who held an aspiration to the social elevation of a country house and estate, and eventually, perhaps, a title. Men who had become rich through wartime contracting, through holding a lucrative government office, or by practising the law, were among those who established new landed families. Thus in the later seventeenth century the wealthy lawyer Sir Harbottle Grimston was willing to lay out the enormous sum of well over £50,000 (equivalent to £1m or more today) in building up his estate in Hertfordshire, quite apart from other properties which he acquired in Essex. Another eminent lawyer, the first Earl Cowper, twice Lord Chancellor in the early decades of the eighteenth century, spent some £27,000 in laying the foundations of his family's Panshanger estate in Hertfordshire, while the financier Peter Walker laid out the huge sum of £116,000 on land, mainly in Dorset.[4] Many other examples, if of a more modest kind, could be cited for other parts of the country as wealth poured into land from its breeding grounds in commercial centres like Bristol, Liverpool and Hull. London, however, as the great centre of government, the law, trade and much of the country's industry, was the largest source of new landed families. One such was the Sperlings, originally fur merchants, with premises near the site of the medieval Hanseatic steelyard in Cannon Street. Beginning with a rural retreat at Chigwell in south-western Essex, only 14 miles from London, the family later moved further afield, acquiring in about 1765 a more impressive estate near the Essex–Suffolk border. This was Dynes Hall, near Halstead, a mansion once owned by the son of a wealthy Essex clothier. This property, with its estate of 500 acres, placed the family firmly in the ranks of the county's gentry, Henry Sperling becoming a magistrate and turnpike trustee, and in 1777 High Sheriff of the county.[5]

There were not a few gentry families whose histories were similar to that of the Sperlings, newly established from mercantile, industrial or professional origins, but quickly accepted into the higher levels of county society. At quarter sessions, at meetings of Commissioners of Sewers and the Militia, at local spas, hunts, assemblies and balls, families of business or professional origins, some of whom perhaps were still closely connected with the primary sources of their wealth, rubbed shoulders with the representatives of much older-established gentry families. Their interests had much in common, extending to landed property, politics and county affairs, and together with connections by marriage, created a homogeneity which was further cemented by a broadly similar form of education. As boys, the wealthier of the gentlemen had a shared experience of public school, followed by university or Inns of Court, while the less well-to-do had known only the local grammar school. But in both an immersion in the classics established a basis of understanding and appreciation of literature and the arts, and not least the ability to pen skilfully worded, polite and witty letters – and in this, greater gentry and country gentlemen of widely varying wealth and background were much on a par.

DIVISIONS IN SOCIETY

There was thus a community of interests which transcended the divisions created by differences in wealth and status. The association of men of different backgrounds found a unifying cause in their concern with landed property. They formed an 'interest', what the eighteenth century called the 'landed interest', a body of propertied men who tended to hold broadly compatible views on social and political questions. They were divided, it is true, on some basic political issues, as between the great Whig landlords, who favoured the Hanoverian succession and the over-riding power of Parliament *vis-à-vis* the Crown; and the Tory gentry, many of them the lesser squires, who still hankered after a Stuart restoration and the divine right of kings, and viewed with hostility the weakening of the Church of England by the rise of Nonconformity. But after the '45 had ended in bloody collapse on the field of Culloden, the Stuart cause fell gradually into oblivion, and time gradually ensured the quiet if grudging acceptance of the *status quo*.

Meanwhile, the rising power of rival interests, those of the merchants and manufacturers, posed an increasingly serious threat to the pre-eminence of the landowners. As the eighteenth century progressed there were greater numbers of wealthy and influential men of business who chose to remain closely wedded to the sources of their income, and whose pretensions to a rural lifestyle rarely exceeded a villa on the outskirts of the town. Since ownership of a qualifying amount of land was a prerequisite to a seat in the Commons, and a peerage to one in the House of Lords, it might be supposed that Parliament remained almost entirely a preserve of the landed interest. Not so. The grant of titles to some new families, especially of successful lawyers, admirals and generals, created greater diversity in the ranks of the Lords, while the property qualification for the Commons was not a sufficiently high hurdle to prevent an increase in the ranks of Members who came from outside the landed interest. Indeed, a much more important obstacle to entering the Commons was the cost of fighting an election, although this was not insuperable if there was access to wealth and patronage. As a result, the number of Members with large commercial interests doubled between 1760 and the end of the century, and came to account for as much as a quarter of the House.[6]

In addition to gaining a louder political voice, the expanding urban élite was establishing its own separate identity through the growth of a recognisably distinct urban culture and way of life. Leading townspeople had the means to support a life-style which could rival that of at least the more substantial gentry, if not that of the great landowners with their country mansions and parks. Possessing, quite commonly, fortunes of over £10,000, and occasionally in excess of £100,000, the urban magnates lived in substantial residences set in their own grounds, with their own carriages and numerous servants. They could afford to give their children an education quite as good as that given to the scions of landed estates, and they were able to support town churches, hospitals and charities at least as well as landowners did their country ones. They had their private libraries, their fine furniture and works of art, and they developed cultural interests which were arguably more useful to society at large than those of the hunting and shooting type of country squire, the rustic bumpkins so sharply attacked by Addison and despised by Lord Chesterfield.

Of particular significance were the urban literary and philosophical societies which met regularly in elegant assembly rooms, where debates might centre on arcane questions of physics, chemistry or mechanics, topics highly relevant to the emerging world of steam power, iron-making and factory machinery. There were of course landowners who had wide-ranging interests in literature, religion, history, geography and botany, even economics and mathematics, but they were for the most part isolated individuals who pursued a purely academic field of enquiry. When landowners met in groups it was mainly to discuss current questions of politics, law and order, county administration or agriculture. A number, it must be said, studying the latest agricultural literature, took a close practical interest in farming, and gave attention to running an experimental farm, attempting to introduce new practices to their tenants, and attending the private agricultural shows mounted by such great enthusiasts as Coke of Holkham and the Duke of Bedford – where at dinner glasses were raised to the initiator of an improved breed of livestock or the author of a pamphlet on manures.

Thus the landed interest and the commercial and industrial interests moved on separate courses, divided not only by the differing sources of their wealth but also by differences in outlook, culture and even in some degree religion – as the urban merchants and manufacturers leaned more and more towards Nonconformity. Many squires, it is true, adopted a broad-minded attitude towards creeds other than that of the Church of England. On a private basis they often maintained close personal relations with Roman Catholics, although in their public capacity as magistrates they might be obliged to fine them for some flagrant breach of the restrictive laws. Church of England clergy were not averse to staying with Catholic friends, and Parson Woodforde once sat down to dinner in the house of his squire with the Bishop of Norwich and some Roman Catholic guests. Further, the sons of aristocrats were encouraged to spend some of their time while on the grand tour in attending the services of Catholics, Jews and others, in order to broaden their understanding of religion. Nevertheless, though some members of the landed class were known for their sympathy with the Wesleyans, even subscribing to their chapels and protecting their preachers, the feeling among most of them was generally hostile. Methodist doctrines, said the Duchess of Buckingham, expressing a common view, were 'strongly tinctured with impertinence and disrespect'. It was truly monstrous, as the Duchess went on, 'to be told that you had a heart as sinful as the common wretches that crawl on the earth'.[7]

The growth of Nonconformity in industrial towns, and indeed in industrialised villages over large parts of the countryside, was one cause of resentment against the newly rich men of trade and industry. But it was their wealth, in not a few instances so great as to vie with that of the highest aristocracy, that was the major irritant. They could argue, as did a wealthy London merchant in a well-known play of the time, Colman and Garrick's *The Clandestine Marriage*, that birth, education and titles were insignificant when set against money. 'Money, money, that's the stuff that makes the great man in this country . . . a rich English merchant may make himself a match for the daughter of a Nabob.' Sterling, the merchant, displays his wealth by ordering turtle and venison, pineapples and champagne for the lavish reception of Lord Ogleby, his daughter's prospective father-in-law. And his lordship, on arrival, is shown the merchant's pleasure grounds, his cascade, Chinese bridge and imitation ruins – which, as Sterling boasts, had just been put in thorough repair at an expense of £150.[8]

The ability to become rich, so rich as to rival the wealthiest in the land, fostered a degree of contempt for even the greatest of landowners. They often were heavy borrowers, who occasionally got themselves so deeply into debt as to have to put their affairs into the hands of trustees, divest themselves of ancestral acres, and enter upon a spartan existence of straitened circumstance. Were men who recklessly gave themselves up to the pleasures of Newmarket, the hunt and the bottle, who lavished thousands on the building of great, comfortless mansions, spent more thousands in pursuit of parliamentary seats, and yet more thousands on the chance of a card or a throw of dice – were these the men to whom the government of the country should be entrusted?

As landowners saw it, the 'sudden accumulation of wealth in vulgar hands' had 'almost levelled every distinction'. The rise of the 'commercial interest' in the Commons had meant wars fought for commercial objectives at the expense of taxes levied on landowners. The waning of the eighteenth century thus became a period of great concern. When the House of Commons was 'filled with moneyed men, speculators and underlings in office' it was seen that the landed interest's opposition to reform of Parliament could not long prevail.[9] And the reactionary John Byng, fifth Viscount Torrington, saw the rising tide of industrialisation as a source of economic instability and as a demoralising influence on the labouring classes:

> The business of agriculture is as permanent and moves as regularly as the Globe. But is that the case with manufactures? May not some event overturn them? And who is to maintain the mechanic? The husbandman works regularly, is sober and industrious, and poorly paid, but the artisan will work (from high wages) but 4 days a week, and wallow in drink the other 3, and if unemployed, will be ripe for and active in any mischief. . . .
>
> I dread trade, I hate its clamour: as a gentleman born, I scowl at their (over) advantages. It is in trading towns, only, where rioting and discords begin: and yet they want representatives; why of all places they are the last that should be represented; for their members will be most falsely, and violently chosen and their towns for ever convulsed by faction. Look at Leicester; house against house! Think of the last election at Liverpool! Old Sarum is a better and honester representation, than any great manufacturing town could produce.[10]

A threat even more extreme made its appearance late in the century. A small number of radicals then began to attack the whole principle of private property, the right of ownership fundamental to the creed and very existence of the landed interest. Thomas Spence, a Newcastle schoolmaster, advocated the public ownership of all land, with the rents to be used for support of the poor, to maintain the roads and to encourage agriculture. Slightly less extreme was the plan of William Ogilvie, a Scottish professor. He attacked the landowners' 'pernicious monopoly' of the soil, and proposed that a government agency should buy up land as it came on the market and let it out to small farmers on favourable terms. Thomas Paine, the best-known radical of the day, proposed a death duty of 10 per cent, out of which the landless population would be compensated for the loss of their 'natural inheritance' of the land, while the aged poor would be helped by annual pensions.

The visions of these reformers seemed at the time to be absurdly Utopian and impossible of realisation, though in fact, of course, the essentials of Paine's plan were proposed, and in some degree realised, in the course of Lloyd George's reforms shortly before the Great War. Nevertheless, far-fetched and preposterous as they seemed at the end of the eighteenth century, these ideas were connected in the minds of the ruling class with the more conceivable extension of the franchise and reform of Parliament – and after 1789 with the bloody upheavals in France. Proposals for land reform, however modest, were viewed as attacks on the constitution and established government. Reformist writings, consequently, were regarded as seditious: Spence was arrested and Paine harried into exile. And although radical views continued to survive the repression of the Napoleonic Wars and their aftermath, they failed to make any great impression on the country at large. It was not until the Chartists became a political force in the early 1840s that the ideal of a revived landowning peasantry enjoyed a brief burst of enthusiasm, and even saw some modest results.

It is interesting that the late eighteenth-century ideas of land reformers appeared in a period when food prices were rising under the pressure of a rapidly increasing population, labourers' living standards were under threat, and the numbers of able-bodied people seeking relief from the parish poor law authorities were on the increase. The landowners, it might be pointed out in their defence, were in some degree taking steps to help expand the food supply by encouraging agricultural improvements and by enclosing commons and waste lands for additional farmland. However, not all landowners took much interest in advanced agriculture, and enclosures of open fields and commons which resulted in the conversion of former arable lands to pasture reduced local farm employment and sometimes meant severe hardship for cottagers and small farmers. Moreover, owners were increasingly using their powers over the land to extend game reserves, and as law-makers and magistrates, to punish poachers. Frequently, what was often the one and only direct face-to-face confrontation between squire and labourer occurred when the man was sentenced to imprisonment, a public whipping or even trans-portation, for the taking of game. The enclosure of the commons, too, meant the disappearance of open spaces where in leisure hours the poor could formerly enjoy a little harmless sport.

But it is possible that the growing hostility towards the landowners owed more to their flaunting of their wealth. When so many were poor, the contrast between the great house with its vast grounds, and the confined, tumbledown homes of the landless, was glaring. Even Byng was moved to make the comparison when he observed near St Neots the new kennels built by a duke for his hounds and the 'miserable mud hovels erected for the sons of Adam'.

> Here is little fuel to be bought, little to be pick'd up, but that is
> punished as theft, no land allott'd them for potatoes, or ground for
> a cow: Agues devouring the children: Despondence overcoming
> the aged. At the mercy of an oppressive farmer, at the beck of
> a domineering overseer. . . It is from neglect, and despair that

Democracy, that Anarchy, spring . . . whilst the unaided paupers
of the country will look at a dog-kennel with envy. . . . I will say
'Something is rotten in the State of Denmark'.[11]

The gentry, it is true, usually did something, sometimes a great
deal, to help the poor of their own villages, and they subscribed to
funds used to provide the poor with food in time of bad harvests.
Moreover, much of the cost of the official poor relief, five times
as great as at the beginning of the century, came ultimately out
of their pockets since their rents were adversely influenced by the
burden of parish rates. Nevertheless, the affluent could have done
much more to help the poor, even if private charity was increasingly
becoming swamped by the rising tide of the numbers of the labouring
classes. Their incomes swelled with rising prices, their country houses
became grander, their life-styles more extravagant. In the end, what
is remarkable is that the sansculottes did not rise and attack the
châteaux of England as they did those of France. And the core of
the answer, probably, is that the English poor, though poor, were
never so desperately so as the poor across the Channel, a difference
remarked on by perceptive foreigners. Only five years before the fall
of the Bastille a visiting Frenchman wrote that all kinds of people
'were well clothed and, above all, of great cleanliness', and that the
homes of the lower classes showed a 'marked superiority . . . over
those of the poor French peasants, which it has so often been painful
to observe'.[12]

The margin between the condition of the English poor and that of
the French peasantry may not have been great, though it was certainly
sufficient to arouse the notice of observant French visitors. They may
not have been aware that there were in England in years of high food
prices riots in market places and attacks on corn dealers, millers and
bakers. But, in general, the English poor accepted their lot, their
poverty and their lowly place in society. The most serious rioting
only occurred after the French Wars, in 1816 and in 1830, when on
both occasions troops had to be used to restore order; but though the
upper classes were alarmed, there was never any real likelihood that
the unrest would swell and culminate in revolution. The ruling class
survived, making limited and gradual concessions on parliamentary
reform, beginning in 1832. But it was in fact another hundred years
before all men and women in the country had the right to vote, and
at that date the landowners, though much reduced in their territorial
power and influence, still enjoyed possession of a large proportion of
the country's land.

LAND AND THE ECONOMY

It is impossible to understand fully the extent of landowners' hege-mony in the politics and government of the nation unless one recalls the multi-faceted role of land in the economy. We do not possess precise figures for the numbers employed on the land in the eighteenth century, nor what proportion of the national labour force they constituted. At the first census of 1801, it is estimated, 1.7m people were engaged in agriculture, forestry and fishing, representing 36 per cent of the total British labour force. Given the rapid growth of non-agricultural employment as industrial and commercial changes multiplied in the later eighteenth century, it is reasonable to suppose that the proportion represented by farm labour was considerably higher in 1750. At that date it may be guessed that the agricultural numbers were something over one million, and represented 45 or 50 per cent of the smaller total labour force. Agriculture was thus by far the greatest single source of employment (as indeed it still remained a century later), much larger than textiles, clothing, coal, iron and shipbuilding put together. It is a chastening thought that the next largest category of labour after agriculture consisted of domestic servants (as again was still the case in 1850).

The employment provided by land is seen to be even more extensive if account is taken of all those country people who, while not involved in farming, still gained their livelihood entirely or mainly from agriculture. The processing of farm produce, for example, employed millers, maltsters and tanners, and the transporting and trading of the produce required wagoners, carters, drovers and the drivers of trains of pack animals as well as the crews of coastal vessels and of canal barges. The trade in farm produce needed also such indispensable middlemen as corn dealers, auctioneers and hop factors as well as petty higglers. The farmers themselves required the services of blacksmiths, carpenters, wheelwrights, farriers and carriers, while landlords' woodlands were exploited by woodcutters, dealers in bark (for tanning), and buyers of the timber required for shipbuilding and housebuilding, as well as the wood needed for the making of a vast number of articles such as posts, stakes, hop-poles, gates, fencing, barrels, tubs, brooms and handles for tools, to mention only a few.

It should be remembered, too, that many industrial workers of the eighteenth century had some land ancillary to their craft or trade, if only for keeping the horses used for collecting raw materials or delivering finished products. Some combined an industrial occupation with a little part-time farming, engaging themselves more fully in their trade in the winter, and in their farms in the summer. Part-time farming of this kind tended to die out as industry became more specialised and large-scale, but it was still to be found in some areas as late as the middle of the nineteenth century. In 1850 Sir James Caird remarked on the survival of weaver-farmers in the West Riding, men who kept dairy cows and a horse to convey their manufactured goods: 'when trade is good the farm is neglected; when trade is dull the weaver becomes a more attentive farmer'. And he noted that on the south bank of the Tyne in Durham some of the most enterprising farmers were those whose main business was as innkeepers or butchers in Newcastle.[13]

Landlords themselves required the services of professional people such as land stewards, country attorneys and surveyors, while the incumbents of country churches relied on their glebe lands and their tithe or tithe-compositions for an income. The homes of landowners and clergy were built and repaired by local builders and their craftsmen, and needed full-time domestic servants, grooms, coachmen and gardeners, and possibly woodsmen and huntsmen. In order to function, the large country house required the services of perhaps sixty or seventy such people, and in some instances even more. Even the more modest establishments of the gentry and clergy might provide work for from two or three to twenty or more persons.

On many landed estates, especially in the northern half of the country, a variety of industrial activities was often to be found. Among them were the mining of coal, lead or iron ore, the making of iron, and brickworks, quarries and lime kilns, tanneries and even textile factories. It is true that often large amounts of the produce of these enterprises were consumed on the estate itself, the coal for heating, the bricks, stone and lime for making repairs to the house and tenants' farms. But not infrequently much was sold off the estate and the industrial activities loomed very large indeed. Some Midland and northern landowners ranked among the leading local industrialists, the Lowthers in Cumberland, for instance, or the Fitzwilliams in Yorkshire. In the Black Country the Dudleys obtained much the largest part of their revenues from their coal mines and ironworks, and the agricultural properties were relatively insignificant.

Further, in order to improve the outlets for heavy and bulky estate products such as coal, timber and iron, and to widen the market for their tenants' farm produce, landlords promoted a variety of transport projects. Some of these were local, and perhaps privately developed, such as the Dudleys' initiation of canals and railways around Dudley and Tipton, [14] but others were major concerns which contributed significantly to regional development. Landlords and farmers helped to finance turnpike roads, and in some instances, such as the Charing Trust of 1766 in Kent, provided the whole of the necessary capital. They put money into river improvements designed to assist in navigation, and subsequently involved themselves in canal building. The Duke of Bridgewater was of course the renowned prototype of landlord involvement in canal construction, but what the Duke did for his Worsley mines was widely imitated, if not on so large or so remunerative a scale. In all, landowners subscribed 41 per cent of all the share capital in canals built between 1755 and 1780, and nearly 22 per cent of those built between 1780 and 1815. [15]

In numerous instances the markets for landowners' coal were distant and could be reached only by sea, and so exploitation involved the construction of docks and harbours. The coal from mines in Cumberland, for example, found outlets in Ireland and continental Europe, a trade which was facilitated by the Curwen family's development of the ports of Workington and Harrington, the Senhouses' founding of Maryport, and the Lowthers' expansion of Whitehaven. [16] Similar projects were undertaken for the South Wales coalfield. There Sir Humphrey Mackworth was concerned in the early development of Neath, and subsequently other families of mineral owners, such as the Tennants and the Llewellyns, involved themselves in the building of canals and railways. In the south-west of Wales Milford Haven was established as a port by Sir William Hamilton and the Greville family, and came to dominate the coal trade of Pembrokeshire. The expansion there of the gentry's mines fostered the local market for timber and led also to the building of iron furnaces and tin works. [17]

For the most part the industrial investments made by landowners were on a small scale, at least in their early stages, although some developed subsequently into major sources of local employment. Collectively, however, they played a significant role in the exploitation of neglected resources, and especially in what were formerly remote and backward regions, bringing such areas more closely into the mainstream of the country's expanding economy. Of course many estates had no minerals to exploit, even in northern England, though everywhere timber, bricks, stone and lime could be important. Even in the coalfields, however, it would be misleading to suggest that landowners universally welcomed transport improvements. There were fears that a turnpike, canal, or railway might reduce the value of property by breaking down a local monopoly arising from inadequate roads, or in the case of a river improvement or canal by causing changes in water levels. Furthermore, farm tenants were often engaged part-time in the business of land carriage, and looked to their landlord to protect their livelihood. Opposition to Bills in Parliament, and hostile measures locally, were mounted by some landowners for more aesthetic reasons, to protect the privacy and beauty of their houses and parks. Thus some nineteenth-century owners refused to sell land and forced railway lines to skirt round their estates. And when it proved impossible to prevent a factory chimney from obtruding on the view, the factory master might be pressed to disguise the unwelcome excrescence as the tower of a fortress. But, in time, the majority of landowners who had no coal or iron of their own came to terms with the rise of industry, and in the nineteenth century there was a tendency for owners to move away from purely agricultural investment towards holding shares in railways, water companies, breweries and similar enterprises.

There were not a few landowners who enjoyed the benefits of diversification of interests through possession of urban properties. Large parts of what eventually came to be central London – Covent Garden, Southampton Row, Bloomsbury, Pimlico and the West End – were held by noble proprietors, as names like Russell Square, Bedford Square, Portman Square, Manchester Square and Grosvenor Square remind us. Through their careful control of development they were able to create London's characteristic environment of great squares, which with their green centres and superior residences still provide welcome relief from the brash commercialism of so much of the capital. And in so doing they also created future sources of vast revenues for the advancement of their heirs. Of course, country landowners' urban properties were not confined to London. They had often extensive holdings in provincial towns, and sometimes deliberately set out to acquire further ones in order to secure a tighter grip on a parliamentary electorate. Some owners, moreover, possessed farm lands that fringed expanding seaports or industrial towns, and these, if enclosed and any small proprietors bought out, could become immensely valuable for building purposes. Others had holdings in spas, like the Duke of Kingston at Bath, or in coastal villages and fishing harbours that, later on, with the railways, might be profitably developed as the craze for visiting the seaside spread to the urban masses. Such varied resorts as Eastbourne, Bournemouth, Folkestone, Fleetwood and Skegness were all examples of landowner enterprise in the making of new holiday resorts.

LAND AND INDUSTRIALISATION

The wider economic significance of land and its produce became more and more apparent as the tide of industrialisation advanced. In the hundred years after 1750 the population of England and Wales trebled, and by 1850 the typical Englishman had ceased to be a country dweller. In the eighteenth century it was London, housing a tenth of the country's people, that was the great magnet for agricultural production. Increasingly, however, industrial areas like the Black Country, the West Riding and southern Lancashire became valued outlets for the foodstuffs and raw materials of nearby farming districts. The growth of these provincial market centres proceeded apace in the nineteenth century. In the fifty years after 1801 the population of Birmingham rose more than three-fold to reach 233,000, that of Manchester four-fold to total 303,000, Glasgow's numbers four-and-a-half times to 345,000, and Liverpool's people by more than four-and-a-half times to 303,000. At the same time the proportion of industrial workers who still had roots in the countryside sank to a very low level though, as we have seen, such dual occupations did not disappear altogether.

British agriculture, with the enclosure of former commons and waste lands, and with the adoption of more productive methods of farming, managed to cope with the larger part of the population increase. True, the prices of farm produce rose after 1750 as population pressure combined with poor seasons to make demand run ahead of supply, and it was of course the high prices, until near the end of the Napoleonic Wars, that provided much of the stimulus for enclosure and agricultural improvement. However, by the third decade of the nineteenth century supply had pretty much caught up with demand, and prices moderated. The price of wheat, for example, settled down as a level far below that which had caused such distress in the war years, and despite an addition of over 6m to the population averaged only about 30 per cent higher than in the 1780s; it remained at about this level, or lower, for the rest of the century.

It is true, of course, that in the meanwhile Britain had ceased to be an exporter of grain and had come to rely increasingly on imports. The changeover from exporter to importer was not, however, very sudden or dramatic. After the exceptional years of 1728–29, the first sizeable import of wheat (of 142,000 quarters) occurred in 1757, though this proved to be an isolated incident since large exports were resumed in 1759–66. The years 1767–68 again saw very substantial imports (totalling 847,000 quarters over the two years), and there then followed five years when the net trade was very small. Large net imports recurred in 1777, 1783–84, 1790–91 and from 1793 onwards, although there were considerable exports again in 1776, 1779–80, 1786 and 1792. Even in the war period of severe shortages, when imports were generally heavy, there was still in every year a modest outflow of wheat; indeed, in 1808 a net outflow. Exports also continued after the wars, amounting in some years to as much as a quarter or a third of the imports.[18]

In fact, Britain moved to the position of a regular net importer of wheat only with the extraordinary run of bad seasons after 1792, and when the rate of population growth was rising towards its peak. In the preceding thirty years there was a balance of imports over exports of 723,000 quarters, an average of only 24,100 quarters a year. This was a very marginal figure when one considers that (assuming an average annual consumption of 6 bushels per head) it would have fed only a little over 32,000 persons, or well under a half of 1 per cent of the population. Even in the thirty years after 1792, when net imports of wheat and wheaten flour averaged a little under 568,000 quarters a year, this represented a supply for 757,000 persons, which in 1811 was only slightly over 6 per cent of the much increased population. And in the next twenty years, from 1823 to 1842, when the population of Great Britain rose by over 4 million, the rising imports of wheat fed an average of under 2 million people, or less than 11 per cent of the 1841 population.[19]

Of course, other grains had also to be imported. The imports of barley were only sporadically large before 1825, but became more consistently substantial thereafter, while in most years from 1790 onwards there were considerable imports of oats, reflecting the large increase in the numbers of horses used for transport, haulage, carriages and pleasure, as well as on farms. Livestock was also imported to supplement the home supply of meat, the imported stock amounting to an annual average of £3.3m in value in the middle 1850s, while imports of butter averaged just over £2m a year in the same period.[20] By this time it had become quite clear that Great Britain was necessarily and increasingly dependent on Irish and foreign producers for a large and growing proportion of its food supplies. The Corn Laws were seen as obsolete when the availability of cheaper food for the non-agricultural population was recognised as economically and politically essential. Agricultural protection had to be sacrificed to wider industrial and social requirements.

But this situation did not reflect the failure of British agriculture to meet the needs of the new industrial society. It is estimated that home farm production rose by over 100 per cent in the hundred years after 1750, a massive increase by former standards, but still one quite dwarfed by the growth of the numbers to be fed. In the same hundred years the population trebled, and there were some 13m extra mouths to be satisfied. Given the limited area of fertile land in Britain, and the necessarily slow rate of progress of improved farming techniques, it was inevitable that such an enormously increased population would have to be fed in part by imported food. In 1851, nevertheless, British farmers managed to supply, under conditions of free trade, some 85 per cent of the country's wheat needs, and a very large proportion of the requirements of meat, dairy produce, fruit and vegetables. And this was done by dint of investing new capital in farming which originated very largely from within the industry, from landlords' rents and farmers' profits; and, furthermore, with a labour force that had declined sharply as a proportion of the country's total. Moreover, landowners, as we have seen, had capital to spare to invest in the non-agricultural activities of their estates, as well as in canal and railway shares and the Funds (or government stock), while the falling proportion of the national labour force engaged in farming meant that there was plenty of labour available for the expansion of non-agricultural employment.

Thus the aristocracy's and gentry's control of some three-quarters of the country's land could hardly be described as inimical to the nation's wider economic interests. A large proportion of landowners' revenues, it is true, went on personal consumption, often of an extravagant kind, while the amounts devoted to agricultural improvements (with the major exceptions of enclosure, and later, drainage) were very small in relation to total income. There were indeed numbers of estates marked by neglected farm buildings, tumbledown cottages and discouraged tenants, and it is clear from Caird's strictures that some landlords were not managing their estates properly and were failing to invest sufficiently in them.[21] Nevertheless, most landowners certainly had an eye to the profitable exploitation of the non-agricultural resources of their property, and took advantage in some degree of the investment opportunities offered by the growth of the wider economy beyond. The history of the period shows that their domination of the country's largest industry, and of its government, posed no serious obstacle to the upsurge in industry and trade; and although it became very clear in 1832 and after that their political power was on the ebb, the landowners could be said to have managed the country's affairs in an age of unparalleled economic change and social upheaval with at least a moderate degree of success.

NOTES

1. **P. Mathias,** 'The social structure in the eighteenth century: a calculation by Joseph Massie', *Economic History Review*, 2nd ser., **X,** 1957–58, pp. 42–3.
2. *Ibid.*
3. **Daniel Defoe,** *A Tour through England and Wales,* Everyman edn, 1926, I, pp. 6, 100.
4. **Christopher Clay,** 'The price of freehold land in the later seventeenth and eighteenth centuries', *Economic History Review*, 2nd ser., **XXVII,** 1974, pp. 175, 185–6.
5. **G. E. Mingay,** *Mrs Hurst Dancing,* Gollancz, 1981, pp. xii–xiii.
6. **R. R. Palmer,** *The Age of the Democratic Revolution,* Princeton University Press, 1959, p. 47.
7. **F. Turner** (ed.), *A Berkshire Bachelor's Diary,* Blacket Turner & Co., Newbury, 1936, p. 46; **J. Beresford** (ed.), *Woodforde,* Oxford University Press, 1935, p. 132; **G. E. Mingay,** *English Landed Society in the Eighteenth Century,* Routledge & Kegan Paul, 1963, p. 150.
8. **John Hampden** (ed.), *Eighteenth-century Plays,* Everyman edn, 1938, pp. 278–9, 283, 292.
9. **J. B. Botsford,** *English Society in the Eighteenth Century as Influenced from Overseas,* New York, Macmillan, 1924, p. 154; **Lord Sheffield,** *Observations on the Corn Bill,* 1791.
10. **C. Bruyn Andrews** (ed.), *The Torrington Diaries,* Eyre & Spottiswoode, 1954, pp. 395, 417.
11. *Ibid.,* pp. 494–5, 506.
12. **Norman Scarfe** (ed.), *A Frenchman's Year in Suffolk, 1784,* Suffolk Records Society, 1988, pp. 4, 110.
13. **J. Caird,** *English Agriculture in 1850–51,* 1852, new edn, Frank Cass, 1968, pp. 287, 344.
14. **T. J. Raybould,** *The Economic Emergence of the Black Country: a Study of the Dudley Estate,* Newton Abbot, David & Charles, 1973, pp. 56, 71.
15. **J. R. Ward,** *The Finance of Canal Building in Eighteenth-century England,* Oxford University Press, 1974, p. 74.
16. **E. Hughes,** *North Country Life in the Eighteenth Century,* vol. II, *Cumberland & Westmorland, 1700–1830,* 1965, Oxford University Press p. 162; **J. V. Beckett,** *Coal and Tobacco: the Lowthers and the Economic Development of West Cumberland, 1660–1760,* Cambridge University Press, 1981.
17. **D. W. Howell,** 'The landed gentry of Pembrokeshire in the eighteenth century', Unpublished MA thesis, University of Wales, 1965, pp. 146–7, 175–7.
18. **B. R. Mitchell and Phyllis Deane,** *Abstract of British Historical Statistics,* Cambridge University Press, 1962, pp. 94–5.
19. *Ibid.,* p. 298.
20. Caird, *English Agriculture,* pp. 490–7.
21. *Ibid.,* pp. 488–94.

CHAPTER TWO

The Landowner and the Village

SOCIAL RELATIONSHIPS

The stereotypical village of the past is sometimes pictured as a cluster of cottages nestling in the lee of the squire's mansion, gathered perhaps round the gates to his grounds or kept at a more respectful distance, giving importance to a road junction or river crossing. There were certainly villages of this kind, though it is doubtful whether they were typical; rather, they formed only a minority of rural settlements. Villages varied greatly in size from hamlets of a few isolated farmsteads and cottages, to those boasting several hundreds of inhabitants and even larger ones which bordered on the status of country town. These larger settlements sometimes straggled for a mile or more along a road or up a hill, with an older portion above which included the church, parsonage and manor house, and a newer, more populous part below which, with its inns, craftsmen's workshops, and butchers and grocers, had grown to achieve semi-independence from squire and parson. Alternatively, however, large villages might consist of several scattered hamlets, half a mile apart, which betokened their origin in separate clearings in a once-enveloping woodland.

Numbers of the larger places acquired importance as way-stations on coaching routes and were the homes of substantial inns and the shops of craftsmen and tradesmen. These essential elements of rural life were widely found, of course, although a certain minimum size of population was required to support a particular craft or trade. In Norfolk in 1836, for example, the figure needed before a blacksmith would be found was 475, for a wheelwright 500, and for a saddler 550. A minimum population of 377 was needed to support a public house, 463 for a village shop, and 498 for a grocer's establishment.[1] These figures may seem small but, of course, many craftsmen and tradesmen were not entirely dependent on their main occupation and had other supplementary ones, such as running a carrier's business, selling coal or wood, or dealing in poultry, eggs, fruit and vegetables.

A large village like Binbrook on the Lincolnshire Wolds, with a population in 1851 of 1,310, housed surprising numbers of craftsmen and tradesmen, and attracted custom from a wide area around. In 1851 there were 109 craftsmen in the village as compared with 251 persons engaged as farmworkers. The craftsmen included as many as fourteen wheelwrights and thirteen blacksmiths, and in addition there were seven millers and five butchers. Ten people described themselves as builders and bricklayers, and another ten as joiners and carpenters. The village was also served by a large number of dressmakers, eighteen of them, as well as fifteen shoemakers and thirteen tailors, while other occupations were represented by a single ropemaker, a tinplate worker, a machine-maker, and a maker of small agricultural implements.[2]

Binbrook remained largely concerned with serving an agricultural population, but in the course of the eighteenth and early nineteenth centuries many villages became industrialised, and often developed into considerable settlements where the inhabitants who were involved in farming formed a distinct minority. In the North and Midlands arose many pit and furnace villages, the homes of miners and ironworkers. And elsewhere, until late in the eighteenth century, the flames of charcoal furnaces lit the skies of the Forest of Dean and the Weald of Kent and Sussex. Black Country villages became dominated by the cottage workers engaged in making chains, nails and other ironware, many of them women and girls. Framework knitting, again a cottage or small workshop industry, spread through villages near Leicester and Nottingham. Textiles were the main support of many of the rural population of the West Country, the West Riding and East Anglia, as on a smaller scale was glove-making in Worcestershire, Oxfordshire and parts of the West Country. The making of boots and shoes occupied many country families in Northamptonshire, while ropes, cordage, nets and buttons were made in Dorset cottages, pillow lace by the village women in Buckinghamshire and neighbouring counties, and straw plait for the Luton hat trade by women and children in Bedfordshire and neighbouring districts.

It is clear from even these limited examples that very many villages existed where the workfolk were in thrall, not to landowners or farmers, but to pit-owners, ironmasters or clothiers, or to the many middlemen who stood between them and the ultimate purchasers of their wares. To them the squire was merely a name, a figurehead, if indeed there were any resident squire at all. Large industrial villages, as also semi-industrial hamlets in woodland clearings – in such forests as Sherwood or Rockingham, for example – very often had no squire, and in them the influence of the landed gentry and of the established Church was small or non-existent. Moreover, some of the settlements in wooded or upland areas derived their notorious character from the very absence of squires and magistrates, being the homes of gangs of robbers, highwaymen, smugglers, coiners and escaped criminals, men too well-armed, too violent and too numerous to be easily awed by the distant and often feeble might of the forces of the law.

Nevertheless, there were still the many agricultural villages and country towns where life largely revolved round the seasons and any crime was usually of a petty nature. Some of these, however, though the land might be in the hands of one or two large owners, still had no resident squire, while in others there was no dominant landowner and the property was divided among several members of the minor gentry. But all farming villages felt the influence of some landowner-magistrate, even if he were not resident, while the owners of the land, whether magistrates or not, exercised some degree of control over the lives of the inhabitants. The justices were becoming considerably more numerous as the eighteenth century advanced, and although the majority were landowners of substance, owning much more than the qualifying £100 worth of land set in 1731, a growing proportion consisted of leading clergymen, prominent tradesmen, clothiers, ironmasters, and the like. Even in remote and sparsely populated Pembrokeshire the thirty-five justices of 1663 had doubled in number by 1727, more than trebled by 1779, and reached nearly 200 by 1790, and 258 by 1836. In that county clerical representation on the Bench, totalling only three in 1727, had grown to thirty-nine by 1790.[3]

Although the Bench swelled in so dropsical a manner, many of the additional justices were really supernumerary, men who accepted the office for its prestige but neglected its duties. The actual work of the justices was frequently done by an active minority of perhaps a quarter of the Bench, and in this minority the clerical justices proved to be among the most energetic. They were especially prominent in the supervision of prisons and the Poor Law, although, rather surprisingly, they also often took the lead in the pursuit and prosecution of criminals. This kind of activity was a factor in the growth of rural anti-clericalism in the century or so after 1750. The considerable powers of the parson-justice were resented by those who regarded the exaction of tithes as unjust, and who believed the clergy were doing too well out of enclosures, where the costs of enclosing and fencing the glebe, and the allotments made as compensation for redemption of tithes, were all met by the other proprietors.[4]

As an active magistrate, the landowner frequently came into conflict with villagers, not only in the enforcement of regulations governing the qualifications of electors and appointment of constables, but also in such day-to-day matters as the number of horses that might legally be used to haul wagons and carts. Apart from their responsibility for maintaining law and order, the justices had many administrative functions, in which supervision of poor relief loomed large, but also included the maintenance of roads, licensing of alehouses, and regulating of fairs and markets and weights and measures. Conscientious justices closed alehouses which were known to be the resorts of robbers and smugglers, and saw that honest innkeepers kept their doors shut during the hours of divine service. They prohibited the activities of fortune-tellers, punished vagrants, and suppressed those village fairs which, in their view, had become infamous as occasions for debauchery, violence and sexual licence. And they might make enemies among village folk by their over-zealous pursuit of poachers, high-handed treatment of parish officers, and indictment of those parishes which neglected to repair their roads and bridges.

On the other hand, there were justices who were conscientious in other ways, who did their best to improve prisons and houses of correction, who went out of their way to help the poor, and who in a year of a bad harvest raised funds to buy supplies of flour to be retailed to the poor at the price of a normal year. The conscientious justice was often lavish in his unpaid service to the community, out several days a week in all weathers on public business. Apart from local petty sessions and quarter sessions in the county town, there was much travelling to attend meetings of Militia Commissioners, charity trustees, Commissions of Sewers, and managing committees of workhouses, Bridewells and prisons. Nevertheless, the enforcement of the law was his primary function, though this was often tinged with mercy. Although the number of capital offences rose markedly in the eighteenth century, and capital punishment was regarded as the only real deterrent to crime, in practice the severity of the law was mitigated in a number of ways. It was a common device to value stolen goods at under their true value in order that the charge of larceny might be classed as 'petty' rather than 'grand', the latter carrying with it the death penalty. In the courts the judges eliminated many capital charges, and juries refused to convict where the law was regarded as too harsh. Even in the rather small majority of cases where the defendants were not acquitted, transportation was frequently substituted for the death penalty – although enforced removal overseas under brutal conditions, the almost certain severing for ever of ties with home, family and friends, was in truth no mild alternative.

Apart from the official capacity which some landowners and clergymen held as justices, the great majority of squires and parsons did much to maintain harmonious relations with the local community. There were feasts and celebrations when the harvest was in or some major task completed on the farms, such as marling or manuring. The squire's birthday, his son's wedding or news of a victory of wartime were festive occasions in the village as well as in the hall. At Christmas both squire and parson provided little feasts for the poor, and there might be distributions of bread, blankets and fuel. At Christmas, 1795 – a very dear year – Parson Woodforde noted in his diary that a total of 90 shillings' worth of bread was baked specially for the poor and paid for out of a collection taken for the purpose, while at Christmas, 1800 – a year when prices were even higher – the parson himself gave a dinner for several poor people and distributed 6d each to fifty-five others (though he rejected two hopefuls who were not of his parish). Each year when his tithes were paid, the farmers could expect a jolly evening in the parsonage when, to Woodforde's chagrin, a decanter or two might be broken by his befuddled guests. The tithe dinner which he gave on 3 December 1776 consisted of a roast sirloin of beef, a boiled leg of mutton, and plum puddings 'in plenty', and the seventeen farmers who stayed to dine polished off six bottles of wine, a gallon and a half of rum 'and I know not what ale'.[5]

In such a village as Woodforde's the squire sometimes took a close personal interest in the inhabitants' welfare. He might, for example, have paid a doctor an annual fee to attend to the village sick, set bones, and provide simple medicines. He might also have been prepared to put his hand in his pocket to pay for repairs to the church – an almost inescapable responsibility when he possessed the advowson, the right of appointment of the parson. Growing numbers of gentry believed in the advantages of education for civilising and enlightening the workfolk, and for making poor children better fitted to earn their living in a respectable and honest manner. Thus they founded a variety of small elementary and industrial schools and helped meet their running expenses. One such innovator was a prominent Welsh gentleman, Sir John Phillips of Picton Castle in Pembrokeshire, who founded a number of charity schools and encouraged other local gentry to do the same.[6] In addition to schools, almshouses and hospitals, the institutions most frequently favoured in their wills, the country landowners of a later period provided village halls and reading rooms, playing fields and recreation grounds.

During their lifetimes, however, public charity was usually a minor concern and absorbed only a very small proportion of the gentry's expenditure, seldom more than 5 per cent, and commonly less. Much of their day-to-day charity, in fact, was of a highly personal and private kind, directed towards particular individuals who were well known to them as old tenants or former servants of the family. A widespread form of this individual charity consisted of reductions in farm rents made to tenants who were known to be elderly, ill, or in reduced circumstances with large families. If the estate were sufficiently extensive for a steward to be employed, this official often regarded it as part of his duties to report deserving cases to his employer. Thus we find Dudley North, a Suffolk landowner, responding to his steward's letters by ordering 5 guineas to be paid to a certain villager who had broken a leg, and 2 guineas to another who had suffered an injured knee. Sir George Saville, a prominent Nottinghamshire and Yorkshire owner, was asked by his steward to approve the loan of a milch ass to a widow who was 'very ill, and she will take care of her'. And a Gloucestershire gentleman told a friend how in the January of 1792 he had rescued Bett Green, an old servant of his family, 'who I thought had been long since Dead; but on enquiry found her in a Cott on the Common, with the Snow on her bed; nearly 90 years of Age, and almost starved, having too much pride for the Workhouse'.[7]

Many landowners accepted that works of charity were incumbent on their elevated social position and income. For these reasons it was a common practice among the greatest landowners to keep their rents at moderate levels, and they thought it below their dignity to seek the highest return that the land could be made to produce. This had more than purely local significance, moreover, since lesser owners over a wide area frequently took their cue from the great estates. When rents were rising they waited to see what size of increase the biggest owners would impose, and when times were hard they waited similarly to see what sort of abatement the great owners would offer.

Rents, however, were often influenced by other considerations. A neglected estate, with dilapidated buildings and land out of condition – one owned, for example, by an absentee landlord – might require low rents merely to attract any tenants at all, and in prolonged periods of low agricultural prices the farmers might look for reduced rents and a range of other inducements to remain on the land. Those owners who had large non-agricultural incomes from mines, canals or urban properties could afford to be generous to their farm tenants, and often felt it appropriate to subsidise their farmers from other revenues. Rents might be kept low also for political reasons, since numbers of tenants had the vote, or because the proprietor was a keen sportsman and found it necessary to give his farmers an implicit *quid pro quo* for the damage done to hedges and fences by the hunt and the depredations of foxes and pheasants. Or a low rent might merely reflect the owner's indifference to increased income or a desire to be popular among his tenants, to be able, as Arthur Young expostulated, to ride round 'his country' and be greeted by 'an extra-low bow and scrape' from the inhabitants.

Another, much less costly, form of largesse was the help offered to poor wayfarers who called at the kitchen door of the mansion. They were often offered food, and some gentlemen's ladies set aside one day a week for cooking for the poor. Alternatively, or in addition, the help might be in the form of cash. Dudley North's records show the considerable sum of 5s (a week's pay for many labourers) given by him to 'a poor Man from Molsford'; sixpence to 'a poor Woman', and the same amount to 'a poor Man what had Losses'. No doubt this casual charity from landowners, parsons and others helped many poor people to avoid the indignity of having to resort to the parish overseers. A more unexpected service was given by squires who accepted deposits of villagers' savings, in the role of banker or trustee. The sums were often considerable, and were frequently accompanied by instructions as to how the money was to be disposed of in the event of the depositor's death, whether to be paid to his widow, for example, or to be used to apprentice out his sons; and in the meanwhile the squire paid interest on the money at the going rate of 4 or 5 per cent. Sometimes these deposits arose from small purchases of land by the squire, the sellers leaving part of the purchase money in the squire's hands at interest, but not all the depositors were farmers or villagers. The Stanhopes, whose estate was near the woollen-cloth manufacturing town of Leeds, received deposits from clothiers and merchants, clothmakers, shoemakers, salters and bakers, while local friendly societies also placed their spare funds with them.[8]

THE AGE OF DEFERENCE

Along with the solicitude for inhabitants' welfare which was exhibited in many squire-dominated villages went a different kind of care, a care for law and order, for respectability, for protection of property, and for deference. To the present age – with its assertion of wide-ranging 'rights', some old-established, some newly claimed, and its insistence on equality, if not fraternity – the social control which country squires exercised in the past smacks of a disparity amounting almost to petty tyranny. Of course, applied to the eighteenth century, this criticism is unhistorical since it takes no account of the general acceptance of the ordered society, the society in which each person had his place and the duties and privileges, if any, which went with it. In this society the relatively small numbers of wealthy and educated people were alone regarded as having the prerequisites for government, both national and local, and for setting rules of behaviour and standards of morality, taste and religion. Moreover, the inequality was in some respects less absolute than might be supposed.

In England, if not in pre-Revolution France, there was in fact equality before the law, even if the peers enjoyed some limited privileges in their right to trial by the Lords. In theory, at least, the meanest tradesman could secure redress for an injury done to him by the greatest nobleman in the kingdom, although in practice a long purse was then, as now, of inestimable advantage in entering the law courts. And in the matter of deference, it was not always the case that a wealthy aristocrat could obtain the obedience of his tenants, nor even their politeness, nor yet prompt payment of their rents. The high turnover of domestic servants is an indication of their liking for independence as well as their propensity for drunkenness, stealing, fornication, and other undesirable habits. And even so exalted a personage as the Duke of Hamilton found it unwise when travelling not to send his servants ahead to reserve rooms at the inn, and could find himself 'obliged to bed upon a parlour floor'.[9]

There were, on the other hand, numerous examples of arrogant excesses of rank and power. Landowners desirous of creating extensive and elaborately landscaped parks round their mansions secured grants of royal forest and common land, and displaced the poor inhabitants. Where necessary they transferred cottages to other sites, and even removed whole villages that stood inconveniently in the way of the view. Such a removal occurred in the case of Lord Harcourt's Nuneham Courtenay, in Oxfordshire, the origin of Goldsmith's *Deserted Village*; though there, and elsewhere, displacement resulted in the provision of new and better cottages for the inhabitants. Some aristocrats required privacy of another kind. Near the end of the seventeenth century the portly Earl of Lincoln had a 'prentice boy beaten to death for gazing at him in the street', and the 'Proud Duke' of Somerset sent outriders to clear the roads of inquisitive plebeians, although it was said that one farmer insisted on peering over his own hedge and held up his pig so that he, too, might see the Duke pass by.

Generally, however, the kinds of deference expected were more modest, though it is true that the subservant classes were very extensive, and included professional men, tenants, servants, tradesmen and workmen of all kinds. Long credit, meaning unpaid bills, were a normal part of the deference expected from wine merchants and tailors in town, from butchers and carpenters in the village. The country doctor, when not on an annual stipend, had also to wait for his bills to be settled, and when visiting the mansion was expected to call at the kitchen door like other tradesmen. Tutors, governesses and schoolteachers employed in the house were often regarded as no more than superior servants (as *Jane Eyre* makes clear) – superior only because of their pretensions to an education more advanced than that of the other servants. In salary they might, in fact, not be paid as much. Even the parson applying for his humble living must needs testify his attachment to the government, must remind how his father 'served at the Election', and in turn must promise to serve 'his Lord in everything in his Power . . . and doe everything he would have him'. Parson Woodforde, who served his church at Weston Longeville for nearly twenty-seven years, never quite overcame his diffidence in dealing with the squire, and felt somewhat honoured and faintly embarrassed when invited to dine with him and his grand friends.[10]

Some landlords expected a good deal by way of deference from their tenants. When a farmer was first admitted to a tenancy he was judged not only in terms of his farming capital and experience but also in regard to his politics, religion and social behaviour. Strongly Anglican landlords would not brook Dissenters or Roman Catholics, while it was generally expected that at least one of the tenant's two votes for the county seats would be at his landlord's disposal at election time. The respectability of the estate had to be safeguarded, and those tenants who were discovered to be drunkards, womanisers or steeple-chasers (a plebeian sport much disliked by landowners), or who were lax in their attendance at church would be warned, and eventually, perhaps, dismissed. The wealthier of the farmers might be expected to turn out with the landlord's hunt, properly dressed

and on good horses, and all tenants were expected to play their part in the preservation of foxes, to discourage poaching, and not to trap or shoot game on their own farms without the landlord's permission. A common provision in tenants' leases required them to board out puppies in order to keep up the strength of the hounds.

Reports on the tenants were sent in by stewards and rent collectors – how well they managed their farms, whether they were in breach of covenants by subletting land, ploughing up permanent pastures or selling manure off the farm, and how regularly they paid their rent. In practice the dismissal of a tenant was unusual, generally resorted to by a landlord only in extreme cases. A mediocre standard of farming would be accepted, particularly where farmers were handicapped by difficult soils or by old age or poverty, and many estates were run with numbers of tenants always in arrear with their rents. But if a large arrear came eventually to be regarded as irrecoverable, or 'desperate' as the contemporary term was, then the tenancy might be ended and a distraint ordered on the man's goods to recover at least some part of the debt. And there were of course obstreperous and deceitful tenants whose behaviour could not be condoned. Such a one was a Robert Archer, tenant to Sir Mark Stuart Pleydell, who in a letter of 1761 described the farmer as 'a greedy cunning dog and will creep about and skulk and lurk in a Hole for Three Years together – exactly like a ————Rabbit'. Some owners' eyes stretched beyond their tenants to encompass the workfolk too. Thus on this same Berkshire estate it was recorded that a Harvest Home supper should consist only of beef and beer, and ought to be confined to 'such as have personally assisted in bringing home ye harvest'. The absence of labourers from work in order to attend a funeral was something that was allowed, but the wages had to be duly abated in these and similar absences. 'The Day lab^s will pretend to make it out on such days, by rising earlier to their work but that is only a pretence wch Mast^s never admit.'[11]

As the numbers of the population grew rapidly from the middle of the eighteenth century onwards, so a greater distinction developed between squire-controlled 'close' parishes, which often remained small, and 'open' ones, which were generally large and grew larger. In the close parish the inhabitants' housing, religion, political views and social habits might all be subject to some degree of influence by squire or parson, even if it were indirect influence. The object might be to restrict the numbers of the inhabitants in order to keep down the burden of poor rates, or it might be to keep it a respectable community by deliberately excluding families who were notorious for

Godlessness, petty crime and violence. The villagers were expected to conform to the political and religious views of the landowner, and sometimes a public house was not allowed; or if allowed, was strictly regulated.

The open village, by contrast, was often a populous and expanding place, where the increase in numbers represented profitable new custom for a multitude of small builders, publicans and shopkeepers. It was often marked by radicalism in politics and religion, where Dissenting chapels had far more sway than did the parish church. Some of these villages, too, were the homes of gangs of robbers, sheep-stealers, footpads and poachers, and daily life was punctuated by irruptions of violent assaults and drunkenness. Each set of inhabitants looked with disdain on the other: the estate workers and farm labourers of the close village thought themselves above the disgraceful ways of the open one; the tradesmen, craftsmen and labourers of the open village scorned the tugging of forelocks which they believed to be obligatory in the close counterpart, valued their independence, and laughed at those who dared not blow their nose without the squire's permission.[12]

Reduction of the widespread offence of poaching might be one reason for the squire's careful control of his close parish. As shooting, and its corollary, game preservation, increased in popularity in the eighteenth and nineteenth centuries, so poaching was the more perceived as a pernicious crime which had to be put down. Before the legalising of the sale of game in 1831, a succession of Acts had imposed increasingly savage penalties on those caught taking game, and even after this date poaching offences remained common indictments in the courts. Previously, neither legal frightfulness nor private terror had proved effective in discouraging this particular disregard for property. Before they were prohibited in 1827, some landowners had recourse to such fearful instruments as mantraps and spring guns, capable of maiming and killing. Paradise Place, an estate near Canterbury, exhibited a notice warning the public of the danger to trespassers. 'A pretty idea it must give us of Paradise', growled a sardonic Cobbett, when he rode by in the September of 1823, 'to know that spring guns and steel traps are set in it.'[13] Owners joined together to form societies to share the cost of bringing prosecutions under the Game Laws, as well as for prosecution of other offences, and some employed private police forces. The numbers of gamekeepers increased, even after the eventual establishment of publicly provided police forces in the counties. Indeed, the peak in the numbers of gamekeepers was not reached until the early years of the present

century, and by 1911 there were twice as many gamekeepers in the rural districts as there were country policemen.[14]

The difficulties of protecting the property of landowners and farmers intensified as populations rose in towns and countryside alike. The worst depredations on game, indeed, were not committed by individual countrymen but by gangs of poachers based in the larger villages and industrial towns. Such gangs were often numerous, armed and organised, and were concerned not with filling the cottage cookpot but with taking large, regular bags which could be profitably sold in distant markets, especially London. And from the late eighteenth century onwards the attacks on rural property, more especially in East Anglia and southern counties, were extended to the burning of haystacks, destruction of barns and machinery, and the killing and maiming of farm livestock. There was no way of completely protecting property that was necessarily scattered and exposed from the alarming attentions of the discontented, and the coming in of the new police force in the middle decades of the century had little effect in this respect. Indeed, so hostile were some county notables towards the new police that even as late as 1856 only about a half of the counties could boast of having a force. By that time, however, the peak of rural crime was past, and the exceptional and frightening lawlessness that had marked eastern and southern districts since the late eighteenth century had subsided, leaving theft and drunkenness as the most persistent of the older types of offences.[15]

However, the causes of this unrest, and the failure in many areas of landowners to control rural crime, raise large and complex issues which we must consider separately. But, very clearly, the existence of widespread poaching, and the upsurge of the more serious arson and destruction of farm property, show that landowners' social control suffered severe limitations, and that when major breaches of the peace occurred there was no alternative but to seek the support of the government and, more particularly, of the troops.

LANDOWNERS AND AGRICULTURE

The most obvious of landowner influence lay in the sphere of agriculture. It is thought that the proportion of land occupied by tenants, rather than by small owner-occupiers, may have risen from about 70 per cent in the late seventeenth century to as high as about 85 or 90 per cent at the end of the eighteenth century. Subsequently the

figure did not change very much for another hundred years, although there were always wide regional variations, small owner-occupiers being numerous in some districts and almost non-existent in others. The landowners' near monopoly of the farmland meant that they were uniquely situated to exert influence on the character and efficiency of agriculture, but it appears that, with a relatively small number of exceptions, they preferred in general to play a somewhat passive role. This seems to have applied also to the institutional owners, the Crown, Church, London hospitals, and Oxford and Cambridge colleges, which generally followed policies similar to those of private proprietors.

There was of course a coterie of landowners who shared a great enthusiasm for the cause of agricultural improvement. They, together with large gentlemen-farmers, leading breeders, and publicists like Arthur Young, created experimental farms, spent their evenings reading, and perhaps writing, agricultural literature, initiated and supported local farmers' clubs, and were to be seen at the prestigious gatherings of leading spirits organised by the Duke of Bedford at Woburn and Thomas Coke at Holkham. It was they, or their successors, who helped establish the Smithfield Club, the Bath and West of England Society, and later the Royal Agricultural Society. One should be careful, however, not to exaggerate their numbers. Young complained bitterly of the paucity of the support given to his periodical, *The Annals of Agriculture* (which was published between 1784 and 1815), lamenting in 1791 that despite its value to gentry and farmers alike it had achieved a regular sale of only 350 copies.

But farmers were never a reading class of men, and more could be done to spread new ideas through practical example than via the printed page. To this end the great enthusiasts held their private shows, and many lesser figures established model farms where the latest crops, livestock and tools were tried out and demonstrated to the farmers. A few owners went to the trouble of importing from another part of the country new designs of tools and men used to working them; more authorised their land stewards to spread new ideas round the estate, while some farm agreements bound the tenant to follow the steward's advice in managing the farm. The 'stewards', later known as 'agents', were often key figures in bringing about local advances, and in the nineteenth century were influential in encouraging their employers to go in for subsoil drainage, up-to-date farm buildings, and leases that required tenants to follow certain rotations or utilise certain manures.

There is a good deal of evidence that the leading farmers, too, were themselves in the forefront of advance, making their own private agricultural tours to see other farmers' practices, and writing to one another about the results of their own innovations.[16] In this way they anticipated the overseas tours carried out by leading breeders of the present time, men who desire to find improved stock to cross with their own herds. In the past there was a great deal of backwardness and ignorant farming, as no doubt occasionally persists today. Agricultural experts of the eighteenth and nineteenth centuries drew a distinction between the enlightened and progressive large farmers (with some 300 acres or more) and the conservative and backward small ones (generally men with under 100 acres). It is evident, however, that the nature and efficiency of the farming had much to do with geographical and geological factors, the characteristics of the soils, and ease of access to good markets; and there were certainly important regional, and even local, differences.[17]

Landowners, too, drew a distinction between their large tenants and their small ones. The large tenants were carefully chosen, with particular attention given to their experience and their possession of sufficient capital for stocking the farm. Large farms had by definition substantial areas of land (up to 2,000 or 3,000 acres in some areas), a varied range of farm buildings, and a farmhouse that in some cases might well be comparable in size and appointments with the residences of country gentry. Large farms were consequently sufficiently valuable for landlords to take the trouble to make a detailed agreement with each tenant, lasting for perhaps fourteen or twenty-one years, and known as the long lease. Small farms, on the other hand, were of much less value and less care was taken in letting them. Frequently, a small tenant was succeeded by his son as a matter of course, or even by his widow or daughter. As a result, although small farms were usually let merely on an annual agreement or 'at will' (six months' notice), it was not uncommon for them to remain in the hands of the same families over very long periods, even for a century or more.

To what extent the leases on which large farms were let included requirements which made for improved farming is uncertain. There were invariably conventional clauses designed to protect the property from being despoiled by a bad tenant; but even where there were also clauses requiring the use of certain quantities of marl or manure, or particular rotations of crops, it is difficult to know how thoroughly these were enforced, if at all. Good tenants, it may be presumed, would farm well in any case, and with changing markets and prices

might find strict husbandry clauses unsuitable and restricting. It appears also that, with the great rise in prices during the Napoleonic Wars and the subsequent post-war depression, both landlords and tenants came to regard leases with distrust. A landlord who happened to let a farm for twenty-one years in, say, 1792, at what was then a good rent, would be chagrined to have lost the opportunity of making large rent increases over the highly inflationary period of the lease. Similarly, a tenant who took on a long lease at a high, fixed wartime rent in, say, 1812, would have made severe losses when prices and rents fell disastrously after 1813. Tenants in this position were in fact bankrupted and forced to give up their leases, and landlords found that the obligations of the lease seemed to fall only on them and not on the tenants. To sum up, it is probable that, in general, landowners' leases for their large farms had at best only a minor influence on agricultural improvement.

Almost certainly more important was the tendency for landlords gradually to change the detailed composition of their farms. This came about because a 'farm' was not regarded as necessarily a unit that was sacrosanct, and it was seen to be convenient and profitable to take whole closes of enclosed land, or acreages in common fields, away from tenants who were inefficient, elderly or incapacitated, and transfer them to the holdings of more efficient, younger and more vigorous men. In this manner more land was put into the hands of the better farmers, and one must suppose that the average standard of farming on the estate would gradually improve. Another effect of these piecemeal transfers was slowly to raise the average size of the farms, and where the figures are available, historians have shown how a very considerable transformation could occur over periods of, say, thirty or fifty years. There can be no doubt that on some estates by the early nineteenth century the farms were on average very much larger than they had been a century earlier, and this, together with the care taken in selecting tenants for large farms, must have meant that a higher proportion of the land was in the hands of better-educated and progressive farmers.[18]

It is now generally accepted that the pace of agricultural improvement was slow and uncertain, and that the term 'agricultural revolution' is inappropriate for a process that stretched over more than two centuries. The earliest-known introduction of new fodder crops, designed to help farmers reduce fallowing, and to keep larger flocks and herds and hence increase their supplies of manure, occurred about the middle of the seventeenth century. Imports of clover and rye-grass seed from Holland came in regularly after 1620, and in a work

first published in 1650 Sir Richard Weston explained the value of clover and turnips, whose cultivation he had seen for himself in observing Flemish husbandry. Turnips, in fact, were already in use in Suffolk by about the time of Weston's publication, and had spread to east Norfolk by 1670. Rape or coleseed was cultivated in the Midlands by 1686, cabbages were in use as a field crop in the 1660s, and potatoes, grown in Lancashire by 1650, were fairly commonplace by 1690. Water meadows, provided in order to produce an early feed for the stock in the spring before the grass in the normal pastures was growing, were numerous in some parts of the country; and 'ley farming', the alternation of land between a succession of arable crops and a period under temporary grass, was practised in the Midlands before 1560.[19]

Other major developments, however, appeared later, in the course of the eighteenth and nineteenth centuries. Among these were the replacement of the unreliable turnip by the hardier swede and mangold; the gradual improvement of livestock by crossing the best types of existing breeds; and the enclosure between about 1760 and 1830 of the surviving common fields and commons, and of wastelands that were worth the cost of taking into cultivation. Three of the most important advances belong more specifically to the nineteenth century: the spread of a wide range of factory-made implements and machines; the introduction from mid-century of subsoil pipe or tile drainage for heavy lands; and the adoption of new effective manures, such as bone-meal, guano and, from 1843, the first widely used 'artificial' or chemical fertiliser, superphosphate of lime.[20]

The initiation and spread of these various advances was the work of many individuals, landowners, farmers, contemporary experts, and implement designers and makers in village workshops and town factories. Much of the necessary work of experimentation was carried out by farmers and breeders, a few of whom, like Jethro Tull, Robert Bakewell, George Culley and the Colling brothers, have received the accolade of a mention in the textbooks. But there were certainly a great many less well-known figures, such as those shadowy Midland breeders, Webster of Canley and Joseph Allom of Clifton, who had laid the foundations of improved livestock before Bakewell; or Arbuthnot and Ducket, two leading experimental farmers, whose names were coupled with that of Bakewell in a memoir written by Young in 1811. Many remain quite obscure, although perhaps meriting contemporary mention as being expert tenants of Coke of Holkham, or featuring in the tours of Arthur Young. An example of the latter is a certain Mr Dann, who farmed at Gillingham in

Kent. Dann evidently specialised in potatoes, using ashes brought from Chatham Barracks to improve his soil, and measuring carefully the produce of each of his fields to see which practices yielded the best results.[21]

Of course, some of the experimental enthusiasts visited by Young were far from obscure, and included famous noble proprietors and leading gentry, as well as less prominent independent gentleman farmers. These were the men who had not only the personal interest but also the money and leisure to try out new ideas. They made up the several hundred visitors who gathered at the annual 'sheep-shearings' or private shows held at Holkham and Woburn about the turn of the nineteenth century. At these shows the latest implements were exhibited and trials made of different designs of ploughs, the best tups were auctioned off for the next season's breeding, and prizes awarded for the best livestock on display. The organisation required to mount these shows, and the expense involved, were very considerable. For example, at the Woburn sheep-sheering held in June 1800, the attendance numbered several hundred, including a member of the royal family as well as English and foreign aristocrats, and the host, the Duke of Bedford, gave public breakfasts and entertained the larger part of two hundred guests to dinner during the four days of the meeting.[22]

In addition, numbers of great proprietors, such as Lords Rocking-ham, Egremont, Portland and Clarendon, kept experimental farms, partly for their own amusement, partly for the more practical purpose of interesting their tenants in new practices. Probably, however, it was only the larger, wealthier of the tenants who reaped much advantage from the examples put before them. The smaller tenants had neither the time nor the resources of money and labour to seek out new designs of implements, experiment with new crops, or go in for costly pedigree stock. They were necessarily cautious and conservative, believing that it was one thing for a great duke or wealthy squire to risk his money on these things, quite another for a working farmer who had but little in his pocket and a family to keep. Moreover, many of the new practices were labour-intensive, involving time-consuming tasks such as the singling, hoeing, harvesting and carting of root crops, or the preparation of a fine tilth in order to put land down to a ley. But the precarious nature of the small man's finances was the over-riding difficulty. Arthur Young showed appreciation of this point when he remarked that, to gain acceptance, any new practice had to be shown not only to work but also to pay. Farmers would not interest themselves in ideas that were not practical nor likely to produce a

return in hard cash. Hence his accounts of farming experiments were accompanied by detailed figures showing the cost and profit involved.[23]

There were, furthermore, practical problems affecting the spread of new ideas, difficulties which went far to justify the farmers' caution. Some of the new crops, like turnips and potatoes, could be grown satisfactorily only on well-drained light soils. Turnips also were liable to damage by pests and were likely to rot in the ground in a winter of sharp frosts and sudden thaws, while the continued cultivation of clover, it became realised, made the soil 'clover-sick' and unable to bear a good crop. On heavy soils, too, it was thought necessary to retain the fallow course in order to have the opportunity of thoroughly cleaning the land of weeds in preparation for the next grain crop. The improved livestock, moreover, were by no means perfect. Bakewell's New Leicester sheep matured early, it was true, but their meat was fat and their wool unremarkable, while they were not suited to exposed situations where the weather was harsh.[24]

The new implements, again, were sometimes more trouble than they were worth, especially when they had to be made locally by a blacksmith or carpenter new to the task and the result was imperfect. When in 1748 the Swedish visitor Pehr Kalm saw a seed drill demonstrated on the farm of William Ellis, a well-known farming writer of the period, he commented that a whole afternoon was spent in tinkering with the device, and in the end not so much as a pint of seed was sown.[25] Those farmers large enough to employ hired men also had good grounds for scepticism. The farmworkers were often fiercely conservative, and set their faces obstinately against any tool or mode of cultivation to which they were strangers. They, too, had to be convinced that novelties were practical, and they were often dangerously inept in their handling of valuable stock and carelessly clumsy with implements. Young once remarked that for him to be assured that a new device was of use it had to be picked up and thrown down on the ground with as much force as a man could muster. If it survived this treatment then it might possibly be of service.

There must, therefore, be room for doubt whether the efforts of landowners to advance agricultural techniques bore much fruit. Even as late as 1850, as we have seen, Sir James Caird found numerous instances of backwardness in English agriculture. The shows and societies, the landowners' experimental farms, and the pioneering work of large gentlemen farmers benefited only a small, if growing, proportion of the country's farming. More, perhaps, was achieved through the private visits made to well-known farmers by some

leading experts, men who conveyed through correspondence with friends their observations and the results of their own experiments.

If the work of experimentation and dissemination of new ideas was slow to take effect, there was indeed a more sweeping change which in the course of some seventy years affected a substantial part of the farmland. This, of course, was enclosure. It proceeded in three ways: first, by piecemeal creation of closes from land taken out of common fields by its owners, a process which already by 1750 had halved the size of common fields in some villages; secondly, by private agreements between proprietors, leading to the enclosure of whole parishes; and thirdly, by private Acts of Parliament which authorised the enclosure by nominated commissioners of the remaining common fields and commons, and often also of the waste lands within a parish. We do not have figures for the first two forms of enclosure, but collectively they must have affected some hundreds of thousands of acres at least. It appears, for instance, that as much as some 70,000 acres may have been enclosed by agreement in the single county of Nottinghamshire during the eighteenth and early nineteenth centuries.[26] For the enclosures carried out by Acts of Parliament we have now a highly reliable figure, some 8.4m acres in England and Wales, amounting to nearly 24 per cent of the total acreage.[27] Taken together, therefore, we are discussing the modernising of the cultivation of perhaps as much as a third or more of the farmland.

The agricultural consequences of the abolition of common fields and common grazings were significant, although in some areas of poorly drained clays it still remained as difficult to introduce new rotations after enclosure as it had been before. Generally, however, the farmers benefited from having their land in compact blocks of enclosed fields rather than in scattered open strips, and from having exclusive rights over the land instead of sharing it with the community. The over-riding advantage was their new ability to use the land in whatever way was most profitable. Thus, where the soils allowed, old, worn-out arable, under the plough for centuries, could be put down to permanent pasture or to leys, while over-grazed and weedy commons could be ploughed up for additional crop land. The fact that rents rose substantially after enclosure is a broad, if inexact, indication of the value to the farmers of the new conditions; and even where no change in the farming occurred, the occupiers were still willing to pay more for their newly compact holding than when it was scattered and subject to the restraints of the old system.

Many of the parliamentary enclosures, especially those after 1790, were concerned with common pasture, and especially the bringing

into cultivation of waste lands. Some 5m acres of former commons, heath, moor, hill and fell, were enclosed, and even if some of this land passed out of cultivation again when the high prices of the Napoleonic Wars came to an end, nevertheless the newly enclosed waste represented a large accession to the farming resources of the country, a major help in feeding a population which trebled in number between 1750 and 1850.[28]

It is much less easy to generalise about the social consequences of enclosure. It can be said with some assurance that enclosure did not usually result in any sweeping change in the size of the farms, for it was always difficult to find farmers with sufficient experience and capital to take on large concerns. Engrossment, as we have seen, was a slow and gradual process, and one which was proceeding in all kinds of villages, old-enclosed, newly enclosed, and those still retaining their common fields. More problematic is the fate of the small owner-occupiers and cottagers. Some authorities believe that small owners were adversely affected by the costs of carrying out a parliamentary enclosure (which varied over the period from an average of about 10s to 65s per acre, plus the considerable cost of fencing), and their argument is supported by evidence, of rather doubtful reliability, taken from land tax records. These records appear to show a large turnover of small owners to have occurred at or soon after an enclosure, but there is no direct evidence that the turnover was in fact due to owners being unable to pay the costs. The costs were not always high in absolute terms, and were generally low in relation to the increased value of the land that enclosure brought about. Further, there were several possibilities of borrowing the money, most obviously by obtaining private loans from relations, friends and neighbours, a practice which we know to have been widespread long before the time of parliamentary enclosures. The apparent high turnover of small owners may have been due in part to sales of land by absentee owners as well as by resident ones; and the purchasers no doubt included other local owners, as well as neighbouring tradesmen and craftsmen who sought a few acres for use with their business, or who simply wanted a sound investment.

It does seem likely, however, that very small owners, men with only a few acres, might have found that after enclosure their holding was no longer viable now that the possibility of grazing on the common had gone. Unless the holding could be used for some specialised or intensive form of production – for dairying, market gardening, or poultry, for example (which would depend on ease of access to good markets) – it might have yielded only a part-time

43

occupation and an inadequate income, though this was also very often the case before enclosure. One of the difficulties in coming to any conclusion on this aspect is that units of ownership were not necessarily the same as units of occupation. In other words, we know that there were small owners who were at the same time considerable tenants, occupying much more rented land than they owned. In such cases the loss of the common grazing might not be very important. Further, there were owners who might have only a few acres in the parish being enclosed, but who had considerably more land in a neighbouring parish.

The position of the cottagers is even more difficult to clarify. Before the enclosure numbers of them, perhaps the majority, had access to the common, in order to keep a cow or perhaps a few sheep on it, to find feed for pigs, gather fuel, collect berries and herbs, and possibly other small uses. The enclosure of the common would of course mean the end of these supplements to a cottager's life, though it has to be remembered that many commons were already much over-grazed before enclosure, or their use strictly stinted or controlled – and the inadequacy of the common was, indeed, often a prime reason for bringing an enclosure in the first place. The effects of the enclosure were as varied as local circumstances differed. The common was not invariably enclosed; and where it was, there might still remain waste land which served some of the same purposes. In some enclosures, also, land was set aside to provide fuel for the poor, and occasionally cow pastures were established which cottagers could rent. If one looks at Young's lengthy and detailed account of the effects in Norfolk it becomes apparent that the lot of the cottagers varied greatly from one place to another: often they were worse off, having once been able to keep cows but now no more, though sometimes they were in a better position to do this than before, and in other instances their conditions were little changed.[29]

In practice it is difficult to distinguish the overall effects of enclosure from those of the other important changes that were going on at the same time. The Midlands, the part of the country in which parliamentary enclosures of common fields and commons were most concentrated, were becoming industrialised, and apart from the growth of large urban centres such as Birmingham and the Black Country, the Stoke-upon-Trent district, and cities like Nottingham and Leicester, many former agricultural villages became dominated by industrial occupations. Furthermore, the growth of the population after 1750 meant that, in industrialising areas, surplus farmworkers could find jobs in other types of work; while where this outlet was too

far off, the rural surplus tended to stagnate in the villages, creating a swollen labour force that agriculture could no longer absorb entirely. Indeed, where a village had been enclosed and the new freedom of land use led to an expansion of more intensive arable farming, or where large areas of waste were brought into cultivation, enclosure must have increased agricultural employment and helped relieve the labour surplus which was developing.

Of course, each village was in some sense unique: the local circumstances which influenced population growth, opportunities for migration, and access to alternative occupations – all varied from place to place. Consequently, it is simplistic to ascribe to enclosure changes, good or bad, which may well have arisen from quite other causes. The enclosures of this period, it must be remembered, affected considerably less than half the country, and further, varied greatly in intensity from region to region, some districts experiencing little or none. In so far as it can be shown that enclosure resulted in socially harmful consequences – and it is interesting that in some villages a lingering folk memory attributed later poverty and landlessness to an enclosure of a hundred years before – we should be careful to weigh the balance of advantage and disadvantage. There were clear gains in the increased production of food and raw materials at a time of rising population and urban growth, and also in the improved efficiency of agriculture and its greater responsiveness to markets. There may have been social loss in the possible decline of small owners and, more certainly, a deterioration in the cottagers' standard of living. But progress can rarely, if ever, be achieved without some casualties, and it is evident that the old farming system could not have coped with the rapid growth of rural population: more and more cottagers would have had to be excluded from commons that were often already inadequate in the early decades of the eighteenth century.

So far as there was social deprivation, the fault must lie mainly with the landowners, who usually, though not invariably, were the initiators of enclosure. The lure of higher rents, a material gain which could be coupled with the unselfish cause of agricultural improvement, were the justifications for the destruction of the old communal system. It may be concluded that enclosure was in some places one element in the deterioration of social relations in the countryside which began to be evident about the close of the eighteenth century, and which culminated in the rick-burning and machine-smashing of 1830. But, again, it is important to remind oneself that enclosure was only one strand in the diverse web of rural social relations, and not necessarily the most common or most

45

vital one. It is indeed highly significant that the riots of 1830 broke out in rural areas little affected by enclosure. Rural society was an enormously varied and rapidly changing organism, and tempting as simplification may be, we must accept its highly complex reality.[30]

NOTES

1. **J. A. Chartres** and **G. L. Turnbull,** 'Country tradesmen' and 'Country craftsmen', in **G. E. Mingay** (ed.), *The Victorian Countryside,* Routledge & Kegan Paul, 1981, I, pp. 304, 321.
2. **R. J Olney** (ed.), *Labouring Life on the Lincolnshire Wolds: a Study of Binbrook in the Nineteenth Century,* Society for Lincolnshire History and Archaeology, Sleaford, 1973, pp. 8, 12–13.
3. **David W. Howell,** 'The landed gentry of Pembrokeshire in the eighteenth century', Unpublished MA thesis, University of Wales, 1965, pp. 271–2.
4. **Eric J. Evans,** 'Some reasons for the growth of English rural anti-clericalism, c.1750–c.1830', *Past and Present,* **LXVI,** pp. 84–109.
5. **J. Beresford,** *Woodforde,* Oxford University Press, 1935, pp. 105, 158, 391, 484.
6. **David W. Howell,** *Patriarchs and Parasites: the Gentry of South-west Wales in the Eighteenth Century,* Cardiff, University of Wales Press, 1986, p. 206.
7. **G. E. Mingay,** *English Landed Society in the Eighteenth Century,* Routledge & Kegan Paul, 1963, pp. 208–9, 271.
8. *Ibid.,* pp. 208, 271.
9. *Ibid.,* p. 287.
10. *Ibid.,* pp. 285–6; Beresford, *Woodforde,* pp. 142, 171–2, 176–7.
11. Berkshire Record Office, D/EPb E4 f.120; E7 f.75.
12. **M. A. Havinden,** *Estate Villages: a Study of the Berkshire Villages of Ardington and Lockinge,* Lund Humphries, 1966 and 'The model village', in Mingay, (ed.), *Victorian Countryside,* II, pp. 414–27.
13. **William Cobbett,** *Rural Rides,* Everyman edn, 1912, I, p. 249.
14. See **F. M. L. Thompson**, 'Landowners and the rural community', in Mingay (ed.), *The Victorian Countryside,* II, p. 459.
15. **David Jones,** 'Rural crime and protest', in Mingay (ed.), *Victorian Countryside,* II, pp. 567, 573.
16. **Stuart Macdonald,** 'The diffusion of knowledge among Northumberland farmers, 1780–1815', *Agricultural History Review,* **XXVII,** 1, 1979, pp. 30–9.
17. **G. E. Mingay,** 'The size of farms in the eighteenth century', *Economic History Review,* 2nd ser., **XIV,** 1961–2, pp. 471–2; **J. Caird,** *English Agriculture 1850–51,* 1852, new edn, Frank Cass, 1968, pp. 19, 23, 42–3, 78, 118, 122, 142.
18. Mingay, 'Size of farms', pp. 478–88; **J. R. Wordie,** 'Social change on the Leveson-Gower estates, 1714–1832', *Economic History Review,* 2nd ser., **XXVII,** 4, 1974, pp. 595–605.

19. **Eric Kerridge,** *The Agricultural Revolution,* Allen & Unwin, 1967, pp. 194, 197, 270–80; **G. E. Mingay,** *The Agricultural Revolution: Changes in Agriculture 1650–1880,* A. & C. Black, 1977, pp. 19–23.
20. Mingay, *Agricultural Revolution,* pp. 27–50.
21. *Ibid.,* pp. 89–91.
22. *Ibid.,* pp. 68–75.
23. **G. E. Mingay** (ed.), *Arthur Young and his Times,* Macmillan, 1975, p. 16.
24. *Ibid.,* pp. 58, 69.
25. Mingay, *Agricultural Revolution,* p. 26; **Pehr Kalm,** *Kalm's Account of his Visit to England on his way to America in 1748,* Macmillan, 1892, p. 341.
26. **J. D. Chambers,** *Nottinghamshire in the Eighteenth Century,* 1st edn, 1932, 2nd edn, Frank Cass, 1966, Appendix II.
27. **John Chapman,** 'The extent and nature of parliamentary enclosure', *Agricultural History Review,* **XXXV,** 1, 1987, p. 28.
28. *Ibid.,* p. 29.
29. **Arthur Young,** *General View of the Agriculture of Norfolk,* 1804, pp. 75–181.
30. Cf. **K. D. M. Snell,** *Annals of the Labouring Poor: Social Change and Agrarian England 1660–1900,* Cambridge University Press, 1985, pp. 138–227.

CHAPTER THREE

The Politics of Land

THE LANDED INTEREST THREATENED

The political power of the great Whig landowners of the eighteenth century rested in part on a succession of events which had advanced and bolstered their position: the 'Glorious Revolution' of 1688 which gave Parliament control of taxation and thus reduced the power of the Crown; and the Hanoverian succession of 1714 and defeat of the Jacobite insurrections of 1715 and 1745, which placed and maintained a Whig-installed monarchy on the throne. More fundamental to landowners' continuing political power, however, was their pre-eminence in wealth, and especially in that most respected and permanent form of wealth, land. And although numbers of landowners had significant incomes from urban properties, from mines and other industrial developments, investments in the Funds, and the salaries of public offices – nevertheless it was, above all, the rents of their landed estates which formed the principal support of their exalted rank, their social status and their political influence.

Between the middle of the eighteenth century and the end of the Napoleonic Wars farming prospered almost continuously, and, as a result, the rents of land rose to unprecedented levels. It is probable that most landowners found their rent rolls swelling by some 40 or 50 per cent in the forty years between 1750 and 1790; while subsequently, during the war period itself, their rents rose even more rapidly and on average probably doubled in the space of a quarter of a century. After 1815, however, farming conditions proved to be much less favourable, and rents either made no further progress or, in some areas, declined by perhaps as much as a quarter below the wartime peak. Taking the hundred years from 1750 to 1850 as a whole, the most recent

estimates suggest that agricultural output in general at least doubled, while rents rather more than doubled. Despite this prolonged era of expansion, however, the share of agriculture in the country's national product declined. This was in part an inevitable consequence of the rapid progress made by industry and commerce – a response to the growth of markets at home and abroad and the changes in technology which speeded up and cheapened output in important sectors of industry. Further, with the prolonged period of warfare, the share of the national product taken up by government and defence was also increased. It is estimated that about 1770 agriculture's share of the British national product may have been about 45 per cent, while by 1811 it had fallen to 36 per cent, though of a much larger national product. By 1851 agriculture was producing only a little over a fifth of the national product.[1]

A similar change may be seen if one considers the proportion of the British labour force which was directly supported by agriculture. We do not know with any precision what this figure was in the mid-eighteenth century, but it was very likely of the order of 45 or even 50 per cent. The early censuses of the nineteenth century are not very accurate, though the estimate in the first census, that of 1801, is 35.9 per cent, while the much more reliable figure from the census of 1851 is 21.7 per cent.[2] This substantial fall in the proportion occurred despite some rise in the actual numbers employed. The 1831 census shows the numbers of males employed in agriculture to be something over 1,200,000, while the 1841 census produced a figure of 1,434,000, and that of 1851 1,788,000. The number fell off slightly in 1861 and continued to fall subsequently, and by the end of the century the figure was 1,339,000, about a quarter below that of 1851. Females employed in agriculture, 229,000 in 1851, declined much more rapidly, by as many as 143,000, or 62 per cent, by 1901.[3] By 1901 the total numbers employed in British agriculture amounted to a little less than 9 per cent of the national labour force, and were then of the same order of importance as other major industries such as transport and communication, metal manufacturing and engineering, and building and construction.

Before 1850 the economic decline of agriculture was a relative one: it was expanding both in output and in employment, but other large sectors of the economy were growing more rapidly. After 1850 this situation changed: from that date agricultural output was still rising, as subsoil drainage, new fertilisers and machinery helped to improve efficiency. But in terms of employment, agriculture was shrinking both relatively and absolutely. The political position of the

landed interest – the landowners, farmers and professions dependent on land – was thus gradually undermined, although the decline in the political significance of landowners was a remarkably slow and gradual process. As late as 1892, 42 per cent of the new recruits to Parliament had landed backgrounds and, although the middle class were beginning to break through into the Cabinet after 1868, between 1874 and 1895 the landed Ministers still retained a majority.[4]

In the eighteenth century, as we have seen, landowners dominated both Parliament and government. Once the Hanoverian succession was regarded as inescapably permanent, there was little to unite the Tory gentry except their common opposition to increased taxation, more specifically the Land Tax, which symbolised the financial burden of wars fought to preserve the balance of power on the Continent and to advance the opportunities for profit of the commercial interest. The Tory country gentlemen, about a hundred strong in the Commons of mid-century, formed a kind of permanent opposition. For the most part they valued too greatly their independence of Ministers and Court to be involved in government, while their concentration on the mundane matters that affected their county interests generally over-rode any concern for what might be termed the grand affairs of state.

Government itself was a kaleidoscope of shifting alliances of powerful Whig factions – Whigs in office and Whigs out of office – divided and brought together by personal hostility and opportunities rather than by differences in principles or doctrine. The leaders were great noble proprietors of territorial empires who, with the prime exception of the two Pitts, headed administrations to which eminent members of the Court or King's party – rarely out of office – gave a degree of stability. Though it is true that the direct political power of the great Dukes was quite limited – in 1760 the Duke of Bedford controlled only four boroughs, the Duke of Devonshire three – nevertheless they and their kind, and most notably the Duke of Newcastle (who controlled seven seats), each stood at the centre of intricate webs of private patronage, producing a political influence greatly disproportionate to their share of the country's land. This network of personal obligations gave them command of the support of lesser figures who held strong regard for the magnates' wealth and long connection with government, and who were bound in a worldly loyalty cemented by favours disposed in the past and favours hoped for in the future. The country houses of these aristocrats – Bowood, Stowe, Woburn, Euston, Houghton, Rainham and Holkham – were the real centres of power and of decision making. Eighteenth-century

England, as R. J. White observed, 'might be regarded as a federal republic of country houses where politics were canvassed, governments made and unmade, alliances and desertions planned and executed'.[5]

The tiny numbers of eighteenth-century electors meant that, in general, they could easily be managed by those who had the ambition and the means. The county electorate (returning a total of ninety-two Members) is estimated at about 160,000, and the total borough electorate (returning 408 Members) at slightly more than half that number. Thus the Commons were elected by only some 245,000 people out of a total population approaching 7 millions. Indeed, only twenty-two of the boroughs had as many as 1,000 or more electors, and the miniscule electorates of some boroughs made it feasible for magnates to buy up sufficient town properties to secure their grip on them. The much more numerous county electorates, averaging 3,000 or 4,000, were a different proposition. In numbers of counties the great landowners, together with their gentry allies, commanded sufficient influence to be certain of at least one of the two seats, but in some parts of the country, in the West and South-west, and also some Midland shires, it was the old-established wealthy gentry who had control, and there a few leading families might represent a particular county over very long periods.

In both boroughs and counties the very high cost of fighting an election led to the conclusion of pacts under which rival factions agreed to share the seats, without a contest, and in the seven general elections held between 1760 and the end of the century only one in ten of all the seats was disputed. Nevertheless, there were instances where the many thousands of pounds laid out in the rents forgone by giving the tenants 'good bargains', and the transporting, entertaining and direct bribing of electors, brought the contestants mounting debts and straitened finances, leading eventually to a crisis when land had to be sold. The Myddeltons of Chirk Castle, for example, disputed the Denbighshire seats with other important local families over a very protracted period, and the costs of persistent indulgence in electioneering, together with other forms of extravagance and a reckless attitude towards accumulation of debt, ultimately forced them to part with some of their lands. By 1797 Richard Myddelton was obliged to face reality, his debts totalling over £174,000, to be met from a gross estate income which, after making payments of interest, amounted to under £5,500 a year.[6]

Despite their ability to control seats, landowners' domination of Parliament was never complete. Up to 1761, certainly, over three-fifths of the Commons consisted of Irish peers, the sons of

English and Scottish peers, wealthy gentry and 'independent country gentlemen'. There were, however, some 150 Members who were principally merchants, army or navy officers, or lawyers – though it is true that many of them had connections with the aristocracy and with land. After 1761 the numbers of merchants and lawyers tended to rise in parallel with the expansion of markets and the growth of the middle classes, and by the early nineteenth century merchants had come to hold about a quarter of the seats. Nevertheless, the old connections with land remained, and in 1832, on the eve of the first parliamentary reform, it could still be said that about three-quarters of the Members were concerned mainly, or in part, with land.[7]

Although land remained firmly entrenched in Parliament and government, the political position of the landed interest was being slowly eroded. Among the changes which contributed to this weakening were the relative decline of the importance of agriculture in the national economy, referred to above, and the corresponding rise of industrial and mercantile cities: London, as of old, but now accompanied by a number of new 'wens' in Cobbett's scornful phrase. Already in 1801 Birmingham, Liverpool and Manchester each housed well over 70,000 people – Liverpool over 80,000; thirty years later, Birmingham had more than doubled to 144,000 and Liverpool topped 200,000, with Manchester only 20,000 behind. These were only the more outstanding examples of the effects of the changing employment and location of much of the population: there were others that were on the same upward trend – Leeds, Bristol and Sheffield, for instance, while not forgetting Edinburgh and Glasgow. Britain was well on its way to becoming a predominantly industrial and urban country; and a political structure that gave representation to sleepy country towns and obscure fishing villages, but not to the new bustling centres of wealth, could not be considered anything but archaic.

Moreover, the landed interest was less unified than in the past. The petty landowners, the small freeholders who between them owned perhaps some 15 per cent of all the land, were no longer quite as quiescent as had been their wont. They had in the past been much ignored and despised. They were shut out of the Commons by the rule that required a Member to own land worth £600 a year (implying in the eighteenth century a minimum property of some 600–1,200 acres). They were even prohibited from shooting game on their own land, unless that land were worth at least £100 a year. But in the later years of the eighteenth century the freeholders showed signs of developing an independent spirit. Both in the counties and in the towns meetings were convened from which flowed a

stream of representations to government concerning waste, taxes and inefficiency. During the disasters of the American War the criticisms grew fierce, and an attempt was made, unsuccessful as it proved, to organise the 16,000 Yorkshire freeholders into a permanent reform association. In truth, there was as yet little conviction that the existing institutions needed radical reform, and the taste for greater democracy and more independence was still not widely established. Indeed, the subsequent excesses of the French Revolution gave grounds for caution, not to say reaction, and a wider satisfaction with the superiority of the British constitution.

It was during the French Wars and their aftermath, however, that the landed interest experienced a decline in popular acceptance of their position in politics and society. As we have seen, rents, the main source of most landowners' incomes, had tended to rise substantially after about 1760, rose very sharply during the war years, probably doubling on average, and fell only to a limited extent in the post-war depression. In the 1820s and after rents were still very much in excess of pre-war figures. The taking of increased rents was seen not as a justified upward adjustment to much higher levels of agricultural prices – and rents had often been very low before 1790 – but rather as an exploitation of the wartime shortages, to the detriment of farmers and consumers. The abolition in 1815 of the wartime income tax, and the passing in the same year of a new, highly protective Corn Law, could also be portrayed as unjust exploitation of the taxpayer and consumer; and the new Corn Law, in particular, was the occasion of considerable unrest. Further, in the post-war period the largest element in government spending consisted of payments of interest on the national debt, much swollen by the wartime borrowing. This meant that through the medium of the budget a transfer was made of income away from the public in general, those who paid the numerous indirect taxes on articles of consumption, to the holders of government bonds, those who were the major recipients of government spending, and who, after 1815, paid no income tax. This was the basis for Cobbett's unceasing attacks on 'fund lords' and 'tax-eaters'.

In fact, the holders of the national debt made up a group far wider than merely landowners, and indeed there is evidence that many landowners held relatively few government bonds, or even none at all. Nevertheless, the landed interest had to give way before the gathering storm. The agitation, which went back to the days of Wilkes and of Wyvill's county associations, was stirred afresh by the rumblings of the corresponding societies and the demand for universal suffrage which Tom Paine had led. In the rising industrial

towns there grew up, too, a middle-class sentiment in favour of more direct representation of commercial and manufacturing interests. And there was some response: enquiries were made into the working of government departments, leading to some abolition of sinecures and a declining role of placemen in pre-reform Parliaments.

Despite the ground-swell of reform and the disturbances which surrounded the presentation of the Reform Bill, the resulting reform of 1832 was in fact a highly conservative measure. The new post-1832 electorate still represented only about the same proportion of the increased population – under 5 per cent – as had existed over a hundred years before. Some concessions were made to the increased importance of the owners of industrial and commercial property, and some new industrial towns gained direct representation for the first time. But the franchise still rested on a claim to property, and was very far indeed from Paine's universal suffrage. There was no general belief in democracy among either the country landowners or the owners of urban assets. Democracy, indeed, was seen as inimical to all forms of property, not excepting the national debt. The reform, according to Grey, was consequently 'the most aristocratic measure that was ever proposed in Parliament', and the reformed Parliament, commented Greville, turned out to be 'just like any other'.[8] Although the middle classes were brought formally into the constitution, they were still subordinate to the landowners. Some infamous 'rotten boroughs', it is true, had been abolished, but the county constituencies were increased, and a large number of country pocket boroughs survived the reform. The landed interest had retreated, but only so far as to quieten the current agitation. Parliament and government remained very much in landowners' hands.[9]

THE CORN LAWS

It was the extremely limited nature of the parliamentary reform that led to a shift in the direction of the radical attack, away from Parliament towards the Corn Laws. It is important to be clear, however, that it was no longer the highly protective – and largely ineffective – Corn Law of 1815 that was at issue. That Law had been replaced in 1828 by a new measure, which substituted a sliding scale for the absolute protection offered by the former Act when the home price of wheat was below 80s a quarter. From 1828 the amount of duty levied on imported corn varied with the price ruling in the home markets. Nevertheless, the 1828 Law was still protective, if

less so than that of 1815. Little foreign corn would come in until the home price was in the region of 70s a quarter (the duty payable was 10s 8d at 70s, 6s 8d at 71s, 2s 8d at 72s, and only 1s when the home price reached 73s or more). In fact, over the fifteen years between 1828 and 1842 (when the scale of duties was reduced) the home price of wheat averaged about 58s 9d, and went over 70s in only one year of the period. The general effect, therefore, was that while the Corn Law kept prices higher than they would have been under free trade, it was nevertheless the size of the home harvest which basically determined the price of wheat. And at an average of a little over 61s a quarter for the whole period between 1815 and 1846, the home price of wheat ruled at about 25 per cent below the average of the war years, 1793–92, and some 30 per cent above the pre-war average of 1780–92.[10]

In practice, therefore, the price of wheat was rarely as high in the years after 1815 as during the wartime shortages. The level of 80s a quarter fixed by the Law of 1815 as the trigger for allowing in imports did not mean that the price at home was kept up to that figure: the price prevailing in the market depended mainly on the harvest and not the Corn Law. In fact, the price exceeded 80s in only two years – 1817 and 1818 – and was above 70s in only five of the thirty-one years between 1815 and 1845; in ten of them it was below 55s. Translated into the price of bread, the effects were further diminished: the four-pound loaf ranged between 7½d and 10½d, and averaged under 10d. In terms of the economic facts, therefore, there was little justification for the demand for abolition of the Corn Laws. True, corn prices would have been lower without them, and historians believe that before 1846 supplies of grain were available from the Continent, though it is uncertain how far home prices would have fallen under free trade. It has to be remembered that in 1851 agriculture was still by far the largest single source of employment, with over one in five of the labour force engaged in it, and the Corn Laws could thus be defended as promoting a major source of employment. Further, agriculture was not alone in enjoying protection from foreign competition: other large branches of the economy were also well protected.[11]

The demand for free trade was based less on the adverse economic effects of protection than on political motives and the contemporary theories concerning the 'natural laws' of economics. Before the late 1830s, while harvests were good, even the political voices were muted, and the forwarding of the argument depended on Benthamite Radicals who had imbibed their ideas of free trade from Ricardo. Although the landed interest as a whole took a reactionary stance, there were also

some thoughtful Whig landowners, like Earl Fitzwilliam, who had come to think that the Corn Laws were less crucial to landlords' interests than was commonly believed, and that they were imposing harmful effects on farmers and their labourers, while also increasing the costs of manufacturers by exerting an upward pressure on wages. But at this period these few advocates made little impression. The attention of Parliament and the public was fixed on other, more momentous issues of the day: Catholic emancipation, parliamentary reform, factory legislation, the Poor Law, municipal corporations. There was also the obstacle posed by a purely practical problem of public finance. In 1830 import duties produced as much as 43 per cent of the government's annual revenue, and it was clear that any major move towards free trade would necessitate replacing this income by some other large alternative source.[12]

The only real possibility, though one that seemed politically unthinkable, was to revive the income tax. At the time of its abolition in 1815 this much detested tax had produced a remarkably high proportion of the revenue, no less than 22 per cent. Its revival would provide the new revenue that might make it financially feasible to remove some major import duties, and in particular those on corn. But what government was prepared to incur the hostility and odium that restoration of this infamous impost would be bound to generate? Little or nothing could be expected of the weak Whig government that was elected in 1837, but it was just at this time that economic conditions began to change and provided the head of water that enabled the stream of free trade to run more strongly. The series of good harvests which had marked the mid-1830s came to an end: in 1837 the price of wheat rose by more than 7s over that of the previous year; in 1838 it rose again to over 64s, in 1839 to over 70s – the highest price since 1819 – and remained not much below this figure in both 1840 and 1841. The arguments against the Corn Laws were seen to be proven. Dear food reduced the purchasing power of the population for manufacturers, while our failure to buy the food exports of our foreign customers prevented them from buying our goods, and moreover, stimulated them to set up their own rival industries. Protection was blamed for the stagnation of British trade, and indeed there was much unemployment in the cotton districts, with starving operatives said to be existing on milk and boiled nettles and sitting at home on stones or boxes, having sold their furniture for food.[13]

The bad harvests led to an upsurge of corn imports, which averaged nearly 3m quarters a year between 1839 and 1842, compared with well under 1m quarters in 1834–36. Gold flowed abroad to pay for

the swollen imports of grain, and the drain of bullion weakened the banking system, causing bank failures and lack of credit. Meanwhile, in 1840, the government's Select Committee on Import Duties produced its famous *Report*. In essence the *Report* argued that many duties could be safely abolished because, in fact, almost all of the customs revenue was produced by only seventeen articles, of which corn and wool were two. In regard to the Corn Laws, the Committee held that foreign tariffs were raised in retaliation to our own, and that duties on imported grain raised the level of wages in Britain and therefore made our export prices less competitive. At the same time, and somewhat contradictorily, it was argued that removal of the Corn Laws posed no immediate threat to British agriculture since, even in years of bad harvests and high prices, experience had shown that imports were small relative to the home production; while in any case a free trade in grain would be healthy for the farmers, who would be encouraged to concentrate less on arable and to turn to other forms of production for which their land was better suited.[14]

The *Report* was in fact a highly biased and contentious document which emerged from a Committee packed with free traders who had placed much reliance on Board of Trade arguments that were supported by little firm evidence. The Committee even contrived to hold its meetings in the summer months when it was known that the few representatives of the landed interest were unlikely to be in London! Nevertheless, it was well received by both press and public, and was widely regarded as an authoritative statement of the rights and wrongs of the free trade controversy. It provided excellent ammunition for the propaganda of the Anti-Corn Law League, an organisation which from 1838 had taken up the cause of achieving free trade in corn. The League, based in Manchester, and heavily supported by the cotton interests, was an early example of the modern political propaganda machine. It employed peripatetic lecturers, published journals and pamphlets, and delivered parcels of tracts to electors. It encouraged its supporters to acquire the necessary property qualification to exercise their votes, and put up its own candidates to fight elections. Soon the thunder of its two great parliamentary leaders, Cobden and Bright, was heard in the Commons itself.[15]

The League, though remarkably effective, did not carry all before it. At a late stage a group of landowners, clergy and large tenant-farmers, first brought together by Robert Baker of Writtle in Essex, formed in 1844 an 'Anti-League' to counter the free trade agitation. Local groups of country gentlemen and farmers coalesced into a national

association, and succeeded in attracting the support of some large owners, such as the Duke of Richmond, while finding publicity in the columns of the *Farmer's Magazine*. The Anti-League took up the case for protection using the same weapons as the League, circulating tracts, employing lecturers, and intervening in the registration of electors; but generally its efforts were much less wholehearted. Its supporters among the gentry and farmers were conservative in their politics and saw an appeal to public opinion as constituting a dangerous precedent and a threat to the preservation of the 1832 settlement of the Reform issue. Consequently, the efforts of the Anti-League made only a limited impact on the Corn Law question, and its effect was mainly to strengthen the opposition to free trade within the Tory party in the Commons.[16]

There were other reasons why the propaganda of the League itself did not convince the nation at large. It was very evident that its political objectives were those of the middle class, and more particularly of the manufacturing and commercial middle class – it was no accident that its headquarters were in Manchester, and that it was associated with Manchester and all that the great cotton centre stood for. The politically aware among the working classes recognised that the League was essentially the organ of a sectional industrial interest, and regarded with suspicion its profession of a humanitarian concern for cheap bread. For them, cheap bread, indeed, might mean lower wages and competition from displaced farmworkers seeking jobs and housing in the towns. In London and the South, especially, the League never achieved much influence; and in Parliament, after all, the landed interest, despite 1832, was still very strongly entrenched.

Many factors in addition to the work of the League led to Repeal, and among the more powerful influences was that of economic depression. The severe downturn in economic activity which marked the years between 1839 and 1842 – the worst depression of the century – brought unemployment in the manufacturing districts and much distress, while the grievance of food continuing dear when conditions were so bad played into the hands of the League. These were the years of the 'Plug' riots in Lancashire, the Newport rebellion, and a peak in the Chartist agitation, as well as demands for factory reform and free trade. The troubles brought also a portentous change of government. The Whigs went out in 1842 leaving the new Tory government under Peel to deal with both the unrest and the legacy of a large budget deficit. New and bold initiatives were required in order to restore prosperity, and to stave off the potential threat that the disorders might swell and escalate into a full-blown revolution.[17]

One of Peel's immediate measures was a new Corn Law, an attempt to take the wind out of the League's sails. The 1842 Act greatly reduced the sliding scale of protective duties which had been in force since 1828, but though temporarily damping down the free trade agitation it failed to weaken its momentum completely. Another urgent concern of the new government was to put the national finances in order. To this end Peel took the critical step of re-introducing the income tax, which even after a lapse of nearly thirty years still aroused bitter memories among those who regarded an impost on earnings as pernicious, and the requirement to reveal the extent of their personal revenues as an outrageous intrusion on privacy. However, opinion was mollified by the proposal that the new tax was to be a temporary measure for only three years (an expectation not to be realised), while the standard rate was set at only 7d in the pound, as compared with the 2s in the pound which was in force between 1799 and 1802, and again between 1807 and 1815. Moreover, incomes of below £150 a year were exempt, effectively removing any liability from the working classes. The new tax produced about £5.5m a year, which represented a little under 10 per cent of the total revenue, and after 1843 this additional government income was sufficient not only to meet the budget deficit but also to provide a margin of surplus.[18]

The importance of the surplus was that it offered the means for making cautious experiments with reductions in duties. In 1845 it was still the position that customs and excise duties together produced a total of £38.5m, two-thirds of the entire revenue. Clearly, it was not possible to make sweeping changes in the duties with a surplus of only some £1.3m in 1844, and of £3.4m in 1845, but some reductions were possible, and indeed those that were made seemed to be beneficial. A combination of lower duties on imported raw materials and manufactured goods, together with better harvests, cheaper food and heavy investment in railway building, saw improvement in the economy, so much so that depression gave way to boom conditions. Peel was emboldened to extend the income tax for a further three years and proceed with further reductions in duties. The changes made, important as they were, nevertheless remained tentative and exploratory. The whole of the tariff reductions achieved between 1842 and 1846 cost the Exchequer only a little over £6m in revenue, and reduced the average proportion of customs duties in import prices only from 31 to 25 per cent.

The logic of the tariff changes, however, inevitably brought again into question the issue of the Corn Laws, the foundation stone of the protection system. The League saw that the government's cautious

measures were working in its direction and stepped up its agitation. Had matters worked out differently, it seems likely that Peel would not have conceded total repeal but might have worked towards a low, perhaps almost nominal, scale of duties on corn imports. In any event, ultimately it would have been morally and politically impossible to remove the protection of industry while leaving agriculture exempt from the full rigour of free competition. As it happened, of course, events hastened to bring matters to a head with unexpected suddenness. The potato blight, which struck widely in both Europe and North America, had particularly devastating effects on large numbers of the Irish population who relied heavily on the tuber for sustenance. Apart from ordering a temporary suspension of the Corn Laws and arranging some belated relief measures, the government seemed unable to respond speedily or adequately to the problems of the Irish famine. The difficulties were compounded by a poor harvest at home, the crop damaged by the rain that 'rained away the Corn Laws'.

But it was essentially political, rather than economic, pressures which brought Peel to contemplate a total repeal of the duties on corn. Together with many of his party, he saw the anti-Corn Law agitation as threatening the constitution, an attempt to mobilise public opinion and over-ride the sovereign power of Parliament. For this reason, it has been argued, he was determined that any change should be made by the existing Parliament, and not after a dissolution and a general election fought on the issue. It had to be Repeal, since suspension of the Corn Laws was only a temporary expedient and offered no solution to the political problem. Repeal was obviously a bitter pill for many landowners and farmers to swallow, and it was with the object of making it more palatable that Peel phased the disappearance of the duties over a period of three years from 1846, and also introduced cheap government loans for landowners to help them adjust to unaccustomed conditions of free trade.

Peel was himself an improving landlord, and he believed that the importance of protection for profitable farming was exaggerated. With many agricultural experts of the day, he argued that there was much scope for making English farming more efficient, and the cheap loans were intended to assist in this respect. Further, it was not the case that all farms were dependent on corn for their cash crop. Large parts of the country were given over to grass, for rearing, fattening and dairying; and as the great agricultural authority, James Caird, pointed out, the trends in consumption were moving more in favour of grassland products than corn – and this trend was to continue long after Repeal. Moreover, Peel believed that

wages did not move up and down with the price of bread, and the labouring classes would therefore benefit from Repeal. And even the corn farmers, if efficient, would benefit from the growth of the home market as population expanded and purchasing power was increased by more flourishing trade.

Politically, Repeal was a strategic retreat, a necessary sacrifice of the bastion of the Corn Laws in order to keep intact the main stronghold of aristocratic power and the limited constitution. Repeal, Peel said in 1847,

> tended to fortify the established institutions of this country, to inspire confidence in the equity and benevolence of the legislature, to maintain the just authority of an hereditary nobility, and to discourage the desire for democratic change in the Constitution of the House of Commons.[19]

And, in fact, Repeal diverted the demands of Radicals to less emotive objectives, such as reform of settled estates and an ending of the monopoly of land, while an extension of the franchise and further reform of Parliament were held back for another twenty years.

Not all the landed interest saw the matter in Peel's light. Opinion was divided; many of the large proprietors, and Members whose seats depended on aristocratic favour, voted for Repeal, while the country gentlemen and farmers, especially in the eastern arable areas of the country, maintained a narrow, reactionary view and clung to protection. The large owners, it might be argued, were in many cases accustomed to bearing the responsibilities of office and hardened to the necessities of politics, and could see the political advantages of Repeal as outweighing its economic disadvantages. Moreover, they were wealthier and more easily able to accept some fall in rents, though in many instances their estates were widely scattered and generally their rents were not always, in fact, much dependent on corn prices. In other instances they were little reliant on agriculture at all, drawing the greater part of their income from coal mines and ironworks, canal and railway shares, urban ground rents and government stock. However, it was not economic interests which necessarily determined their view of Repeal, for a number of the chief coal owners and urban proprietors were among those who regarded the ending of the Corn Laws as a great betrayal. Ultimately, political views were paramount. The division was primarily between those who saw that a concession was necessary to adjust to the industrial and commercial society that was growing up and to enable landowners to

retain their role in government; and those more conservative proprietors who believed that a weakening of the economic strength of the landed interest would inevitably bring about the eclipse of its political power.

DECLINE OF THE LANDED INTEREST

In the event, Repeal did not spell the immediate decline of arable farming. There was, it is true, a brief post-Repeal depression between 1849 and 1852, when the average price of wheat fell to below 40s the quarter for only the second time since 1780; but thereafter prices rose again, and in the twenty years after 1852 wheat averaged nearly 55s, only some 3s a quarter less than in the twenty years before Repeal. In the same post-Repeal era the prices of meat and dairy produce rose substantially, more than offsetting the small effect that, as yet, free trade had wrought on corn prices. Grassland farmers prospered, and those arable farmers who were sufficiently flexible in their production shifted more towards expanding the livestock element of their mixed farming output. Helped by cheap government loans, landlords and farmers together invested in subsoil drainage and new buildings, and with improved breeds of stock, better implements and new manures endeavoured to raise the yields of much of the farmland. Meanwhile, as prices remained favourable, the full economic effects of foreign competition were not apparent, and were not to be felt, in fact, until the painful era after 1878.

After Repeal the composition of both Parliament and governments changed quite slowly. True, the second Reform of Parliament in 1867 added nearly 1m new voters, mainly the better-off skilled artisans and tradesmen in the boroughs, to the miniscule electorate of 1832. Even then only a minority of the adult male population had been given the right to vote, though there was a further redistribution of seats and the urban franchise was now politically very significant. The third and last Victorian extension of the franchise came in 1884, bringing the property qualification for electors in the counties into line with that which had existed in the boroughs since 1867. The electorate was expanded from about 2.6m to some 4.4m, though the latter figure represented only 28.5 per cent of the adult population since not all males were as yet enfranchised, and until 1918 no females possessed the right to vote.

More significant for many landowners than the widened franchise was the abolition of the old public hustings, which had made it possible for pressure to be put on those electors who were tenants

of farms or of landowners' urban properties to vote as their landlord desired. The Secret Ballot Act of 1872 was a first, if ineffective, step towards ending owners' power to control elections, and the subsequent Corrupt Practices Act of 1883 went further towards breaking it completely. However, there remained many voters who continued to believe that there were means by which the landlord could find out how they had voted, and they tended to be cautious in exercising their new independence. But generally the country moved into an era when the influence of private dependence of electors, personal loyalties and local matters all declined, in favour of group loyalties and class solidarity, now influenced by national issues such as cheap food and more egalitarian taxation.

The attacks of nineteenth-century Radicals on the landed interest went considerably beyond the protection of corn. Before Repeal there was considerable agitation over the preservation of game. A succession of Game Laws, stretching back to the Middle Ages, had always restricted the right to hunt game, but with the popularity of shooting in the eighteenth century landowners became more interested in creating and maintaining preserves, and new Game Laws placed tighter limits on who might, and who might not, take deer, pheasants, partridges, hares and rabbits. From 1671 to 1831 freeholders of less than £100 a year, and leaseholders worth less than £150 a year, were barred by law, and as poaching increasingly caused depredations on game, so the penalties were raised to a ferocious level. An Act of 1803 made armed resistance to arrest punishable by death, and in 1817 armed poachers caught at night were liable to seven years' transportation. It was about this period also that some landowners reinforced the severity of the law by private means, not only by employing more gamekeepers and organising local associations of owners to bring prosecutions and offer rewards to informers, but also by setting dangerous spring-guns and mantraps in their woods. Intruders were likely to be fatally injured by accidentally tripping the wire of a gun, or be maimed for life by the teeth or heavy jaws of a steel trap, one type of which was euphemistically named the 'Bruiser'. Every year saw murderous affrays between keepers and gangs of poachers, men who hailed from nearby industrial towns and went poaching on a commercial basis for the profits to be made out of illegal sales of game.

The harshness of legal and extra-legal measures having failed to curb poaching, a more responsible approach to preservation set in among landowners from the later 1820s, associated with some falling-off in the popularity of shooting. Spring-guns were outlawed in

1827, and reduced penalties were introduced for convicted poachers in the following year, while in 1831 the sale of game was legalised and restrictions on the right to take game were relaxed. Poaching still thrived, nevertheless, and there was still the glaring anomaly of accused men appearing before magistrates who were themselves game preservers, perhaps the ones immediately involved. 'There is not a worse-constituted tribunal on the face of the earth', remarked Brougham in 1828, 'than that at which summary convictions on the Game Laws constantly take place; I mean a bench or a brace of sporting justices.'[20]

The sacrifice of justice to sport, and the association of landowners with heavy-handed protection of a species of property limited strictly to themselves, were only two of the adverse aspects of game preservation. For a long time past, the careful guarding of game birds, and of foxes too, was a source of grievance to small landowners and to tenants of estates whose crops were ravaged by pheasants, partridges and rabbits, and whose livestock was stolen or savaged by carefully protected foxes – all to give the landlords and their friends an entertaining day of sport. As another stick with which to belabour the landed interest, the opponents of the Corn Laws seized upon farmers' complaints in the hope of driving a wedge between landlords and their tenants. Bright collected evidence from farmers, and in 1845 launched a biting attack in Parliament. At the resulting Select Committee, Grantley Berkeley, a well-known figure among sporting squires, appeared as the chief defender of the landowners. He was able to argue that tenants suffering damage from game received compensation from their landlords and enjoyed their farms at beneficial rents. He also argued, less convincingly, that game birds helped keep down insect pests and so were actually an advantage to farmers. In the end the Select Committee reported inconclusively, and the issue was swept aside by the clamour of the Corn Law repeal.[21]

The popularity of shooting recovered after mid-century and the sport entered on a period of renewed activity. The *grande battue*, when exclusive parties of distinguished gentlemen gathered at a country house to shoot over a period of days, became a high point in the social calendar. The huge bags were carefully recorded in game books, and leading sportsmen posed for photographs by enormous piles of dead birds. Even when some landowners were obliged to give up the sport for reasons of ill-health or economy, there were always others, especially among the *nouveaux riches*, who could afford to take over, perhaps renting the shooting and the house itself for the purpose. It was not until 1880 that, at last, Gladstone's new Liberal government

of that year brought in a measure to allow tenants of estates the right to shoot hares and rabbits on their farms without the landlord's permission, thus removing a long-felt grievance. Poaching, however, remained a severe nuisance, and this despite a massive increase in the employment of gamekeepers. At the end of Victoria's reign more than 17,000 keepers guarded the preserves, as compared with about 8,000 at its beginning. Moreover, there were grounds for suspicion that the rural police supplemented, at the public expense, the work of the private gamekeepers in warding off poachers, a suspicion reinforced by the Night Poaching Act of 1862, which authorised police to search merely on suspicion of poaching. The preservation of game was not only the most widespread and most rapidly growing country pursuit of landowners, it was also the activity which caused the most friction between them and the rural community: 'the point at which landowners mobilized the maximum amount of directly coercive power and displayed most nakedly the legal and physical force which maintained the rights of the propertied over the propertyless in the countryside'.[22]

In addition to game, another line of Radical attack, especially after Repeal, was aimed at the landowners' monopoly of the land. There was no doubt that, collectively, landowners controlled much the greater part of the countryside. In 1873 an official return (known as the 'New Domesday Survey') showed that more than 1m people owned some land in the United Kingdom. It also showed, however, that fewer than 7,000 persons owned together four-fifths of that land, so that the remainder of the million shared only a fifth between them. Another analysis showed that some 70 per cent of England and Wales was held by private owners in estates of more than 300 acres; and at about the same time that some 85–90 per cent of the country was held by owners both private and institutional, who were not the occupiers.[23] However, the complaint of the Radicals was not merely that land was monopolised but that, in addition, landowners deliberately prevented land from being owned more widely by means of the legal device known as the 'strict settlement'. This was a formal agreement between members of a landowning family that attempted to ensure that land passed intact from the present generation to succeeding generations; and it involved limiting the powers which the owner at any one time had over selling land or borrowing on its security. The point was a fair one, since landowners in general were loth to sell land, and were always on the lookout for further land to add to their existing estates. There was a great desire to try to ensure that estates that had been painstakingly built up over a long period should not pass into the

hands of a spendthrift, who piled up large debts which might in the end be discharged only by selling land. The strict settlement was the legal instrument by which this object might be most effectively secured.

Nevertheless, the strict settlement could not prevent some families from accumulating large debts – not merely through personal extravagance, but also by engaging in politics or in unsuccessful industrial and commercial ventures, or by rebuilding the family mansion and developing its park on an excessively grandiose scale. In such cases it might eventually prove necessary to sell land, though usually it was the land that had been in the family the shortest time or was remote from the main estates that was chosen for disposal. In more extreme cases, however, it might prove necessary to secure an estate Act to break the settlement and allow the owner to sell settled land as well. Not all sales were for the purpose of discharging debts, however, as some owners followed a policy of selling outlying lands in order to buy land nearer to the main core of the family property, or perhaps in order to diversify into industrial projects such as mining and ironworking, or into stocks and shares. Further, usually only a proportion of the total acreage of an estate was settled, perhaps only a half or less, and the owner was free to do as he liked with the remainder.

The result was that, in fact, a considerable market in land existed even before the agricultural depression of the years between 1879 and 1914, when land fell sharply in value and many owners were anxious to sell. It is true that prior to this period most of the land offered for sale was in the form of entire estates, requiring a very large investment by a purchaser of outstanding wealth who recognised the political and social value placed on landed property as distinct from its often modest value for agricultural production. In the period after 1879, however, it was not only the agricultural value which declined but also the political and social advantages of landed estates. There were now fewer purchasers interested primarily in acquiring these declining advantages, and more who wanted smaller properties merely to establish a modest country residence accompanied by adequate space for pleasure grounds and sport. The country house was being replaced by the house in the country. The great houses and parks, with their costly upkeep, and their associated farming properties, which yielded a very low return and might even be difficult to let, were seen more as liabilities than assets. It is ironical that when in 1882 Gladstone's Liberal government passed its Settled Land Act, to enable settled land to be freely sold or let on long building leases, it came to the rescue of those very families who in the past had been blamed for monopolising land. Many such owners were now anxious to sell, and to them the new Act

was welcome. Their difficulty, rather, was that the market for country property was tending to dry up as large mansions and farmland were seen to be a much poorer investment than in the past.

A further criticism associated with monopoly of land concerned landowners' management of their estates. It had always been the case that some estates were neglected, their farmhouses dilapidated or even ruinous, the farm buildings antiquated, primitive and inadequate, the farmland subject to winter flooding or lacking in drainage, or badly farmed with worn-out arable and weed-infested pasture. Such defects were often associated with owners so embarrassed by debt as to lack the relatively small funds necessary for maintenance and improvement; or with owners who were absentees, who left the running of the estate to an agent who was incompetent, lazy or venal. Many of the large estates were widely scattered, and there neglect might occur on outlying properties which were in the hand of a local attorney or farmer and were but rarely inspected. Before the middle of the nineteenth century such neglect might be a subject for comment in the local community but rarely went further. By 1850, however, the standards of the best estates had reached unprecedentedly high levels, and with landowners' control of so much of the country under attack, poor management came under wider scrutiny and was subject to criticism by well-known public figures.

Particularly eminent among these was the leading agricultural writer, Sir James Caird. In 1850 and 1851 Caird carried out an extensive inspection of English farming for a series of articles which were published in *The Times*, and later collected into a substantial volume, *English Agriculture in 1850–1851* (1852).[24] His comments on contemporary estate management were harsh and trenchant. Farm buildings, stated Caird, were 'generally defective' and were 'a reproach to the landlord'. If landlords were unwilling to grant their tenants long leases – for reasons of maintaining political control, it was often suggested – then they should provide the permanent improvements that tenants at will could not be expected to make. It was important for the landlord to be professional, to have practical knowledge of the management of land, and to appreciate the benefits of improvement to his tenants and, no less, to himself. If the extent of the estate made essential the appointment of an agent, then he should be selected with the utmost care. An experienced and sensible agent, Caird went on, brought to an estate a 'general air of comfort, activity, and progress which animates all classes'. One other great barrier to improvement was the indebtedness of landlords who, pinched by debt, were unable to find the money for the necessary improvements

to their farms. The solution to this, argued Caird, was to make the transfer of land 'as cheap and easy as that of stock in the funds'. This would not only give landowners the opportunity of reducing the burden of debt and enable them to afford improvements, but would also raise the value of land in general. Such a measure, he claimed, would be more beneficial to the rural community 'than any question connected with agriculture that has yet engaged the attention of the legislature'.[25]

Another consequence of the scarcity of long leases, Caird continued, was that the capital invested by tenants in the farms was not adequately protected. A system of 'tenant-right' had grown up in some areas, whereby the tenant leaving a farm was able to obtain compensation from the incoming tenant for 'unexhausted improvements', such as expenditure on manures, drainage, fencing, and the cleaning and fertilising of worn-out land. An independent valuation of such improvements was made, and the appropriate sum was paid over by the incoming farmer. The system was capable of working fairly and well, but it could be subject to fraud and, moreover, tended to perpetuate obsolete practices while placing a heavy financial burden on the incoming tenant. He, in turn, might expect compensation in the form of a reduced rent from the landlord. It was remarkable, Caird claimed, that the system flourished where standards of farming were inferior, and it would be preferable to abolish the system altogether than to extend it to the whole country by legislation. The alternative was for landlords to offer long leases, though Caird recognised that very often they were attractive to neither tenant nor landlord, and in such cases there might be an agreement on a certain basis for the tenant to be adequately compensated. It was true, Caird conceded, that many instances could be found of tenants making long-term improvements without the security of a lease, there existing a strong bond of mutual confidence between tenant and landlord. Nevertheless, the tenant was entitled to ask for effective security, and it was regrettable that changes in the farming climate, notably the removal of protection from corn imports, had added to the lack of confidence which both landlords and tenants had shown in long leases since the depression which ended the Napoleonic Wars.[26]

This particular problem of estate management remained unsolved, and indeed the sharp decline in the profitability of grain production which set in from 1879 intensified the distrust of leases, and in fact made it difficult for landlords in some arable areas to find any tenants at all. One last aspect of the attack on the landed interest was the growth of official enquiries into the working of agriculture. The

nineteenth century saw the introduction of official investigations of many controversial questions, such as the Royal Commissions which looked into the Poor Law, the employment of women and children in factories and mines, education, housing, and numerous other subjects. Agriculture was not exempt from this concern to gather evidence and lay it open to the public, and a long series of enquiries probed into many aspects of this great branch of the economy. Beginning with a Select Committee on agricultural wages in 1824, the more extensive investigations included another Select Committee on agriculture in 1836, Royal Commissions on the employment of women and children in agriculture in 1843 and again in 1867–70, enquiries into agricultural depression in 1882 and 1896, farm labour, 1893–94, and the earnings of farm labourers in 1900 and 1905. Other subjects for investigation included the Game Laws, agricultural customs, improvement of land, rural housing, allotments and smallholdings, agricultural land use and production, and the decline of the agricultural population.

These enquiries, of course, were much wider in scope than the question of the landowners' role in agriculture. In some of the most important ones the sins of commission or omission were largely those of the farmers. It was the farmers, for example, who were mainly concerned in farmworkers' wages and working conditions, and especially the employment of women and children, often under shameful conditions. The provision of allotments for labourers was also primarily a matter for the farmers, who were widely opposed to the notion. Much of the worst rural housing was that owned by small property-owners in the country towns and villages, craftsmen and tradesmen, publicans, widows and the like, while that provided by landowners was frequently, though by no means always, of a superior kind. Criticism, especially of housing, came from a number of sources in the decades before 1914: from Medical Officers of Health concerned with unfit dwellings, from private amateur investigators who published their findings in widely read books on the subject, and, most extensively, from the unofficial Liberal Land Enquiry Committee, which published its evidence in 1913. Public concern over the 'flight from the land' became widespread in the closing years of the century and was the motive for further investigations of rural conditions, both official and private, and indeed underlay much of the concern about rural housing. Politically, the attack on the landed interest was taken to the House of Lords which, after a momentous struggle over Lloyd George's budget, with its higher rate of income tax, a new super-tax, and alarming new taxes on land, found its powers greatly reduced by the Parliament Act of 1911.

This was the logical and inevitable consequence of the earlier shift in political power to the urban voter.

Overall, the effective results of the enquiries, both official and private, were quite small. There was legislation concerning the scandalous employment of women and children in gangs, and measures were passed dealing with insanitary housing, allotments and smallholdings, and education. For the most part, however, the interventions were of limited scope, were poorly enforced, if at all, and were often easily evaded. The attempt to close or demolish insanitary dwellings, for example, was blocked by the inadequate supply of country housing for the rural poor, and the unwillingness of rural district councils to build new houses, as well as by a reluctance to add to the rates and to cross swords with local owners of influence. There was no legislation concerning farmworkers' wages or male workers' conditions, although these were often deplorable, nor any regarding farm rents. The agricultural depression of the last quarter of the century brought two Royal Commissions but only a few minor palliatives from government – the effective answer, a return to protection, was no longer politically feasible. Agriculture continued to decline and suffer under the effects of free trade, while *laissez-faire* prevailed in most of the important questions which investigations had revealed as requiring attention. The ultimate progress to wide-ranging intervention was not to come until the First World War, when suddenly home food supplies and agricultural labour both assumed a new and urgent significance; and eventually the shift in national policies back towards protection, together with greater industrial and social regulation, brought into being a controlled and subsidised agricultural industry. In this process, as we shall see, the political and economic eclipse of the landowners, already far advanced before 1914, implied the demise of the 'landed interest' as that term was understood in former times.

NOTES

1. **Phyllis Deane** and **W. A. Cole,** *British Economic Growth 1688–1959,* Cambridge University Press, 1962, pp. 156, 161; **B. R. Mitchell** and **Phyllis Deane,** *Abstract of British Historical Statistics,* Cambridge University Press, 1962, p 366.
2. Deane and Cole, *British Economic Growth,* p. 142.
3. Mitchell and Deane, *Abstract,* p. 60.
4. **J. V. Beckett,** *The Aristocracy in England 1660–1914,* Basil Blackwell, 1986, pp. 463–4.

5. **R. J. White,** *The Age of George III,* Heinemann, 1968, pp. 29–39.
6. **G. E. Mingay,** *English Landed Society in the Eighteenth Century,* Routledge & Kegan Paul, 1963, pp. 37–41; **J. H. Plumb,** *England in the Eighteenth Century,* Penguin, 1950, pp. 37–41.
7. **M. Ransome,** 'Some recent studies of the composition of the House of Commons', *University of Birmingham Historical Journal,* **VI,** 2, 1958, pp. 139–42.
8. **Derek Fraser,** 'The agitation for parliamentary reform', in **J. T. Ward,** (ed.), *Popular Movements c. 1830–1850,* Macmillan, 1970, pp. 50–1.
9. **E. L. Woodward,** *The Age of Reform 1815–1870,* Clarendon Press, 1938, pp. 84–6; Fraser, 'The agitation for parliamentary reform', pp. 50–1.
10. **D. G. Barnes,** *A History of the English Corn Laws,* Routledge, 1930, *passim*; **J. D. Chambers** and **G. E. Mingay,** *The Agricultural Revolution 1750–1880,* Batsford, 1966, pp. 148–9.
11. Mitchell and Deane, *Abstract,* pp. 488, 498; **S. Fairlie,** 'The Corn Laws and British wheat production 1829–1876', *Economic History Review,* 2nd ser., **XXII,** 1, 1969, *passim.*
12. **D. Spring,** 'Earl Fitzwilliam and the Corn Laws', *American Historical Review,* **LIX,** 1953–4, p. 291.
13. Woodward, *Age of Reform,* p. 113; Mitchell and Deane, *Abstract,* p. 488.
14. Mitchell and Deane, *Abstract,* p. 95; **Lucy Brown,** *The Board of Trade and the Free Trade Movement 1830–47,* Clarendon Press, 1958, pp. 70–5, 141–213.
15. **N. McCord,** *The Anti-Corn Law League,* Oxford University Press, 1958, pp. 103–7; **G. Kitson Clark,** 'The Repeal of the Corn Law and the politics of the forties', *Economic History Review,* 2nd ser., **IV,** 1951–2, p. 5.
16. **G. L. Mosse,** 'The Anti-League: 1844–1846', *Economic History Review,* 2nd ser., **XVII,** 1947, pp. 131–42; **Mary Lawson-Tancred,** 'The Anti-League and the Corn Law crisis of 1846', *Historical Journal,* **III,** 2, 1960, pp. 162–83.
17. Woodward, *Age of Reform,* pp. 128–35.
18. **S. Dowell,** *A History of Taxation and Taxes in England,* Longmans Green, 1884, III, pp. 120–2; Woodward, *Age of Reform,* p. 107.
19. **Betty Kemp,** 'Reflections on the Repeal of the Corn Laws', *Victorian Studies,* **V,** 3, 1962, pp. 195–204.
20. **J. L. Hammond** and **Barbara Hammond,** *The Village Labourer,* Longman, 1978, p. 134.
21. **Chester Kirby,** 'The attack on the English Game Laws in the forties', *Journal of Modern History,* **IV,** 1932, pp. 22–5, 29.
22. **F. M. L. Thompson,** 'Landowners and the rural community', in **G. E. Mingay,** (ed.), *The Victorian Countryside,* Routledge & Kegan Paul, 1981, II, p. 459.
23. Beckett, *The Aristocracy in England,* pp. 50–1.
24. Reprinted in a new edition, Frank Cass, 1968.
25. **J. Caird,** *English Agriculture in 1850–51,* 1852, 1968 edn, Frank Cass, pp. 490–5.
26. *Ibid.,* pp. 503–9.

CHAPTER FOUR

The Clergyman and his Parish

THE CLERGYMAN AND THE COMMUNITY

In the eighteenth century a large stake in the country's land was held by the Church of England. In addition to the glebe – a portion of the village land set aside for the clergyman – there were the tithes, often highly valuable. Nominally, the tithes represented the right to a tenth of the produce of the land, though in practice the incumbent's income was often very much less than this. The situation was frequently a complicated one, since the glebe varied in size and value, and might even be non-existent, while the clergyman might be entitled to only a part of the tithes or, not infrequently, none at all. Rectors were entitled to receive both the great tithes, usually those of corn, hay and wood, and the small tithes, which were all the rest. Vicars were usually entitled to only the small tithes, although the division between great and small was not fixed and varied with local custom, while much depended on whether new crops, such as turnips, swedes and potatoes, were judged to be great or small. However, in many parishes the great tithes, and possibly the small also, had come to be appropriated by a lay personage, an impropriator as he became known, who from his receipts paid a fixed money 'pension' to a curate to perform the offices of the Church.

The parish clergy of the early eighteenth century were generally poorly paid. There was certainly a well-to-do minority whose incomes might be £500 a year or more, making them the equivalent in income of minor country gentlemen, or better off even than many so-called squires in more remote regions. But the great majority earned much less than a tenth of this figure. While a small number of parish clergy were thus gentlemen of some consequence, living

in an ample parsonage house with carriage and servants, there were thousands of others, most of them curates, who toiled on their glebe like common farmers or sought additional work in order to augment their inadequate stipends. Pluralism, the holding of two or more livings at the same time, was one common answer to meagre stipends, though this did not mean that all pluralists were well off. There were in the eighteenth century numerous livings worth less than £20 a year, even some less than £10, so that a curate who held three such livings was still worth only about the same as a small farmer. Other paid work which was compatible with a curacy included tutoring the children of gentry families, teaching school, the administration of local charities, and taking up farming on some scale by renting land additional to the glebe. There were indeed some noted farmers among the clergy, but a combination such as prevailed at Chapel en le Frith, Derbyshire, where James Clegg served as parson, farmer and local doctor, was not very uncommon.[1]

The most common answer to insufficient incomes, however, was pluralism. Studies of individual counties have shown that near a half of all clergymen might be pluralists, the majority of them through necessity.[2] A study of the Bishop of Ely's benefices, for instance, shows only one clergyman to have had a stipend exceeding £400, though it is true that this was not a wealthy area. There were twenty-nine of between £50 and £100, and twenty-two worth less than £50. However, many of the pluralists were able to enjoy incomes of between £150 and £500, providing them with a comfortable, if not luxurious, existence.[3] Generally, the poverty of the living was reflected in the church itself: a small, cold, damp and tumbledown building, holding only a few rough benches instead of pews, and a simple kitchen table for communion. The curates were not infrequently of a piece with the church, poorly educated, unrefined, and inclined to be over-fond of sport and the bottle. In Cumberland, tales were told of parsons who worked in the fields all day, and caroused and quarrelled in the inn on a Saturday night before reeling home to prepare a sermon for the next morning. At Wastdale Head it was not unknown at one time for the sexton to appear at the door of the tiny church and announce to the congregation: 'No sarvice today. Parson's gone fishing.'[4]

Pluralism meant not only the serving of churches by ill-paid assistant curates but also non-residence. This in turn meant neglected church buildings and dilapidated parsonages. Cobbett was to remark angrily on empty and neglected parsonages in his *Rural Rides*, and it is interesting that the Revd David Davies, the author of a celebrated

study of rural poverty published in 1795, was obliged to rebuild the parsonage house when he became rector of Barkham in Berkshire in 1782, the old building being no more than a 'mean Cottage badly situated'. Fortunately, the living was worth £160 a year, which was supplemented by a further £60 paid him by the family of Viscount Cremorne, whose son he had tutored. Helped by this income Davies was able to build a new, if modest, parsonage at a cost of over £400.[5] Non-residence was widely blamed for the Church's lack of moral influence, for poor attendance in many parishes, the backwardness of education, and the prevalence of communities deeply infected by crime, brutality and immorality. The Church, if properly served by a resident parson and well-supported by an attentive squire and his tenants, was held to exercise a great power for checking violence and imparting good behaviour in the parish, instilling respect for the established social order as well as sobriety and industriousness. But particularly in heavily wooded or remote upland areas, where resident squire and parson were both absent, lawbreakers gathered and carried on their nefarious activities with impunity. Such areas were the homes of scattered groups of small farmer-craftsmen, men who combined the rearing of a few livestock and cultivation of a little piece of arable with perhaps a part-time occupation in cloth-making, mining or ironworking. But they were also sometimes the haunts of gangs of robbers, smugglers, coiners and poachers.

In those many villages which housed a resident squire he often played a major part in supporting the role of the Church, not least by attending regularly himself and expecting his tenants and servants to do the same. In many instances the squire possessed the advowson, the right of appointing the parson, and quite naturally he tended to choose a man who was congenial in the style of his services and also in his private life, one who held the same religious and political views as the squire, and who was likely to be useful in helping control the local electorate. Sometimes the parson was a relation, who was thus provided for, and sometimes the squire might offer his advowson to oblige a local magnate, accepting his choice of incumbent as one of the many elements in the intricate network of patronage and obligation. Very often the community of interest between squire and parson was based on a common enthusiasm for sport. There were parsons who became keen sportsmen in their own right, who rode regularly to hounds, and might even, if wealthy enough, keep their own packs of hounds. Occasionally, when no suitable candidate appeared, a presentation was put up for auction, one such advertisement referring to

a most valuable living in one of the finest sporting counties. The vicinity affords the best coursing in England, also excellent fishing, extensive cover for game, and numerous packs of fox-hounds, harriers etc. The surrounding country is beautiful and healthy and the society elegant and fashionable.[6]

On the other hand, there were scholar-parsons, men widely read and cultured, pillars perhaps of local literary societies and leading spirits of a private circulating library. Many had wide interests, though some chose to specialise in a particular branch of knowledge – divinity obviously, but frequently natural history, law, local history or current social questions. A number took their studies so far as to publish them in books or pamphlets which might attract a considerable readership. Among well-known examples the name of Gilbert White, appointed curate of Selborne in 1751, comes readily to mind; and mention has been made already of David Davies and his pioneering *The Case of Labourers in Husbandry*, a work praised by, among others, the Revd John Howlett, vicar of Dunmow in Essex, who was himself a well-known authority on social matters at the time.[7] The curate of Teddington and absentee rector of Porlock, the Revd Stephen Hales, was a great amateur botanist, also distinguished by his somewhat horrifying experiments to discover the force of blood in a variety of animals. And of course there were poets. George Crabbe, curate of Stathern, near Melton Mowbray, the mecca of hunting men, though not a sportsman himself dressed like his neighbours in a velveteen shooting jacket, breeches and gaiters, while numerous other poets and writers of renown, Addison, Coleridge, Cowper and Tennyson, were nurtured in English parsonages, to say nothing of the Brontë sisters. There were also diarists, men obscure in their own day, like Parson Woodforde of Weston Longeville, near Norwich, and Francis Kilvert, who described village life in parts of Wales. Both painted highly detailed pictures of rural communities, the one in the later eighteenth century, the other in the seventies of the last century, documents that record much that would otherwise escape the historian.[8]

It was perhaps a short step, though sometimes a bold one, to move from gathering knowledge in one's own study to going out and imparting it to the wider village community. In the nineteenth century there were numerous parsons and their wives who established classes for the young, perhaps in their own parsonage or in a rented barn, or even in the church itself. Penny readings, meant for a wider audience of young persons and adults, represented an attempt to carry an appreciation of popular poems and novels to people who

might otherwise never have known of them, just as magic lantern shows brought scientific subjects, natural phenomena, exploration and exotic lands to a society little exposed to the wider world. Of considerable advantage to village housewives who found it difficult to put any money aside for future consumption, were coal clubs, clothing clubs, Christmas clubs and the like, established by thoughtful parsons and their ladies.

Even more practical were allotment schemes, introduced in order to give labourers the opportunity of raising their own vegetables and perhaps feeding a pig into the bargain. Village clergy were specially notable in initiating and supervising such schemes and in overcoming the preliminary problem of persuading landowners and farmers to set land aside for the purpose. A leading figure was the Revd Stephen Demainbray, rector of Broad Somerford in Wiltshire, who told a Select Committee in 1843 that he had begun allotments in his parish as far back as 1806. The obvious benefits of allotments in helping to alleviate poverty and keeping the poor off the parish led to legislation in 1819 and 1831, when parishes were authorised to acquire land for letting to labourers. The legislation was only permissive, however, and probably much more was achieved through the efforts of individuals, especially village parsons. It was established in 1833 that 42 per cent of all parishes had some form of allotments, although this figure is somewhat misleading since the proportion varied greatly from one area to another, and in many instances only a handful of labourers had any access to allotment land.

Other concerns of nineteenth-century parsons were health and housing, the two often closely associated. Parsons and their wives, like many squires' ladies, kept stocks of simple remedies for treating common illnesses, and dispensed advice and medicines at the kitchen door. Some went further in attempting to seek out the causes of chronic ailments and epidemics, and although the true causes of diseases were obscure and little understood, it did not take much imagination or observation to detect connections between damp and insanitary homes and suspect water supplies and such terrible diseases as typhoid, cholera, typhus, tuberculosis, bronchitis and rheumatism. Thomas Pearce, vicar of Mordern, Dorset, from 1853 to 1882, was appalled by the state of the insanitary and dilapidated cottages there, and set about sinking new wells at his own expense as well as starting village clubs and founding a school. Charles Kingsley, the celebrated author of *Hereward the Wake* and *Westward Ho!*, did much to improve life in his Hampshire parish of Eversley. He found an empty church with the farmers' sheep grazing in the churchyard, and a rectory

unrepaired for over a century. Long hours were spent in visiting the sick in the cottages, and he attacked complacent cottage owners in a series of sermons on 'Who causes pestilence?'. Boot and coal clubs were founded, a loan fund began, and also a lending library. Kingsley held adult classes in his rectory, which together with his cottage readings took up six evenings a week. And a promising youngster was sent off to Winchester Training College to become a schoolmaster.

The problem of poverty could be alleviated somewhat by allotments, savings clubs and little private charities, so reducing the numbers of desperate poor who were driven to seek the uncertain aid of the Poor Law and perhaps obliged to enter the forbidding portal of the workhouse. Alleviation, however, was no solution. Numbers of reformers, including some of the clergy, saw only too clearly that poverty could be significantly reduced only if wages were raised and unemployment lessened, and that so long as families were large and much of the labour force immobile, the inexorable law of supply and demand would operate to keep wages down to inadequate levels. A solution much in vogue during the nineteenth century was to encourage both internal migration and emigration overseas, and funds from official and private sources were forthcoming to help move the poor from areas where there was insufficient work and wages were at or below subsistence to find better conditions elsewhere. A number of charitable bodies originated their own schemes, as eventually did trade unions in towns and villages, and in addition a number of clergy interested themselves in the matter.

Their difficulty, however, was that attempts to reduce the local labour supply through migration ran counter to the interests of landowners and farmers, who were concerned to keep labour plentiful and cheap. The squire and his tenants were among the most influential supporters of the church, owned most of the cottages, and also dominated local charities, so their hostility might make the work of a conscientious clergyman very difficult, if not impossible. Even the introduction of an allotment scheme could give rise to friction, as many farmers opposed any change which might make labourers more independent, while objections were raised that the men would be spending their strength on their own piece of land rather than on the farmers' fields, and would be tempted to steal seeds and fertiliser. It can readily be understood that few clergymen were prepared to imitate the Revd Edward Girdlestone, who in the later 1860s organised the movement of between 400 and 500 men, many with families, from the acute poverty of his parish of Halberton,

near Tiverton in Devon, sending them to areas of better employment prospects in the North.[9] Since Church of England clergy were thus handicapped by their close association with squires and wealthy farmers, it is not surprising that it was a Congregational minister of Stalbridge in Dorset, George Rodgers, who in 1872 initiated one of the most ambitious of private migration projects. This was a scheme to send a batch of eighty prospective settlers from the Yeovil area to a remote part of Minnesota. But even Rodgers' precaution of travelling out himself beforehand to examine the area and choose a site could not prevent failure. The combination of a terrible winter, scarcity of wood, bad water and distance from markets, together with an unsuitable choice of emigrants, proved disastrous. Within a few months half the settlers had abandoned 'New Yeovil', to be replaced by hardier Germans and Scandinavians.[10]

Although clergymen of conscience strove to bring some element of civilisation and comfort to intellectually moribund and poverty-stricken villages, there was a negative side to their efforts. The Church was seen by its principal supporters, the gentry, middle-class professional men, wealthy tradesmen and large farmers, as a means – in some instances the only means – of securing acquiescence in the existing social order and of instilling respect for the law. The parson and his lady – no matter what they did in establishing schools and clubs or visiting the sick and distributing gifts of coal and blankets at Christmas time – were nevertheless superior and educated persons whose background and way of life were those of the ruling class rather than of the ruled. The difference was emphasised where the clergyman was a close friend of the squire, dined with him regularly and participated in his hunting and shooting, and also where the parson was sufficiently well off to live in a rectory or vicarage that, in point of size, grounds and amenities, was comparable with the leading houses of the neighbourhood.

Moreover, in attempting to bring improvement to the village, the clergyman was often seeking to alter ingrained moral and social habits in a conservative and complacent community, one hostile to all change. Thus, it was only with difficulty that old traditions and superstitions, going back to very early times though still strong in the early nineteenth century, were discouraged, and were rarely stamped out. Villagers still practised folk medicine, both for themselves and their livestock, with some customary remedies involving a supposed transference of the complaint from the sufferer to an animal or to the earth. Accordingly, a child with whooping cough was made to cough into a hole in the ground which was then rapidly covered

up, or a sufferer might be advised to drink from a horse trough or take some of the cat's milk after it had drunk from it. Even some well-educated persons, clergymen among them, tried remedies of this sort. And although the old village sports, brutal as they often were – cockfighting, cock-throwing, bull-baiting, dog fights, cudgels and the like – were frowned upon and eventually outlawed, they still survived clandestinely with or without the parson's approval. The parson was associated also with those who urged the ethic of work, sought the reduction of holidays, and advocated the prohibition of the annual feasts and fairs which were once a high point of village life.

The breach between the labouring class and the parson was widened further where the clergyman was elevated to the Bench of magistrates. The numbers of clerical magistrates grew considerably in the course of the eighteenth century, reaching a peak in the early decades of the nineteenth century as more clergymen acquired sufficient substance to become qualified for the office. In this development the rise in the value of farm produce and, consequently, of tithes in the half-century after 1760, had great effect. Though poor clergy still abounded, there were now larger numbers of well-to-do parsons. Not a few became significant landowners, particularly where enclosures had resulted in the conversion of rights to tithes into ownership of land and on notably favourable terms for the former tithe-holder. The clergymen-magistrates, furthermore, were often the more active members of the Bench, whereas a large proportion of the lay magistrates had always been inactive, rarely taking the trouble to exercise their powers. Both in administrative functions, in regulation of alehouses, markets, fairs, pedlars, and weights and measures, for instance, and also in the supervision of houses of correction and workhouses, clergymen-justices were among the most enthusiastic, and they were not behind either in the pursuit and punishment of robbers, vagrants, poachers and other wrongdoers. It is not surprising, therefore, that parsons were among the unpopular local figures sought out for attack by the Swing rioters of 1830, and parson-farmers were perhaps as likely as any to have their ricks and barns set alight in the unrest of the years after 1815.

REFORM OF THE TITHES

When they angrily confronted local parsons, the Swing rioters had a clear understanding that the clergyman's income from tithes was at the expense of the farmers, and they evidently believed that the

consequent reduction in the farmers' profits was one of the reasons why their own wages as labourers were so low. For centuries the tithes had been a bone of contention between the Church and the farmers.

As the Revd William Jones, Vicar of Broxbourne, Hertfordshire, confided to his diary in 1803, 'the word "tithe" has ever been unpleasing and odious to farmers especially, as "cuckoo" to the married ear'.[11]

From medieval times, it is true, some rights to tithes had got into lay hands, a transfer that was much extended by the dissolution of the monasteries in the time of Henry VIII. From the farmers' point of view the right to tithes, whether in the hands of the Church or lay persons, meant the giving up of a part of their produce, and was in effect a tax on the yield of the land. The more efficient the farmer and the more advanced his methods, the higher was the yield and the greater the amount that had to be surrendered in tithes to someone who had played no part in securing the increases. Tithes gave rise to many vexed and protracted disputes and were often a source of animosity and bitterness in the village, even if (as in Parson Woodforde's parish) the pill was sweetened by the parson giving the farmers an annual dinner of a highly alcoholic character.

The tithes proved most contentious when they were still paid in kind, for the assessment of the tithe depended on a judgement of the size of the crop and there were many opportunities for fraud and sharp dealing. Payment in kind was inconvenient and costly, not only to the farmer but also to the tithe owner. If the latter were the incumbent he would have to have carts or wagons available at the appropriate times and also provide storage facilities, and he would become involved in the time-consuming business of marketing the produce.

The complications in a dairying village, where a large part of the tithes might consist of milk, or butter and cheese, or in a grazing district, where the main product was livestock, can easily be imagined. In practice, it was simpler and more convenient for the tithe to be valued and converted into an annual money payment, and where it was the landlord who owned or leased the tithes then a certain sum was added to the tenants' rents in respect of tithes. Professor Eric Evans, the authority on the subject, estimates that about one-third of all tithes were owned by lay impropriators. Many of these, however, received only a 'modus' or small cash payment in respect of a particular crop or kind of livestock. The moduses represented past agreements to receive cash instead of kind, the agreement going

back perhaps to medieval times when the sums fixed were worth very much more. Often they related to lesser tithes which were of uncertain value and difficult to collect, such as milk, eggs, young livestock and garden produce. Disputes and grievances could arise over every kind of tithe payment, whether paid in kind or in cash, and in the later eighteenth century the complicated and inequitable nature of tithes became more troublesome as the markets for farm produce expanded, new crops were introduced and agricultural methods were gradually improved.[12]

It was for these reasons that when the parliamentary enclosure of open fields, commons and wastes became widespread after 1760 the opportunity was often taken of converting the right to tithes into an allocation of land, or alternatively into a corn-rent or annual cash payment. It is estimated that 70 per cent of the enclosure Acts passed between 1757 and 1835 included provisions for tithe commutation. No doubt the figure would have been higher still but for the exorbitant demands of some tithe owners, who held out for such large compensation that the landowners decided they would have to proceed with the enclosure without any exoneration of the tithes. As it was, exoneration was often expensive since it became established practice for the landowners to meet the tithe owner's share of the costs of carrying out the enclosure, as well as paying for his ring fence. Moreover, the land allotted in lieu of tithes was greater than one-tenth of the whole, since tithes represented a tenth of the produce when ready for market and made no allowance for the farmers' costs of production. A mere tenth of the land would not therefore be a fair exchange, for the tithe owner would now have the production costs to meet (or, in practice, the rent he could charge for his land allotment would reflect the costs of production). Hence the tithe owner demanded not one-tenth of the land enclosed but as much as one-eighth or one-ninth, and by the 1790s an allocation of so large a share as one-fifth of the arable land was standard. The less profitable tithes of the pasture lands were frequently commuted at one-eighth of the meadow land and one-ninth of other pastures.[13]

The result was that where the incumbent was the tithe owner he emerged as a major landowner in the parish, sometimes indeed the largest landowner. This was one of the reasons why more clergymen were appointed to the Bench of magistrates in the later eighteenth century as men of the cloth rose in wealth and status. This effect of enclosure should not be exaggerated, however, for although between 1750 and 1850 some 4,000 Acts of enclosure were passed, the area affected by them was less than a quarter of the total acreage. If

the figure of 70 per cent, mentioned above, is reasonably accurate, then appreciably less than 20 per cent of the country's acreage had the tithes commuted at the time of parliamentary enclosure; and of course the tithe owner was often not the parish incumbent but some higher Church dignitary or a lay person. A more significant change in many respects was brought about by the Tithe Commutation Act of 1836. This Act ended the payment of tithes in kind, where this was still practised, and substituted money payments based on a rent-charge. The rent-charge was not a fixed sum but varied with the average prices of wheat, barley and oats over the previous seven years. Separate arrangements were made for tithes of hops, fruit, garden produce and coppice wood.[14]

For the tithe owners the compensation made under the 1836 Act was much less generous than the exoneration settlements which had been provided under Acts of enclosure. The rent-charge was not a tax on yield as tithes had been formerly, and the rent-charge would not necessarily increase as agricultural output expanded, as tithes had done before. Rather, the tying of the rent-charge to corn prices left the tithe owner at the mercy of market fluctuations, even though the effect of price changes was damped down by taking a seven-year average. For over forty years from the passing of the Tithe Commutation Act there was no serious problem. Corn prices fluctuated, of course, but their general trend was for stable or slightly rising averages. Then, however, the long-term effects of Corn Law Repeal began to be felt. The price of wheat, which had been as high as 64s in 1867 and 1868, never rose above 59s in the 1870s, and fell sharply in the 1880s to reach a nadir of 22s 10d in 1894; barley and oats fell, too, if less precipitously. The consequence was that many clergymen found their incomes sharply reduced, and by 1901 they were receiving only 67 per cent of the rent-charge payable at the time of commutation. The impoverishment of parish clergy was a factor in the decline of the clergyman-magistrate and, more widely, resulted in a loss of status and influence. Burdened by the upkeep of a rambling rectory with its extensive grounds, restricted in his life-style by the nature of his profession, education and background, the parson was now more often to be seen perambulating his parish on a push-bike when his more affluent parishioners clattered by in their carriages.[15]

The 1836 Act had not succeeded in preserving the incomes of the tithe owners. Nor had it made tithe rent-charges acceptable in all parts of the country. In Wales, in particular, the Church of England was regarded by many as an intrusive, alien institution, and the payment of the rent-charge was greatly resented. Openly expressed

hostility led to the Act of 1891, when the responsibility for paying the rent-charge was clearly laid upon the landowners. Subsequent Acts, in 1918 and 1925, attempted to grapple with the problems created by the steep upswing in corn prices during and immediately after the First World War, and the subsequent post-war collapse. A further Act in 1936, influenced by renewed hostility to rent-charge payments in arable districts, tried to get over the effects of low prices by converting the rent-charge into 3 per cent government stock which was transferred to tithe owners. This proved a source of new and disastrous financial problems after 1939, when corn prices rose again while 3 per cent government stock fell in value as interest rates rose.[16]

NONCONFORMITY AND THE LAND

The Church's tithes, and after 1836 the tithe rent-charge, were sources of disharmony, amounting on occasion to active hostility, in many districts of England and Wales. A more pervasive cause of friction, however, flowed from the rise of Nonconformity. The conflict between Church and Chapel was fed by many contentious sources, differences in belief, of course, but also resentment over payment of tithes and church rates by Nonconformist farmers, the parson's hold over village schools, and not least the ministers' radical views and espousal of reforms which challenged the orthodox conservatism of the Church. The parsons' belief in the moral superiority of the upper classes divided them from the majority of their flocks, although some privately recognised that the ministers, with their humble origins and much closer connections with the working classes, possessed a far better understanding of the lives and spiritual needs of ordinary village people.

'The great age of Dissent in England', writes Professor Alan Everitt, 'lasted from the Restoration till the First World War.'[17] Non-conformist chapels were built and rebuilt, and according to the somewhat unsatisfactory figures of the Census of 1851, as high a proportion as 44 per cent of the English population were Dissenters at that date. There had clearly been a great expansion in their numbers since the modest beginnings of Dissent, the growth being most notable at the time of the Evangelical movement of the later eighteenth and early nineteenth centuries. The Census figures also indicated marked variations in the geographical distribution of Non-conformity, suggesting that the movement was stronger in the North

than in the South, and especially strong in counties which experienced much industrial growth, while being weak in the counties which remained more purely agricultural. On closer examination, however, the North-South industrial–agricultural divisions proved not to be clear-cut. There were, in fact, 'areas of counties like Sussex and Suffolk where Dissent was nearly as strong as in a Nottinghamshire mining village or a West Riding clothing town'.[18] In detail, the spatial distribution of Dissent as a whole, and that of its component elements, raises many questions about its compatibility with certain types of village society, differing local economies, and lines of social class.

Despite the generally accepted connection between Nonconformity and urban growth, the evidence suggests that in the seventeenth and early eighteenth centuries the bulk of its support sprang from country towns and villages, rather than large towns. Examination of the figures for Kent taken from the Compton Census of 1676 suggests that a powerful influence in the fostering of Dissenting communities was the nature of the local agricultural economy. Parishes in forested districts held numerous Dissenters, while those in the downlands relatively few; and similar patterns can be seen in areas like the West Riding dales, east Devon, south-east Lancashire, and Rockingham Forest, compared with, for example, the wolds of Lincolnshire and Leicestershire. Relevant factors appear to be the exceptional size of the parishes in forest districts and the scattered nature of the settlements, both having the effect of discouraging regular attendance at a distant parish church, accessible in winter only by an arduous journey over atrocious roads. Additional factors included the distinct scarcity in forest parishes of resident gentry, and the tendency for the local population to grow rapidly as newcomers found it easy to appropriate land for squatting on, a practice made the easier by the absence of strong manorial control. It is possible, considers Professor Everitt, that in such areas the older and more stable communities encouraged the more traditional forms of Dissent, while the new communities of squatters were more receptive to the later Millenarian kinds of sect. Certainly, near the end of the nineteenth century some 30,000 or more chapels were in existence in England and Wales, although of most of them very little is known.[19]

The religious force focused on the chapel was undoubtedly very potent when it is considered that congregations were seldom larger than 200 souls, and included few, if any, members of wealth. Such congregations, usually lacking any endowment, managed not only to build the chapel in the first place (modest as it often was), but also to rebuild and perhaps enlarge it later on; managed also to find

the funds to maintain it, and to pay their own minister without any form of financial support from outside their own ranks, no support from tithes or rent-charges, no munificent patron, and no support from the village community at large. Rural Methodism, in particular, placed considerable responsibilities on the shoulders of the laymen, not only as stewards, trustees and class leaders, but also as preachers. Full members of the Wesleyan or Primitive connections were expected to attend weekly class meetings for prayers, hymns and instruction, and in the early days, for testifying to spiritual experiences. Absence from classes required an explanation; repeated absence might result in expulsion. The practice of giving testimony led on to selection of class members as prayer leaders and prospective preachers. In Niddersdale in 1851 the two sects together held a total of forty-seven weekly services in twenty-four chapels, and additional services were held regularly in eleven outlying places. Only a large reservoir of preachers and ardent congregations could maintain so many services spread over widely scattered rural communities. In addition to services and classes there were occasional camp meetings, and individual chapels held Sunday schools and organised social events like outings, teas, bazaars, concerts and lectures.[20]

The strength of Nonconformity was that its members had the faith with which to withstand hostility, even in places where the numbers were few. While some landowners accepted Nonconformists as tenants, perhaps expecting from them only lip-service to the established Church as a token of social solidarity, there were other owners who would not countenance as tenants any who were not whole-hearted supporters of the Church of England. This was one reason why Nonconformity was stronger in districts of small farms, among men who owned their own land or rented but little, and also among craftsmen and tradesmen in villages where they were little dependent on large proprietors for custom. These three groups together – farmers (especially the more substantial ones), craftsmen and tradesmen – made up the majority of stewards, class leaders and lay preachers among the Methodists in rural areas. The labourers, though not unimportant in the chapels, held a minority of offices. The case was different in the Primitive connection, however, for there the labourers were dominant, and indeed the growth of Primitive sects was 'in some ways a reaction to the growing respectability of Wesleyan Methodism'.[21]

In parishes where the Church of England was strong the Dissenting labourer was in a weak position, for he might well depend for his livelihood on a large farmer who was a pillar of the parish church and

perhaps also a trustee of village charities. To cross him, as equally to offend the parson, by preferring to attend chapel rather than church, was to risk being shut out from what parochial charities existed, and to be omitted from the squire's or parson's distribution of coal and blankets at Christmas. This became a matter of more than slight importance when the labourer became advanced in years and liable to ill-health, and helps to explain a tendency for elderly farmworkers to return to the Church's fold in later life.

The chapel, however, offered compensations of a different kind. By the responsibilities thrown upon the individual, by the possibility of rising to become a class leader or lay preacher – by no means unlikely, especially in the Primitive sects – the labourer could feel he was someone of importance among his fellow men. Badly paid he might be, disgracefully housed, and disregarded by his employer and the superior personages of the village; nevertheless, in the chapel he enjoyed status and respect. Experience in organising chapel meetings or travels as an itinerant preacher inspired self-confidence, an independent attitude, and a wider outlook than was likely to be acquired through lowly submission in the church congregation, where he was relegated to obscure benches in the rear, or by humble forehead-knuckling to squire and parson when they passed by. It is not surprising, therefore, that Nonconformity in general, and lay preachers in particular, played a major role in the agricultural labourers' unions which enjoyed a brief efflorescence in the 1870s. Joseph Arch, the leader of the union movement, and eventually a Member of Parliament, was by profession only a skilled hedger and ditcher; but he was also a lay preacher who had the ability and experience to hold the attention of an audience. Thomas Hardy once heard Arch address a crowd of Dorsetshire labourers and remembered vividly his moderation of tone, his power of drawing a picture of a comfortable cottage life as it should be, that was so well within his listeners' imagination as to elicit an immediate response among men of severely circumscribed knowledge and education[22].

Though after its brief heyday unionism declined and for years disappeared from large parts of the countryside, it left a legacy of hope of progress, and a greater sense among working men of ability to stand on their own feet. Especially in places where union branches had survived, some villagers, labourers, tradesmen and craftsmen were sufficiently self-assertive to stand for election with union support to the new parish councils when they first appeared in 1894. In Warwickshire, Arch's county and an early stronghold of unionism, fifty-four farmworkers and thirty-seven artisans and

tradesmen were elected. The connection, however, of unions and workers' independence with Nonconformity was a long-standing cause of the opposition shown by landowners and clergy. Owners and their large tenants complained that the paternal relationship between master and man was being broken down, and clergymen believed that the infection of unionism had brought about diminished congregations and irregular attendance.[23]

DECLINE OF CHURCH AND CHAPEL

The church building itself was one reason for the falling-off in attendance among working people. Very often in the course of the eighteenth century the larger part of the nave had been divided into private pews, reserved for the families of note among the congregation, while the inferior folk were left to occupy the hard, uncomfortable benches behind or in the aisles or gallery. The elevated partitions of the pews were designed to offer privacy to the occupants, and the pews were made comfortable with carpets and cushions to relieve the damp cold of winter Sundays and help pass the tedium of prolix sermonising. Pews were graduated according to status, and bitter disputes broke out over rights to the most favourably situated ones, or on occasions when one family sent a carpenter to enlarge their pew at the expense of the neighbour's.[24] The lower elements of the congregation stood outside these quarrels, of course, though they might find some wry amusement in them. What they resented was the assumption of superiority before God of the wealthy and their bringing of class divisions into the services. They resented being required to bow or curtsey to the squire and his lady, and even to the parson's wife, and they disliked being counted by the squire, who would send his servant to find out the reason for absence. They objected to innovations such as the replacement of the cheerful, if untuneful, village band by a dull harmonium or solemn organ, and the abolition of the responses once made by the parish clerk. The parson's discourse, often uninteresting, rambling or obscure, his language and accent bordering on the incomprehensible, served only to bring home their own lack of education. No wonder, then, that the Census taken in March 1851 (admittedly on a Sunday when weather and illness kept the numbers unduly low) showed that nationally only a quarter of the population attended the morning service; even less, only 17 per cent, the later ones. Those ordinary villagers who chose to attend neither church nor chapel spent their Sundays in family gatherings

or digging their gardens, in a little fishing or rambling in the woods for rabbits, or in taking a walk with neighbours to a pub in the next village, commenting on the crops and standard of the farming as they went. Or, towards the end of the nineteenth century, they rode out on bicycles and of an evening read (often with some difficulty) the spicy stories retailed in Sunday newspapers such as *Reynolds News* or *The News of the World*.

Church and Chapel together had to meet increasing indifference as working people felt a stronger sense of independence, and as more varied opportunities for leisure became available. Much of the villagers' conduct, and many of their ideas, were not of a kind likely to be approved by vicar or minister. Traditional superstitions and practices survived into the nineteenth century, and indeed lasted throughout that century to a surprising degree. Wife sales, for example, an illicit but cheap and simple form of divorce, were still fairly common down to the middle of the century and were by no means unknown thereafter. As late as 1847 the *Stamford Mercury* reported that at Barton the town crier had announced the sale by auction in the market place of the wife of a certain George Wray. The lady in question appeared with a new halter tied round her waist, and was knocked down to a William Harwood, waterman, for the sum of 1s 1½d, returned 'for luck'. 'Harwood walked off arm in arm with his smiling bargain, with as much coolness as if he had purchased a new coat or hat.'[25] The sum paid at Barton was not untypical of many similar bargains, and often the woman was passed over for as little as a shilling or two, with a gallon of beer thrown in – in a period when the corpses illegally used by surgeons for dissection fetched as much as £8 or £10. Wife sales were commonly held in a market place or in a cattle market (at Smithfield in London), and at hiring fairs and inns: and the sale itself, degrading as it was, followed on a parade of the woman drawn by a halter through the public streets.[26]

Parsons and preachers might condemn the practice, and the superior orders regard it as an archaic survival from barbarous times, but it could not easily be forced out of existence. The same could be said of many other old customs. 'Wise men' were still being consulted even as late as the 1880s, and fear of witchcraft continued even longer. Indeed, the spells and rituals of wise men were sought out not only to charm away the ordinary ills of humans and farm animals but also when some extraordinary misfortune was thought to be due to witchcraft. It may readily be understood that when the resources of formal medicine were limited, when qualified doctors were often hard to find, and even qualified doctors groped blindly in a fog of misconceived and

sometimes absurd theories, that many people – and not only the poorer groups of society – would readily resort to folk remedies. What is surprising is that folk cures, often of a bizarre and horrifying description, should survive even into the twentieth century.[27]

Although some popular superstitions had been whittled away by the various forms of Protestant activity, as well as by many other influences during the seventeenth and eighteenth centuries, belief continued to be strong in the existence of unnatural forces abroad which impinged, for good or evil, on daily life. This belief lay behind the rituals which surrounded birth, marriage, and death, and were extended even to daily occupations. Charms and potions were used to attract a lover or to cure a sick animal, and apparitions of persons about to die might be seen in the churchyard on St Mark's eve or All Saints. Folk-tales told of disasters which occurred to those who broke a taboo, such as killing a robin, or failure to placate the fairies with a dish of cream, or who committed sacrilege by felling certain trees.[28] J. R. Mortimer, a Yorkshire archaeologist, recalled that during his boyhood in the Yorkshire Wolds in the middle of the nineteenth century, almost every village had its reputed witch. At Fimber, where he lived, anything that went wrong was ascribed to the evil eye of a certain Mrs Rachel Kirby. It was strongly believed that a dog howling near the home of a sick person was a certain sign of approaching death. The crowing of a cock at the back door indicated the near approach of a stranger, and a horseshoe was nailed to the door to keep the witch away and bring good luck. When someone died it was the custom to deck the beehives with black crêpe and give the bees some ale on a plate to ensure the continued well-being of the hives. Mortimer recalled an occasion when a neighbouring farmer attempted to cure his father's rheumatism by making passes over the parts affected. The farmer said he had enjoyed many successes with persons who had faith; but apparently Mortimer's father did not have faith sufficient, and he received no benefit.[29]

Even clergymen were sometimes inclined to ascribe a mysterious series of misfortunes to the influence of a witch. Early in the nineteenth century, the Revd William Ettrick of Toner's Puddle in Dorset suffered the unaccountable loss of a horse and a pig, the failure of his garden crops, and the illness of his son, which always got worse when one of his servants, Susan Woodrowe, was nearby. He recalled that she had asked for some hair from the horse's tail, and had tended the crops which failed, and he became convinced she was a witch. And, sure enough, when she was dismissed the misfortunes ended.[30] Writing 150 years later, in 1956, George Ewart Evans told of

elderly villagers he knew in East Anglia who believed that stones grew in the ground, and held that women who cut their hair at the time of the new moon would ensure that their hair would grow thicker as the moon waxed. There were people who believed a corpse should have company and light, candles being required to humour the devil. A dish of salt placed on or below the corpse would make sure 'it doesn't start rising'. Mirrors had to be covered in a thunderstorm, and a slice of onion placed in the room of a sick child served to draw the child's complaint into itself. When the child was better the onion had to be burned.[31]

That superstitions of these kinds lasted into at least the middle of the twentieth century indicates the tenacious nature of the grip they held on the minds of country people. Nor were they confined to the poor and ignorant, but were accepted and complied with by numbers of parsons as well as squires and farmers. It is probable that not a few of those who worshipped regularly in church or chapel paid tribute to alien supernatural forces once they were beyond the ken of the clergyman or minister. Indeed, the churchyard itself was associated with some traditional rituals, while some elements of Methodism were absorbed into the popular culture which the chapels contested. Methodism, it has been said, 'did not so much replace folk-beliefs as translate them into a religious idiom.' John Wesley himself believed in ghosts and witches, and early Methodism was the more acceptable to country people because it did not attempt to demand a rational view of the world – only that inexplicable events, fortunate or unfortunate, were to be ascribed to providence, the will of God, whose purposes could not be known or questioned.[32]

Thus the nineteenth-century village was riven between established Church, Nonconformity and the remnants of the traditional alternative religion. The Church's influence declined as the status of the clergyman himself waned when his income failed to keep pace with that of other professions, and especially when it declined absolutely in the latter part of the century. The status of the vestry declined also as hostility grew towards vestry-levied Church rates in the 1830s; its diminishing influence was finally emasculated by the Local Government Act of 1894. Compulsory church rates formed an element of division between Church and Chapel, though Nonconformists had other serious grievances concerning their access to parochial graveyards and the much-debated question of disestablishment. The last was especially strongly felt in those parts of the country, like Wales and much of the north of England, where Nonconformity was strong and the Church weak. Why should

Nonconformist landowners and farmers pay a rent-charge to help finance a Church to which they did not belong and did not want? And why, after 1870, should they pay school rates for a school which promoted the precepts of the established Church in its religious teaching and ignored other doctrines? These were not merely parochial squabbles but assumed a national significance as Nonconformists gave votes, organised support, and added moral fervour to the Liberal cause, providing in Gladstone's words, 'the backbone of liberal democracy'.[33]

In the end both Church and Chapel went down together as a more secular age seized the opportunities for leisure and travelling afield offered first by the railways and, subsequently, the motor car and motor cycle. Sabbatarianists attempted to check the trend – and succeeded in obliging some railway companies to cease running services on Sundays – but their efforts eventually came to naught in face of rising incomes, shorter working hours and paid holidays, as well as the distractions offered by newspapers and magazines, and ultimately radio and television. Improved education and greater access to the advances of science, notably Darwinism, further weakened the hold of religion on the people. Although in 1957 a Gallup poll found that 78 per cent of its sample claimed to believe in God, only 27 per cent were zealous enough to attend a service. And although over half of the believers claimed affiliation to the Church of England, fewer than one in ten of them took the trouble to go to church. In the countryside chapels were closed and eventually sold to be converted into secular meeting halls or private residences, and even parish churches were thought ripe for closing as congregations dwindled and the Church's finances became more straitened. The vitality of a previous era had been sapped by the Church's divorce from the land, by religious, political and social schisms, and not least by the emergence of a hedonistic society which lacked religious conviction and replaced both superstition and belief in God by a cynical rationalism.

NOTES

1. **Eric J. Evans**, *The Contentious Tithe: the Tithe Problem and English Agriculture, 1750–1850*, Routledge & Kegan Paul, 1976, p. 3; **Vanessa S. Doe** (ed.), *The Diary of James Clegg of Chapel en le Frith 1708–55, Part I 1708–36*, Matlock, Derbyshire Record Office, 1978.
2. Evans, *The Contentious Tithe*, p. 4.
3. **Rosalind Mitchinson**, 'Pluralism and the poorer benefices in eighteenth century England', *Historical Journal*, **V**, 1962, pp. 188–90.

4. **William Addison,** *The English Country Parson*, Dent, 1947, pp. 72–3.
5. **Pamela Horn,** *A Georgian Parson and his Village: The Story of David Davies (1742–1819)*, Abingdon, Beacon Production, 1981, p. 16.
6. Addison, *English Country Parson*, pp. 141–2.
7. Horn, *A Georgian Parson*, p. 29.
8. Addison, *English Country Parson*, pp. 83, 144.
9. **F. G. Heath,** *The English Peasantry*, Warne, 1874, pp. 140–6, 153–6.
10. **John L. Harnsberger** and **Robert P. Wilkins,** 'New Yeovil, Minnesota: a Northern Pacific Colony in 1873', *Arizona and the West*, **XII,** 1, 1970.
11. **Michael Brander,** *The Country Divine*, Edinburgh, Saint Andrew Press, 1981, p. 129.
12. Evans, *The Contentious Tithe*, pp. 8, 18–19, 36.
13. *Ibid.*, pp. 95, 97–9.
14. *Ibid.*, pp. 128–32, 163–4.
15. **Alan D. Gilbert,** 'The land and the Church', in **G. E. Mingay** (ed.), *The Victorian Countryside*, Routledge & Kegan Paul, 1981, I, pp. 50, 55.
16. Evans, *The Contentious Tithe*, pp. 164–7.
17. **Alan Everitt,** 'Nonconformity in country parishes', in **Joan Thirsk** (ed.), *Land, Church and People*, Supplement to *Agricultural History Review*, **XVIII,** 1970, p. 178.
18. *Ibid.*, pp. 180–2.
19. *Ibid.*, pp. 183–93, 197.
20. **Bernard Jennings** (ed.), *A History of Nidderdale*, Chichester, Phillimore, 2nd edn, 1983, pp. 433–4, 437.
21. **J. H. Porter,** 'The Development of rural society', in **G. E. Mingay** (ed.), *The Agrarian History of England and Wales, VI 1750–1850*, Cambridge University Press, 1989, pp. 888, 890.
22. **Thomas Hardy,** 'The Dorsetshire Labourer', *Longman's Magazine*, July, 1883, p. 12.
23. **Pamela Horn,** 'Labour organizations', in G. E. Mingay (ed.), *The Victorian Countryside*, Routledge & Kegan Paul, 1981, p. 108.
24. **A. Cronk,** *The Life and Times of William Mariott Smith-Mariott of Horsmonden*, Chichester, Phillimore, 1975, p. 25.
25. **R. J. Olney,** *Rural Society and County Government in Nineteenth Century Lincolnshire*, Lincoln, History of Lincolnshire Committee, 1979, p. 92.
26. **Samuel Pyeatt Menefee,** *Wives for Sale*, Basil Blackwell, 1981, pp. 36–8, 167.
27. **Charles Phythian-Adams,** 'Rural culture', in G. E. Mingay (ed.), *The Victorian Countryside*, Routledge & Kegan Paul, 1981, II, pp. 616–7.
28. *Ibid.*, pp. 619–22.
29. **J. D. Hicks,** *A Victorian Boyhood on the Wolds: the recollections of J. R. Mortimer*, Beverley, East Yorkshire Local History Society, 1978, pp. 8–10.
30. **Christina Hole,** *Witchcraft at Toner's Puddle*, Dorchester, Dorset Record Office, 1964, p. 4.
31. **George Ewart Evans,** *Ask the Fellows who Cut the Hay*, Faber, 1956, pp. 210–18.
32. **John Rule,** 'Methodism, popular beliefs and village culture in Cornwall, 1800–50', in **Robert D. Storch** (ed.), *Popular Culture and Custom in Nineteenth Century England*, Croom Helm, 1982, pp. 63–4, 67.
33. Gilbert, 'The land and the Church' pp. 50, 55.

CHAPTER FIVE

Poverty and the Poor Law

POVERTY AND PAUPERISM

The poor, as we know, are always with us; and despite the modern growth of affluence there remain even today a great many people who live in conditions of deprivation. 'Poverty' is a shifting concept, and one that is hard to define; and it has changed so greatly over the years that what is considered poverty today would have been regarded as comfortable circumstances a hundred years ago. However, we have first to distinguish between poverty and pauperism. The unskilled labouring classes of the past were commonly described as 'the poor', by no means always a term of scorn. They included many families who, although living at a low and simple standard, were able to subsist on their incomes. They might only rarely, if ever, require public relief, and then only in exceptional circumstances of accident, illness, temporary loss of employment, harvest failure and, more commonly, old age. Those who resorted to public relief were known by the more degrading epithet of 'paupers'. They were destitute, or nearly so, and in the era before the later eighteenth century consisted mainly of the aged, the sick and lunatic, orphans, and deserted wives and widows with young children. The able-bodied unemployed, only temporarily out of work, were tided over with short-term relief in money or in kind, while those with no prospect of early employment were set to work by the parish. However, those persons categorised as vagrants and work-shys or, in the Elizabethan phrase, 'rogues and vagabonds', were very likely to be placed in a house of correction and whipped.

Publicly provided relief for paupers, as distinct from private charity given to the poor in general, goes back to an Act of 1536; compulsory

rate-financed relief, the essence of the Poor Law, was first established by an Act of 1597. England was unusual among European countries in providing relief through national legislation so early as the sixteenth century. It is interesting also that the growth of legislation concerning the Poor Law seems to have been particularly influenced by periods of population increase which coincided with rising food prices. The sixteenth century, when the legislation began, saw four major Acts followed by the codification of the various measures in the great Poor Law of 1601; and again the period between 1782 and 1834 saw two highly influential Acts as well as the introduction of the Speenhamland system of outdoor relief, and in addition much debate and experimentation in methods of relief. Both were periods of increasing population and of high or rising prices, when the supply of labour tended to run ahead of the demand for it, and dear food put pressure on the living standards of the poor. It is argued that an important reason for the Poor Law legislation of the sixteenth century was government concern to maintain law and order, not overlooking measures to curb the unrest and crime that were ascribed to the alarming growth of 'sturdy rogues and vagabonds'; in the later period the prime concern was to cope with the rise of poverty among able-bodied adults in employment, who could not live on their wages through dearness of food.

This is not to say that Poor Law issues were dormant in other periods; far from it. There was important legislation in 1662 and 1722, and, since the administration and financing of relief was a matter for each parish, there was always much diversity and local initiative. Nevertheless, it is clear that more intense concern with poverty began to mount towards the end of the eighteenth century. There was a tendency among contemporary observers of that time to regard poverty as mainly an urban matter. Travellers like John Byng, fifth Lord Torrington, compared the uncertainty of manufacturing employment and the idleness of town workers with the sober and industrious husbandmen whose work was 'as permanent and moves as regularly as the Globe'.[1] Similarly, the agricultural writer Arthur Young was surprised to find on close examination that poverty was increasing in rural parishes, since he believed, with many others, that agriculture occasioned very few poor. Indeed, in many villages in the past it had only been necessary for the parish occasionally to rent a cottage as a 'poor house' for the benefit of the one or two elderly and infirm people who needed help.

However, towards the end of the eighteenth century conditions began to change more rapidly as the rate of growth of population

took a sharp upward turn. The first serious attempt to examine the new problems of rural poverty was an investigation by the Berkshire parson, David Davies, who published his findings in 1795 (although his material was collected a few years earlier).[2] Davies' work included a number of actual budgets of working families, which showed that their outgoings exceeded, or at best were perilously near to exceeding, their incomes. Even some which showed a surplus of income over expenditure did so only because expenditure on food other than bread and bacon was miniscule, because economies were made such as using home-made rushlights rather than expensive candles, and because the budgets omitted some essential items such as clothing and boots, beer, and expenditure on medicines and burials.

A more extensive study was published two years later by Sir Frederic Morton Eden in his *The State of the Poor*. The appearance of both works owed a good deal to the rise in flour and bread prices which marked the years after 1792. In particular, 1795 (which saw the adoption of the Speenhamland system) and the following year were exceptionally dear, though prices were to rise even higher during the continued wartime shortages after 1798. Bread was of great importance to the poor, accounting for a high proportion of their expenditure on food, but the prices of other items of consumption, such as cheese, bacon and meat, also rose sharply. As a result, Eden, examining the years 1794 and 1795, found much evidence that the labouring classes had been 'subjected to great distress, from a rise, unexampled within the present century, in the price of necessaries of life'. It is true there were places, like Kegworth in Leicestershire, where things were better and the labourers in general seemed 'comfortable', while in some villages where poverty was acute substantial private charity was forthcoming. At Nuneham in Oxfordshire, for instance, Lord Harcourt provided the poor with potatoes every winter; and he also allowed a guinea a year to 'such families as behave well' for the fourth and subsequent children until the age of ten (when many children went into service). Poor families at Nuneham also received free schooling for all their children, and every parishioner was allowed to buy flour and bread at prices below the market level. Similarly, near Hornsey in the East Riding, where many cottages were 'miserable hovels built of mud and straw', the employers supplied their labourers 'with corn, etc., much below the market prices'.[3]

Historians have tended to overlook the extent and importance of private charity in relieving the lot of the poor, especially in hard times like the mid-1790s. Such assistance was, of course, local

95

and haphazard, variable in amount, and not always reliable. It was also often directed at particular individuals: given by the squire to his old tenants or servants, for example, and not to the community in general. Further, even where the relief was more general, it was not uncommon for it to be withheld from families who were known to be idlers or drunkards. Food, and perhaps a few pence in addition, were given to the poor travellers who called at the better houses. And in numerous villages private bequests had established almshouses, schools for poor children, funds for poor people needing fuel at Christmas, and similar charitable purposes. A minority of enclosure Acts specified that a certain piece of land should be vested in trustees to provide fuel for the poor, though this was at best only a partial substitute for the resources of an extensive common which had disappeared, having been merged into the farms. More widespread was the kind of emergency measure taken in very bad times to relieve a short-term crisis. To cite but one example, on 15 February 1795 Parson Woodforde recorded in his diary the 'forty shillings worth of brown bread [that is, of the cheaper kind] given to the Poor of Weston on Tuesday last, and fifty Shillings worth of the same given this day, from the late Collection for the poor'.[4]

All in all, it appears that in normal times private charity enabled some of the poor never to have to resort to the parish, and that collections taken in crisis years to provide food or sell subsidised flour to the people were in some places sufficient to cope with a temporary problem. It is clear from Davies and Eden that the extent of poverty varied from one district to another, from village to village, and from family to family. As regards the individual family, much depended on its size, the number of very young children, and the number able to earn. Destitution might be brought on, among other causes, by sickness and accidents, by the death, unemployment or desertion of the husband, and by poor household management and fecklessness. Locally, the nature of the farming, the size of the crops to be harvested, processed and transported, the availability of winter work and of by-employment in men's and women's crafts were all influential.

On a broader regional scale, important factors were the condition of the cottages and the cost of fuel. Southern labourers generally enjoyed larger and better-built housing than in the North and West, but on the other hand were adversely affected by the dearness of coal. This compelled the use of unsatisfactory substitutes such as turf and furze, and also meant that southern families economised in the use of their ovens. Consequently, they were often condemned not

only to live in cold and draughty homes and put on damp clothes each morning, but also to eat a great deal of cold food. However, matters might be improved where plenty of wood was to hand, and where housewives cooperated by each lighting up an oven in turn, taking in their neighbours' baking. It is clear that numbers of Davies' southern labourers brewed their own beer and were able to cut and collect wood for fuel. Ground for growing vegetables and keeping a pig was also more commonly available in the South.

Families varied much in size but frequently numbered between five and seven persons. In large families the older children could earn a few pence by helping in the fields or working at some household craft, like the nineteenth-century ones of straw-plaiting or bone lace, and it was common for children of ten or older to be put out to service. When they left home to become young farm servants or domestic servants, or apprentices to some craft or trade, the family was relieved of growing appetites and, moreover, the inevitable overcrowding in a two- or three-room cottage was reduced. Labouring families went through a fluctuating cycle of poverty as their circumstances changed. Young unmarried men and women in employment were relatively well off and could if thrifty accumulate a small nest-egg in a savings bank. Then, when they married and started a family, they often found themselves in straitened conditions, and in bad times might need help from the parish. Later, as the children grew up and left home, the couple would become better off, though eventually infirmities and old age might bring them back once more to the tender mercy of the Poor Law.

How extensive was severe poverty is difficult to gauge, though it was undoubtedly widespread in southern counties during the high prices of the Napoleonic Wars and the unemployment of the post-war depression; that is, between 1793 and the early 1820s. An idea of the extent of pauperism in this period may be obtained from statistics of Poor Law expenditure, which show figures for twenty-eight southern counties rising from 2s 10d per head in 1750 to 16s 8d in 1812, and then falling somewhat to 14s 6d in 1821; and for thirteen northern counties, from 1s 4d to 9s 4d in 1821.[5] This increase, great as it was, has to be seen in the context of the exceptionally high food prices which prevailed over a large part of the period, a rapidly growing population, and regionally severe agricultural depression and unemployment after the Wars. The major increase in pauperism was of a new kind, occurring among able-bodied labourers with families, men who even when in full employment found it impossible to live on their wages. Figures for 1802–3 (not peak years of high wartime

prices) show that 35 per cent of relief recipients in that year consisted of able-bodied adults, and that of the total of 11 per cent of the population receiving relief (about 1 million persons), the greater part lived in the South.[6] Apart from questions about the reliability of the statistics themselves, it has to be remembered that some of the poor who would have been entitled to claim relief failed to do so, and that numbers of the poor were kept off the parish by private charity. It is relevant here that some charitable aid and schemes of self-help, like the provision of allotments to rent, were available specifically on the strict condition that the participants made no claim upon the parish.

Later investigations into housing and public health, such as that of Edwin Chadwick in 1842,[7] revealed the sinister connections which existed between insanitary housing, disease and poverty. Chadwick, indeed, began his career as a Poor Law reformer and administrator (being responsible in large part for the Poor Law Amendment Act of 1834), and shifted his interests into public health as he realised the significance of the links between the two. Although historians have given most of their attention to the problems of urban housing, there is no doubt that rural slums, though less concentrated, were very extensive throughout the countryside and were just as hazardous to health. Bad housing, and a shortage of housing of any kind, were reasons why rural labourers quitted the country in search of better homes in the towns. Large numbers of the rural poor were housed in dwellings that had fewer than four rooms, consisting often enough of wayside hovels or 'mushroom halls'; or they were put in old farmhouses and converted farm buildings, divided into tenements, and often constructed of crude and flimsy materials. Such dwellings were frequently severely dilapidated and overcrowded, and lacked either water supply or sanitation that could be described as adequate. Water had sometimes to be drawn from a well contaminated by seepage from nearby privies and middens, or was even collected in buckets from a stream or pond. The houses were frequently far from watertight, having unrepaired thatch for roofs, porous walls, and only damp earth or a layer of bricks for floors, and lacking any but the most rudimentary forms of heating and cooking facilities.

Eventually, towards the end of the nineteenth century, legislation was brought in as the seriousness of the situation was better understood. However, the process of pulling down hopelessly insanitary cottages and of improving others was a slow matter, and the inadequacies of rural homes were still exercising the minds of the authorities even after the Second World War. The effects of bad housing on health and longevity had an unmeasurable but certainly

large impact on poverty, and in all, the consequences of disease and shortened working lives for the supply of labour and the efficiency of the labour force must have been very great.

Similarly, bad diet, meaning both insufficiency of food and inadequate nourishment, was responsible even in modern times for much sickness and poor physical development among rural children, as also among town ones. Nineteenth-century observers commented on the low output of work common among low-paid and badly-fed southern labourers, as compared with the brisk activity of better-paid and better-fed northern ones. It was argued then, and historians now believe correctly, that a vicious circle operated whereby low wages gave rise to insufficient nourishment, resulting in a slow, lethargic pace of work, which in turn produced so little as to justify the payment of starvation wages. An American visitor, Elihu Burritt, commented that, as plantation-owners in the American South had learned, low wages were a false economy: better-paid men produced better work.[8] When labouring men lived on little but bread, cheese and perhaps a little bacon, sometimes only on bread and an onion (onions were held to be good for health), when the women and children perforce made do with even less, and their tea consisted of burnt toast soaked in hot water, it is surprising that people were able to get through a day's work, even at a snail's pace.

Dietary deficiencies were not solely due to poverty, of course. Sometimes a lack of suitable cooking facilities or scarcity of fuel contributed to the problem, and there was also lack of time when the wife was eking out the husband's earnings by working in the fields, plaiting straw, making bone lace or sewing gloves. Ignorance played its part, too. Cottage housewives were censured for their inability to prepare simple nourishing soups and stews as did their French counterparts, and among all classes there was little understanding of the need for balanced diets and the value of fresh vegetables, milk and fruit. Moreover, much of the food to be bought in village shops – as in town ones – was adulterated or contaminated. Alum was added to flour to whiten the bread, dust was mixed with tea to make it go further, and much of the milk came from the 'iron cow' – that is to say, it was watered, and often with water of doubtful purity. Surprisingly, milk was often difficult to obtain in the countryside, and even when a dairy was to hand its cows might be tuberculous, a fact well-known from the later nineteenth century onwards, but of disputed significance. Canned milk was preferred as cheap and more easily kept in warm weather, but early varieties were almost totally deficient in vitamins and helped cause rickets among children fed on

it. The late nineteenth-century roller-ground flour was also deficient in vitamins, and indeed vitamins themselves were not discovered until late in the century.

The nineteenth-century panacea for poverty (and for unrest) was education. If ignorance were dispelled and the children of the poor brought up in habits of industry, then thrift and sobriety would replace idleness and fecklessness. Self-help was also advocated, and in the villages took the form of allotments, friendly societies, building societies and savings banks. Farmers' agricultural societies were encouraged to award prizes not only for the best stock, but also for those labourers who had brought up a large family without ever having to seek the aid of the parish. It was rarely conceded, however, that even the most virtuous of labourers could not overcome an absence of work; or when in work, that poverty resulted from the extreme lowness of the wages paid in some areas. Farmers, moreover, opposed the setting of land aside for allotments as encouraging a spirit of independence among their workpeople, while village friendly societies and building societies experienced a high failure rate because of inadequate funds and acceptance of undue risks – as well as defaulting treasurers.

Even schooling for the children of the poor was opposed by farmers as likely to encourage the movement off the land, so diminishing the supply of labour. The teaching of geography was thought to be particularly pernicious in this respect. In any event, whatever the supposed advantages of education, schools, even bad ones, were totally lacking in a number of villages before the last quarter of the century. Many children, especially boys (who left school for work at an earlier age than girls), had only a very limited education at a Sunday school, a private dame school or a charity school of some kind. A very few had sufficient teaching to develop natural ability so as to catch the eye of a kindly teacher or parson, and be selected to go off to train as a teacher or clerk. Before the closing years of the nineteenth century the majority became only barely literate, just enough to be able to get through a Sunday newspaper; or perhaps they met that criterion proposed by Robert Lowe, Secretary for Education in the 1860s, by becoming sufficiently educated to realise that, compared with their superiors, they were hardly educated at all.

More effective than education for reducing poverty was migration. There was a realisation that, in the more purely agricultural districts where wages were low, the farmworkers' pay could never rise to satisfactory levels unless the numbers seeking employment were reduced. Part of the movement off the land, which began to be

fairly strong in the second quarter of the nineteenth century, was due to assistance offered by government funds, and to charitable efforts and the propaganda of American emigration agents, while at a later stage village unions and clubs set up schemes to finance the emigration of families to Canada, Australia or New Zealand. Within Britain, however, most of the short-distance internal migration was of a purely individual and independent kind, much influenced by proximity to a growing centre of alternative sources of employment, by letters from relations or friends who had already moved away, and by a greater knowledge of the wider world gained from newspapers. Here education did play a significant part. The motives for moving included the desire for better wages, more varied and more reliable employment, and dissatisfaction with country work, its low pay and lack of prospects. Country girls went off to towns to work as domestics, and, it was said, the boys followed the girls.

The movement was considerable, and was reflected in some degree in the diminishing numbers of men and women employed in agriculture after mid-century. In addition to the flow to the towns there was some movement of farmworkers into other kinds of employment within the countryside, perhaps in small market towns, into such positions as grooms, railway porters, carters, warehousemen, council men, brickmakers, quarrymen, building workers and the like. In all, through a wide variety of factors – of which migration was one of the more important – the extent of rural poverty diminished in the second half of the century. The economy as a whole was expanding and diversifying, means of transport were revolutionised by railways and steamships, and many towns were greatly expanded. Pauperism, too, declined, since Poor Law policies were such as to discourage all but the destitute and desperate from seeking relief. Increasingly, in fact, the extent of pauperism – dependence on public poor relief – became a more imperfect indication of the extent of poverty.

Nevertheless, however measured, poverty remained significant. The Poor Law figures, certainly, give little idea of how the poor fared. Late nineteenth-century estimates of the extent of poverty, made for large cities like London and York, suggest that some 10–12 per cent of the population existed in acute deprivation, and that, altogether, more than twice this number lived in some degree of poverty, incapable of maintaining 'physical efficiency'.[9] What the figures were for the countryside we do not know, and it is not impossible that they were substantially better, if only because of more regular employment and

the healthier nature of the surroundings. At all events, compared with the urban estimates of poverty, the national figures for *pauperism* seem very small. As a proportion of the population in receipt of official relief, the 11 per cent of 1802–3 had fallen by mid-century to 5.3 per cent; by 1900 to only 2.4 per cent. We should remind ourselves that these figures do *not* measure poverty. What they indicate is that poor relief was becoming less and less significant in assisting the poor. Nevertheless, the decline in pauperism deserves explanation, and its decline, together with changes in relief policies, are the concern of what follows.

THE OLD POOR LAW AND THE PARISH

The Old Poor Law is the name given to the assortment of relief measures which were in force before the passing of the Poor Law Amendment Act (the 'New Poor Law') in 1834. The Old Poor Law hardly merits the description of a 'system' since the provision varied both from parish to parish and from time to time, and there were considerable differences in the use made, for example, of workhouses ('indoor relief'), and of payments in cash or in kind made to paupers living at home ('outdoor relief'). Nevertheless, certain principles can be distinguished which gave some common basis to the complex pattern of relief.

In the first place, relief was based on the parish, and each parish paid for its own poor by means of a poor rate levied on the property-owners. There were, it is true, the national Poor Laws, which provided a legal basis for the various forms of relief; while the activities of the parish overseers were supervised by county justices, in much the same way as the work of the parish Surveyor of the Highways on the upkeep of roads and bridges was liable to the justices' inspection. Parish administration of relief, it has been pointed out, had both advantages and disadvantages. On the positive side, the parish overseers could be expected to have a close knowledge of individual claimants and be able to judge the respective merits of each case; in consequence, they were able to provide the form of relief most appropriate to the circumstances. On the negative side, it could be objected that the overseers commanded undue arbitrary power over the poor and could make themselves into petty tyrants, treating deserving claimants unfairly should they happen to dislike them, and behaving stingily where their prime objective was to keep down the poor rates.[10] They might, alternatively, be careless, dilatory, and

wasteful of the ratepayers' money. On the whole, however, it may be urged that the parish basis was a sensible, flexible and economical system for the administration of relief when the population was small and the majority of people lived in little market towns and villages, and when the numbers of claimants were generally few and their needs quite various.

Secondly, a major result of the parish basis was the natural concern of each parish to ensure that it gave relief only to those who belonged there, and not to newcomers or strangers. The need to establish rules for deciding who belonged to a parish – who had a 'settlement' there – led to the passing of the Settlement Act of 1662 and to subsequent legislation which modified its provisions. So far as the parish poor were concerned, the effect was to establish three main grounds for claiming a settlement: birth, residence and employment. Having been born in a certain parish was, of course, the original right to a claim (a married woman, however, took her husband's settlement if it was different from her own). Residence in a parish for forty days, or employment there during a whole year, provided alternative grounds for a claim. Those persons who became 'chargeable' – that is, in need of relief, but who had no settlement in the parish – could be removed to their own parish. This might be an expensive matter for the authorities, however, and so frequently the parish of settlement preferred to acknowledge the liability and pay a 'pension' or regular sum of money to the first parish in order that the chargeable pauper could remain there and the costs of removal be avoided. Again, the flexibility of the system was increased by the use of certificates. The certificate was a guarantee, granted by a justice, which gave assurance that should the person named in it become chargeable, his own parish would meet the costs of removing him. Armed with such certificates harvest gangs could move about the countryside, and unemployed individuals could look for work in specified places. The Settlement Law, though certainly restrictive, was thus much less of a bar to the mobility of labour than might be supposed.

A study of the examinations made by Poor Law officials when enquiring into the circumstances of poor persons, and more particularly, into their place of settlement, shows there to have been marked seasonal patterns of unemployment. It is also argued that the evidence indicates a decline in the economic independence of rural workers and a reduced role for women in the workforce. The seasonal patterns of unemployment, it is contended, were due to an expansion of large-scale grain production in eastern and southern England, although the statistical basis for the argument is substantially weakened by

the circumstance that the sample of persons examined changed substantially from 1795 onwards. Before that date, both *potential* claimants as well as *actual* ones were examined; after 1795, only those actually seeking relief could be removed to their place of settlement and so required examination. Further, the fact that seasonal unemployment appears to have increased also in non-agricultural occupations suggests that some much broader influence, other than a growth of grain farming, was at work.[11]

Undoubtedly, the growth of population, which became rapid towards the end of the eighteenth century, had the effect of producing a surplus of labour in many districts of the southern half of the country where new, alternative occupations were lacking, and where old alternatives, such as textiles and iron-making, were in decline. The labour surplus showed itself in under-employment, and particularly in a lack of sufficient winter work. The increased insecurity and poverty of the southern labourer, together with any decline in female employment, were due more to this than any other factor, though it has to be remembered that changing economic conditions, affecting markets and prices, and some purely local influences, were also significant.

It is true that from the later eighteenth century the gradual replacement of farm servants (farmworkers who lived in with the farmer and were hired by the year) by day labourers (living in cottages and hired by the day) added to the deterioration in labour conditions, though since the great majority of farm servants were youngsters under the age of twenty-one, the bulk of farmworkers were unaffected by the change. It is very likely the case also that the rise in the labourers' numbers made for greater difficulty in obtaining settlements as employers grew increasingly conscious of the mounting pressures on the poor rates of a swelling workforce.[12]

In any event, the desire of the authorities to keep down poor rates was not new, though it may well have been intensified by the mounting population pressures of the later eighteenth and early nineteenth centuries. The Settlement Law, and associated legislation such as the Bastardy Act of 1733, had long encouraged watchful parish officers to take harsh, even inhuman, measures in order to keep down the poor rates. Property-owners pulled down old cottages when they became vacant and did not rebuild, so that some of the labour employed in the parish had to live elsewhere. Farmers sacked their regular men and left them unemployed for one day in the year so that they could not gain a settlement in the farmers' parish. To prevent a pregnant pauper woman from producing a new burden

on the rates she might, when near to giving birth, be loaded into the parish cart and transported at dead of night across the parish boundary, so that the responsibility for the infant pauper would fall on the neighbouring parish. A further iniquitous manifestation of the officials' regard for the rates was the compulsory marriage. If a pregnant, unmarried woman swore on oath before a justice that a certain man was responsible for her condition, the parish could require the man to give security to indemnify the parish or else go to prison. Alternatively, the man could marry the woman and thus overcome his inability to indemnify the parish. Parson Woodforde recorded in his diary an occasion in January 1787 when he officiated at just such a wedding ceremony:

> the Man being in Custody, the Woman being with Child by him. The Man was a long time before he could be prevailed on to marry her when in the Church Yard; and at the Altar behaved very unbecoming . . . I recd. of the Officers for marrying them 0. 10. 6. It is very disagreeable to me to marry such Persons.[13]

Many of the needs of paupers were met by payments in kind or in cash. The homeless were provided with a room in a poorhouse, the destitute with food, clothing and fuel, the sick with the services of a doctor or nurse. Up to the seventeenth century there were parishes which paid for sufferers from the 'king's evil' (scrofula) to journey to London to be touched by the monarch in the hope of effecting a cure. In the eighteenth century some parishes went in for preventive medicine, when funds were provided for all the children to be inoculated against smallpox. However, parish assistance was often quite marginal in helping the poor to live, and sometimes was not called upon. Late in the century, as Davies reported, some families, as at Sidlesham in Surrey, helped to keep their heads above water without resort to the parish by taking in lodgers, 'for whom the wives wash and mend'. At Holwell in Somerset men in employment, but with large families, had their house rent paid by the parish, while fuel cost them nothing, 'being procured by gathering cow-dung, and breaking their neighbours' hedges'. In Merioneth unemployed men, women and children occupied themselves in knitting coarse woollen stockings, knitting as they walked, talked and begged; the trade was considered unprofitable, it was reported, since they 'were obliged to beg to make up the deficiencies in their earnings'. Widows and their families also supported themselves by begging from door to door, though they received a parish dole of oatmeal. The poor in

Merioneth could not afford tea, and to eke out their soap resorted to 'chamber-lye' (urine). At Marsham, in Norfolk, 'the usual parish allowance to a man advanced in years' was 2s a week in addition to clothing, fuel and, if necessary, use of the poorhouse. A widow without children was allowed 1s a week together with house, rent and fuel, though if she was 'past doing any labour' 2s was given; a widow with one child received 1s 6d, if two children 2s, and so on.[14]

It is clear that payments in cash, not only to the 'impotent' poor but also to men in work with families, were commonplace by the later eighteenth century. The introduction of the Speenhamland system of 1795, under which labourers' wages were subsidised, was therefore not quite so novel as is sometimes supposed. Indeed, the novelty of Speenhamland lay in the sliding scale of payments which varied the relief according to the price of bread and number in the family. This form of relief, in effect a food subsidy, was named after Speenhamland, near Newbury in Berkshire, where the magistrates met at the Pelican Inn to decide on how best to relieve the employed poor in a year of very high bread prices. In fact, the Berkshire magistrates were not the first to hit upon the scheme, for those in Buckinghamshire and Oxford had issued scales three months earlier, and the Dorset authorities had used a scale in 1792 in response to a local emergency. Earlier still, in 1785, the Cambridgeshire justices had met the problem created by a deficient crop by ordering that all wages be brought up to 6s a week.[15] Although never a statutory part of the Poor Law, versions of the bread scale, or sales of food below market price, were widely adopted in southern counties during the high prices of the war period.

The scales of 1795 had been introduced as a short-term measure to meet the dear food crisis of that year, and were partly financed by voluntary subscription; but the continuation of high prices during the following two decades meant that many southern parishes employed similar schemes for the whole of the war period, though not necessarily consistently, and consequently a heavy burden fell on the poor rates. When prices moderated at the end of the Wars the bread scale became less frequently used and preference was given to alternative means of relief for the able-bodied.

These alternatives were concerned with the able-bodied unemployed, who posed an increasing problem in the South as the population rose and opportunities for work outside agriculture either declined or failed to expand sufficiently to absorb the increase in the labour force. One old-established alternative was the 'roundsman system', which in some places was already in use before 1795. Overseers mindful

of the obligation to set the able-bodied to work, and concerned also that the burden on the parish should be minimised, used this as a means of finding at least some paid work, if pitifully paid, for the unemployed, especially in the winter months. The men were sent round the parish to seek work from employers, the parish supplementing whatever wage was paid; if no work was to be found, or insufficient, then the parish provided what relief was considered appropriate. The practice became known as 'going the rounds', and the people concerned as 'roundsmen'. A variation of this practice, already used in the eighteenth century, was to allocate the unemployed to the farmers and other employers by means of a ballot, or according to the acreage of the farmer, the parish again making up the wages as necessary. Or the unemployed labourers might be auctioned off to the highest bidders, with the parish again making up the wages offered. More sophisticated was the 'labour rate', where the ratepayers were offered a reduction in their rates depending on the number of extra men employed and the wages paid.[16] These schemes had the merit from the parish's point of view of reducing the burden of relieving the unemployed, and from the farmers' point of view of enabling them cheaply to undertake labour-intensive projects such as drainage, clearing waste land and growing root crops.

Where these expedients failed or were inadequate, the unemployed might be put to work on repairing the roads and drains, or in cultivating a parish farm by spade labour – again devices which had been resorted to occasionally in the seventeenth and eighteenth centuries. Once more, the twin objects of putting the able-bodied to work and obtaining some advantages for the ratepayers were dominant. The difficulty with these parish work schemes, however, was that of providing proper supervision. If the paupers were not closely supervised they were only too likely to down tools and smoke their pipes, or go off into the woods for rabbits or pheasants. Consequently, direct employment by the parish was never very widespread or successful, and sometimes the only work available consisted of such degrading tasks as collecting pebbles or breaking stones for road repairs.

The workhouse, as the name indicates, was originally an establishment designed to comply with the requirement in the Act of 1601 that the paupers be set to work. Each parish was supposed to provide a supply of implements and raw materials for the purpose, and it was hoped that the goods produced in the workhouse could be sold to defray the expenses. In some areas, notably in East Anglia,

the authorities in the eighteenth century let the workhouse and its inmates to private contractors who expected to make a profit out of the goods produced, but such schemes rarely succeeded for long. As might be expected, the products were generally of poor quality and the output erratic, while independent workpeople outside the workhouse complained of unfair competition.

In addition, workhouses provided a refuge, temporary or permanent, for the homeless poor, the sick, aged, lunatics, and waifs and strays. Over time, this aspect of the workhouse, relief of the 'impotent' poor, tended to dominate over that of putting the poor to work. That there were problems in maintaining discipline and good conduct in the workhouse is obvious from the frequent reports of disputes and assaults, and also from the very detailed regulations which were issued. These required, for instance, the careful keeping of records and accounts by the master and dame in charge, the prohibition of distilled liquors, the setting of strictly limited periods for smoking, and of regular hours for rising, going to bed, and mealtimes, weekly attendance at church, and daily readings from the Bible.[17]

Workhouses were mainly to be found in towns, where the numbers of paupers were such as to justify their provision. Until 1722 the legality of the workhouse was in fact doubtful, but in that year an Act removed this doubt and also allowed the parish authorities to group together to provide a workhouse, and to contract for its management. Thus the union of parishes, an important feature of the Poor Law Amendment Act of 1834, was already authorised over a century earlier. Another supposed innovation of the 1834 Act, the 'workhouse test', was also legalised by the Act of 1722. From the date of that Act it was perfectly lawful for overseers to refuse relief to those who declined to enter the workhouse, and this 'proof of need' served to allow overseers to penalise the idle and, incidentally, to over-rule those magistrates who were thought over-generous to undeserving cases.[18] The Act of 1722 led to the formation of a number of unions of parishes in order to establish workhouses, and the movement was further encouraged by Gilbert's Act of 1782, which, however, was permissive rather than compulsory. It was in fact a watered-down version of what Gilbert, the reformer, believed was necessary, but it is interesting that the Act specified that workhouses were to be only for 'such as are become indigent by old age, sickness or infirmities', together with children, accompanied where necessary by their mothers.[19] In this way Gilbert's Act indirectly encouraged the expansion of various forms of outdoor relief as alternatives to the workhouse.

THE ATTACK ON OUTDOOR RELIEF

With the huge rise in food prices during the Napoleonic Wars, and the rise in the numbers of paupers as the population increased, the cost of relieving the poor mounted sharply. David Davies' book included a report from Marsham in Norfolk for 1790 that poor rates there had averaged 9s in the £ rent over the previous seven years. This meant that a farm rented at £100 a year paid £45 in poor rates, in addition, of course, to the church and highway rates.[20] Later reports, in the 1820s and 1830s, mentioned poor rates as high as a pound in the £ rental, and in some cases actually exceeding the rent of the land. Clearly, this heavy burden of local expenditure, although paid initially by the tenant, ultimately fell on the landlords who found their rents correspondingly depressed. Expenditure per head of the whole population was 8s 11d in 1802, and reached a peak of 13s in 1818; it then fell and averaged 9s 6d between 1822 and 1832. In terms of total expenditure on poor relief in agricultural counties, the peak was reached in 1817, when the figure was nearly double that of 1802. There was a relatively low period in the years 1821–28, when food prices moderated somewhat and many parishes had resorted to more stringent control of expenditure, but it is significant that the years 1829–32, which led up to the passing of the Poor Law Amendment Act, were again ones of high expenditure.[21]

Although there was some concern about supposed high living among paupers lodged in workhouses, the main thrust of the reforms of the early nineteenth century was directed at outdoor relief, and particularly relief of the able-bodied. Much of the blame for the rise in expenditure at that time was laid at the door of the Speenhamland bread scale, although historical research of recent years has shown that this was misplaced. Well before the New Poor Law of 1834 the bread scale had been widely abandoned in southern counties where it had once predominated. Two years before the new Act, in 1832, only 21 per cent of all parishes in the South of England operated a Speenhamland type of relief, and indeed the labour-rate system was more commonplace. Speenhamland had largely been replaced by allowances given to large families, and in the South nearly half of all parishes had some form of child allowance.[22]

The supposed evil effects of making up wages were held to be numerous and pernicious; although if this were true, by 1832 they were largely a thing of the past, as we have seen. One argument was that to subsidise wages was to keep them low; abolition of the subsidy would force employers to pay their men a living wage.

Wages, however, responded more to the supply and demand for labour than to any subsidy from the parish, and indeed wages remained miserably low in many districts for many years after Speenhamland-type relief was abolished by the Act of 1834. Rather, it was true that Speenhamland was itself a reaction to low wages, and not a cause of them.

Another supposed evil of the making-up of wages was the encouragement it was thought to give the poor to enlarge their families, for every extra child meant an increase in the relief doled out by the parish. It is extremely unlikely that this inducement was ever effective in causing labourers to have larger families, since the additional amount of relief was hardly commensurate with the costs of feeding and clothing an extra child. Further, specific research has shown that parishes which operated a Speenhamland system of making up wages had in fact lower birth rates than those which did not.[23] Other complaints concerning the frequency of 'imprudent' marriages, and of idleness and fecklessness among the labourers, may, if valid, be attributed to causes other than the form of poor relief, such as the changing character of rural society and deteriorating relations between rich and poor in the countryside.

THE NEW POOR LAW

Criticism of the supposed evils of the Old Poor Law was reinforced in the 1820s by a number of local experiments in which reformers succeeded in reducing both pauperism and the poor rates. This was achieved by establishing repellently harsh regimes in the workhouse, accompanied by a revival of the 'workhouse test' – the refusal of relief outside the workhouse – as the acid proof of destitution. The Swing riots of 1830, though only partially influenced by the niggardly and degrading nature of the relief grudgingly dispensed by some over-bearing overseers, appeared to provide additional evidence for the weaknesses of the old system. The primary causes of the riots – low wages, under-employment, acute poverty and the threat to winter earnings posed by the introduction of threshing machines – were associated in the public mind with the defects of the Poor Law. Reform was seen to be needed in order to restore the independence of the labourer and to bring social stability to a troubled countryside. Outdoor relief for the able-bodied – and more precisely, allowances in aid of wages and the use of scales – was identified as a major evil,

and the *Report* of the Royal Commission appointed in 1832 went out of its way to gather ammunition for use against such relief.[24]

Drawing on the evidence in the *Report*, and gaining support from the complaints of aggrieved landowners and farmers about excessive poor rates, the Poor Law Amendment Act of 1834 envisaged a radical reform of the old system. For able-bodied men outdoor relief was to be abolished, and the only kind of relief to be available was to be in the workhouse. The workhouse test was to be strictly applied, and the workhouse itself to become a place of such strict discipline and minimal comfort as to deter all but the desperate. For the able-bodied, therefore, the twin principles of the new regime were to be the workhouse test and a workhouse in which the condition of the pauper was to be less 'eligible' – that is, less comfortable – than that of the lowest class of independent labourer. As the *Report* expressed it, 'every penny bestowed, that tends to render the condition of the pauper more eligible than that of the independent labourer, is a bounty on indolence and vice'.

The objective of 'less eligibility' was to be achieved by making the workhouse a place of 'wholesome restraint'. It was recognised, however, that there would be practical difficulties in making the diet and accommodation inferior to those of the worst-paid independent labourers, workpeople who were condemned by the lowness of their wages to eke out a miserably bare subsistence in insanitary hovels; and to offset the superiority of the workhouse in these respects the main deterrent would lie in making daily life similar to that of a prison, with strict regulations, the wearing of pauper uniform, the requirement of arduous and monotonous labour, the prohibition of luxuries such as beer and tobacco, and not least, the separation of wives from husbands, of children from parents, each to be confined in separate parts of the workhouse.[25]

Where existing workhouses could be adapted to the purpose, as in Norfolk, extensive new buildings were not needed. Elsewhere new workhouses were built, usually in a market town, to serve a 'union' consisting of a dozen or so surrounding parishes over about a 10 mile radius. Since new workhouses were costly to build and staff, and since the objective of most Boards of Guardians was to achieve economy in expenditure, the original intention of providing separate buildings for different categories of paupers was fulfilled in only a few places. What generally resulted was a single, large, mixed workhouse, often with some surrounding land, in which separate quarters were allocated to the men, the women, children and the aged. Able-bodied men were put to cultivating the workhouse land,

or breaking stones for the roads and crushing bones for manure; the women were required to attend to the cleaning and cooking, and looking after the sick. A school was provided for the young inmates, and an infirmary for the sick, the latter supervised by a visiting medical officer appointed from among the qualified doctors of the district, who also looked after the pauper sick on outdoor relief.

As a deterrent the new type of post-1834 workhouse was effective, causing widespread abhorrence and hatred among the poor. Fear of the 'house' long continued, even though, over time, conditions were slowly improved, at least for the elderly and the sick. Those able-bodied poor who found the forbidding nature of the workhouse unacceptable were necessarily forced to accept whatever work they could find, or to take to the road as vagrants and beggars. Thus, in the reformers' eyes, the new law was successful in reducing an artificial surplus of labour which, it was believed, had been created by the former allowance system. It was only the incorrigibly idle and work-shy who would enter the reformed workhouse. What was not accepted was that local surpluses of labour arose from causes other than idleness: from inadequate opportunities for the year-round employment of a growing rural labour force, and the limited mobility of the labouring poor (though some attempts were made to remove poor families from southern districts to industrial areas of the North). In this connection it is important to note that the old parish-based settlement system was not reformed in 1834, and it was only in 1865 that the union was made the basis of settlement; though, as was the case before 1834, it is doubtful how far the settlement system restricted the movement of labour.

The New Poor Law, assisted from the mid-1840s by an expanding economy, accomplished a gradual reduction in the proportion of the population that was granted public relief. Already by 1851 that proportion had fallen from the 1803 proportion of nearly 15 per cent in the Speenhamland counties of the South to only 6.3 per cent; and in counties which had never adopted allowances or scales, from 10.4 per cent to 4.8 per cent. The average expenditure per head on the poor fell from 9s 1d in 1834 to 5s 5d in 1837, and then after a slight rise during the depression years of 1839–43, levelled out at a little over 6s in the mid-1840s. In the long term, the gap between the large numbers of the very poor and the numbers of paupers widened, until eventually the latter represented only a quarter or less of the former. In particular, the new regime reduced significantly the numbers of able-bodied among the pauper host. What the new Act significantly failed to do, however, was to make much impact on the

numbers on outdoor relief. Despite some ambiguity in the *Report*, the continued provision of weekly doles to the aged, the infirm, widows with dependent children, and orphans, was expressly authorised by the Act of 1834. Indeed, the Guardians, knowing that outdoor relief was less costly than institutional maintenance, found ways of keeping paupers out of the workhouse – even able-bodied persons who could be reported as supposedly ill in their own homes. In the 1840s the percentage of paupers receiving outdoor relief averaged some 85 per cent.

The 1834 Act instituted not only a new policy regarding the able-bodied and the workhouse, but also a major administrative reform. A Board of Guardians, elected by the ratepayers, controlled the provision of relief in each union of parishes, subject to the instructions of a permanent Commission in London. The relief measures adopted by the Guardians were open to inspection by regional Assistant Commissioners, and the union's finances were made subject to approval by an auditor appointed by the Commission. Thus central control of policy and of expenditure, a principle which was to become the bedrock of local government generally, was introduced through the New Poor Law. The centuries-old independence of the justices, and under them the parish authorities, was thus removed, though the justices, together with the landowners and large farmers, served as Guardians and therefore retained a large degree of local initiative and the supervision of day-to-day relief. Moreover, particularly because of weaknesses in the Act of 1834, the Commissioners' regulatory regime was neither as powerful nor as persuasive as might be supposed. Boards of Guardians, notably in Wales and in industrial areas in the North of England, were able to delay the local introduction of the Act and to hinder the operation of the new policies. Even in the South of England, where the new measures were introduced rapidly, the Guardians did not always comply complaisantly with the instructions from London; nor was the Commissioners' central control sufficiently effective to avoid gross errors from being made – as is shown by the infamous Andover Workhouse scandal of 1845.[26]

In the South of England, however, the support of the propertied classes for the reform withstood the workers' hostility to the new Act, expressed in a considerable number of riots and attacks on the new workhouses. The impetus for reform was such that by 1839, only five years after the Act, as many as 331 unions had new workhouses already in operation or under construction. In industrial areas of the North, however, where able-bodied pauperism was less acute and its causes rather different, there was a much less rapid response.

Nevertheless, over the whole country, by 1854 only eighteen unions had neither a new nor an adapted workhouse, ten of the eighteen being in Wales, where there was particularly strong resistance to the change.[27]

How successful was the 1834 Act in enforcing on able-bodied men the harsh discipline of the workhouse test – the refusal of outdoor relief for those who would not enter the workhouse? In practice, the operation of the Act was very considerably watered down, first by the Guardians' natural preference for the more economical outdoor relief, and secondly by the various exceptions which the central Commission allowed in its Orders restricting outdoor relief, exceptions so large that the Guardians had 'loopholes wide enough to drive a coach-and-four through'.[28] In particular, the Guardians took advantage of permission to grant outdoor relief not only to an adult male suffering from sickness, accident or infirmity, but also where a member of his family was so affected. In the years 1848–59 over a half of all adult able-bodied paupers in six eastern counties were relieved through this provision.[29] Further, funds drawn from the highway rates and from private voluntary rates were used in some areas to provide outdoor relief for able-bodied men and their families without the cost falling on the poor rates. Lastly, from 1842, where workhouse accommodation was insufficient to house all the applicants for relief, Guardians were authorised to apply a task-work test to able-bodied males, and to provide outdoor relief to those accepting the test. This was indeed a most significant departure from the philosophy of 1834.[30]

It may be concluded that the Act did succeed in ending relief given to the able-bodied on a Speenhamland type of bread scale, although it should be observed that this form of relief had been in decline for some time before 1834. It is likely also that allowances in aid of wages, not given according to a scale, were cut back substantially, especially in the 1850s. However, as we have seen, outdoor relief continued to be made available to able-bodied men and their families, as well as to the other categories of the poor whose right to it had not been in doubt. It is difficult to generalise on the matter because there were wide regional and local variations in the ways in which Guardians reacted to the Orders of the central Commission, and local practices were influenced by changes in the economy of the district and by the pressures of vested interests. In some rural areas in the North neither scales nor allowances in aid of wages had ever been used, so that the shift of policy after 1834 made little difference. In the South the loopholes in the Orders were freely

exploited to continue outdoor relief to the able-bodied, though even here there were numbers of unions which were wholeheartedly in favour of rigid application of the workhouse test. The Godstone union in Surrey even went so far as to abolish outdoor relief for the aged.

In Wales, Guardians had difficulty in getting the farmers to pay poor rates at all, and funds were insufficient for building workhouses unless the Guardians went heavily into debt. Resistance to the new regime persisted as farmers protested over the salaries paid to officials and agitated against the influence of Anglican clergy in the workhouse, while it was claimed that the paupers lived better than did some of the ratepayers. The New Poor Law thus became a focus of discontent, and rioters attempted to destroy newly built workhouses. Overt hostility of this kind occurred also in southern and eastern districts of England, if on a much smaller scale than that which marked the introduction of the new Act in Wales and in industrial areas of the North of England. In Kent and Sussex there were at least ninety-three recorded incidents, and at Faversham in north Kent rioting extended over a period of eight days. Rioting also broke out in East Anglia, although as in Kent and Sussex, the most common offences consisted of attacks on the property of Guardians, Inspectors and Relieving Officers.[31]

Generally, the able-bodied were highly resistant to attempts to impose the workhouse test and the new indignities of the reformed workhouse, and they also reacted violently against changes in outdoor relief itself. The various forms of outdoor relief, it has to be remembered, had through long usage come to be regarded in some areas as traditional rights of the poor. It is hardly surprising that attempts to transform in a few years relief practices which had grown up over half a century or so, and in some instances over much longer periods, should have been deeply resented by those affected; nor is it surprising that they resorted to protests of the kinds that the poor had always used to resist unwelcome change, by avenging themselves on the individuals deemed responsible, and by concerted attacks on the symbol of the changed order of things, the new workhouse.

THE MODERN POOR LAW

As the legal basis for the operation of poor relief, the Act of 1834 continued in force for almost a century, indeed until 1929. After the 1840s outward signs of hostility against the new law diminished.

The economy improved, there was more employment, wages slowly began to rise, and living standards rose too. The poor remained very numerous, of course, and a significant proportion of them remained severely under-nourished, poorly clothed and wretchedly housed, trying as best they could to subsist on incomes which, by any standard, were grossly inadequate. To these desperately poor, the Poor Law, as it has been remarked, became increasingly irrelevant. The ratio of pauperism to population was down to under 3 per cent in the late nineteenth century, by 1912–13 to only 2.15 per cent. Public relief was sought mainly as a last resort when the struggle to live in independence became impossible to sustain. In the countryside, land and property, as represented by the ratepayers, allowed the Poor Law to relieve only a fraction of the village poor, and those only meagrely. For the rest, the answer was Victorian 'self-help'; painful accumulation of savings, and subscriptions to often unsound friendly societies; or education, designed to produce a more sober and frugal working class; or it was movement off the land to find better opportunities in towns or abroad. A combination of mounting numbers of poor with, among the propertied, a harsher attitude towards poverty, prevented the rural economy from providing adequately for all who laboured in it.

Over the years the operation of relief gradually departed further and further from the principles of 1834. Outdoor relief continued, and conditions in the workhouses were slowly ameliorated. This did not, however, change the public perception of the Poor Law. 'Help from the parish', as it was termed, was regarded as shameful and degrading, and the workhouse remained very widely feared. The rural aged, when bereft of family and friends, and too infirm to live on in their cottages, dreaded removal to the 'house'. There they underwent the trial of the first bath of their lives; and bodily clean, dressed in clean clothes, and sat in a clean room, they pined miserably for the squalor of their familiar surroundings. Outdoor relief remained highly bureaucratic, so that it might take many hours, even days, to obtain the Relieving Officer's authority and then secure the attendance of the union doctor at a sick-bed.

Wholesale reform of what had become an outdated and inappropriate system was postponed by measures in the early twentieth century which went far to break up the scope of the Poor Law. From 1908 the elderly were helped by old age pensions, and from 1911 workers were increasingly provided with unemployment insurance and medical assistance through a national insurance scheme. Widows' pensions were introduced in 1925, but family allowances to help

parents bring up their children not until 1945, despite the evidence collected since the later nineteenth century that large families were an important cause of poverty. Other measures dealt with the blind and other handicapped persons. And after the Second World War, of course, much broader universal schemes of national insurance and free medical treatment were introduced.

The Poor Law itself, reformed in 1929, when the unions and Guardians were swept away, and again in 1948, when national provision replaced the 1929 county basis, was still needed to provide for the residual poor – still a very numerous category. It included the aged who could not subsist on inadequate old-age pensions, the long-term unemployed, single-parent families, and those employed who could not provide for families on their low wages. The relief, known from 1929 as 'public assistance', and from 1948 as 'national assistance' (now 'income support'), was dispensed from 1945 according to national scales and varied with individual circumstances. In a broad sense it could be said that the wheel had turned full circle. Speenhamland, writ large, had returned, and it was as if the Act of 1834 had never reached the statute book.

NOTES

1. **C. B. Andrews** (ed.), *The Torrington Diaries*, Eyre & Spottiswoode, 1954, p. 471.
2. **David Davies**, *The Case of Labourers in Husbandry Stated and Considered*, London, 1795.
3. **Sir Frederick Morton Eden**, *The State of the Poor*, 1797, abridged edition by **A. G. L. Rogers**, Routledge, 1928, pp. 115, 118–20.
4. See **G. E. Mingay**, *English Landed Society in the Eighteenth Century*, Routledge & Kegan Paul, 1963, pp. 208–9, 271–5; **John Beresford** (ed.), *Woodforde*, Oxford University Press, 1935, p. 391.
5. **J. P. Huzel**, 'The labourer and the Poor Law', in **G. E. Mingay** (ed.), *The Agrarian History of England and Wales, VI 1750–1850* Cambridge University Press, 1989, pp. 762–6.
6. *Ibid.*, p. 763.
7. **Edwin Chadwick**, *Report on the Sanitary Condition of the Labouring Population of Great Britain*, London, 1842; new edn, **M. W. Flinn** (ed.), Edinburgh University Press, 1968.
8. **Elihu Burritt**, *A Walk from London to Lands' End and Back*, Sampom Low, 1865, p. 123.
9. See **G. E. Mingay**, *The Transformation of Britain 1830–1939*, Routledge & Kegan Paul, 1986, pp. 200–3.
10. **J. D. Marshall**, *The Old Poor Law 1795–1834*, Macmillan, 1968, p. 9.
11. **K. D. M. Snell**, 'Agriculture, seasonal unemployment, the standard of living, and women's work in the south and east, 1690–1860', *Economic*

History Review, 2nd ser., **XXXIII**, 1981, pp. 411, 430; **Norma Landau**, 'The regulation of immigration, economic structures and definitions of the poor in eighteenth-century England', *Historical Journal*, **XXX**, 3, 1990, pp. 569–70.

12. Cf. **K. D. M. Snell**, *Annals of the Labouring Poor: Social Change and Agrarian England*, Cambridge University Press, 1985, ch. 1.
13. Beresford, *Woodforde*, p. 240.
14. Davies, *Labourers in Husbandry*, pp. 173, 179, 181, 191.
15. **Geoffrey W. Oxley**, *Poor Relief in England and Wales, 1601–1834*, Newton Abbot, David & Charles, 1974, p. 111.
16. *Ibid.*, pp. 110, 117; see also Huzel, 'The labourer and the Poor Law', pp. 780–2.
17. See regulations for Dartford Workhouse in **Elizabeth Melling** (ed.), *Kentish Sources: The Poor*, Maidstone, Kent Archives Office, 1964, pp. 97–8.
18. Oxley, *Poor Relief*, pp. 81–2.
19. *Ibid.*, p. 82.
20. Davies, *Labourers in Husbandry*, p. 173.
21. Marshall, *The Old Poor Law*, p. 27.
22. Huzel, 'The Labourer and the Poor Law' p. 776.
23. **J. P. Huzel**, 'Malthus, the Poor Law and population in early nineteenth century England', *Economic History Review*, 2nd ser., **XXII**, 1969, p. 444; 'The demographic impact of the Old Poor Law: more reflections on Malthus', *ibid.*, **XXXIII**, 1980, pp. 371–5, 377.
24. Huzel, 'The labourer and the Poor Law', pp. 792–3.
25. *Ibid.*, p. 793.
26. Huzel, 'The labourer and the Poor Law', pp. 796–803; **Ian Anstuther**, *The Scandal of the Andover Workhouse*, Geoffrey Bles, 1973, pp. 151–2.
27. *Ibid.*, p. 791.
28. Quoted by Huzel, *ibid.*, p. 799.
29. Quoted by Huzel, *ibid.*, p. 799.
30. *Ibid.*, pp. 800–1.
31. *Ibid.*, pp. 801–5.

CHAPTER SIX

The Landowners

THE GREAT LANDOWNERS

Land was the prime support of the ruling class down to the later nineteenth century – until the decline of agriculture reduced the value of landed estates, and the landowning class itself was weakened by successive reforms of the franchise and the arrival of new representative institutions in local government. Land supported not only those who had the main say in government but also a cultural élite, whose taste and standards were felt in art and music, in dress and manners, in sport and entertainment, in landscaping and gardening and, not least, in architecture – even the early factory buildings reflected the influence of country-house styles. The beliefs, opinions and prejudices of no more than a few thousand landowners permeated much of English life, and their power was felt, if only remotely, by all sorts and conditions of men.

Their sway, it is true, was not universal: it declined or ceased at the boundaries of the majority of industrial towns, and there were rural parts of certain counties where land was monopolised more by small occupying owners rather than by distant magnates. Nevertheless, there were still many towns, though mainly small ones, where aristocratic ownership was dominant – as, for example, Folkestone, Eastbourne, Reigate, Chester and Fleetwood. Much of central London, came to be dominated by the Dukes of Bedford, Portland and Westminster, by the Earls of Southampton, and by numerous others who gave their titles to many of the capital's streets and squares. And a minority of industrial towns, such as Nottingham, Cardiff, Stockport and Barrow, owed at least some part of their development to great landowners. Generally, however,

the towns were the expanding empires of the middle class: an enquiry of 1886 indicated that only 69 of 261 provincial towns had some significant part of their land held by great landowners, while a half of the towns reported having no large ground landlords at all.[1]

The English peerage numbered some 260 in 1800, and some 520, twice as many, in 1900. Of the ranks below the peerage there were nearly 800 baronets and 160 knights at the first date, and over a thousand baronets and some 500 knights at the second.[2] No doubt some part of this increase in titled persons represented families who held no significant amount of land, although many of the newly ennobled, wealthy men of the later nineteenth century, industrialists, manufacturers, merchants and bankers, secured their *entrée* into landed society by purchasing an estate. Even in earlier periods there had been titled families without large land-holdings, as there had also been great owners who had not succeeded in acquiring a title. It was generally true, however, that the greater the title the greater the estate, but this coincidence was by no means pervasive, and became less so with the passage of time. Nevertheless, it was certain that the major part of the land was in very few hands: the 'New Domesday' enquiry of 1873, while not pretending to perfect accuracy, indicated that fewer than 7,000 persons possessed as much as four-fifths of the country. What was for long the nation's major resource was concentrated in the grasp of a tiny proportion of the population.

It is not a simple matter to calculate the proportion of land held in the different ranks of estates, but it has been estimated that in 1883 some 24 per cent of England was held in estates of over 10,000 acres, and another 29.4 per cent in estates of between 1,000 and 10,000 acres.[3] When country gentlemen with fewer than 1,000 acres are added in, and allowance is made for the extensive areas owned by institutions such as the Crown, Oxford and Cambridge colleges, old-founded London hospitals, and numerous bodies of charity trustees, then the total owned by landlords of all kinds must have approached some 90 per cent of the whole. Certainly, the proportion owned by farmers in the later nineteenth century was only about 10–12 per cent,[4] meaning that the remainder, 88–90 per cent, was that of landlords who, in normal circumstances, did not themselves farm their land commercially.

The great landowners were the most conspicuous monopolisers of land, though the effect of this was moderated by their estates often being spread over a number of perhaps widely scattered counties, a

consequence of a lengthy process of accumulation through marriage and inheritance. None the less, they frequently had their greatest concentrations of property in the district with which they were most closely associated, where the principal mansion was situated, and where they resided when not in London or abroad. Thus the Duke of Bedford had his principal estate round his house, Woburn Abbey, in Bedfordshire (though he also owned large properties in Cambridgeshire, Devonshire and London); similarly, the Duke of Northumberland had a dominating influence with his 134,000 acres in that county, and his ancestral home at Alnwick Castle; and in the eighteenth century the second Duke of Kingston had his principal mansion at Thoresby, among the 'Dukeries' of north Nottingham-shire, while the old family home, Holme Pierrepont, sat among another cluster of properties in the south of the county, and the Kingston estates stretched away into Derbyshire, Lincolnshire, York-shire, Buckinghamshire, Somerset, Wiltshire and Hampshire.[5] In some instances it was urban property which came to be a major support of ducal magnificence, as the London estate was for the Dukes of Bedford; while the fortunes of the Grosvenors, once modest Cheshire squires, were transformed by their extensive property in London's West End, inherited through a fortunate marriage, making them in the nineteenth century Dukes of Westminster and among the wealthiest families in the land. And to increase their influence in their home county some owners followed a policy of deliberately selling off more remote property and buying land nearer home, as the Earl of Leicester did in Norfolk.

But what made a great landowner great? Primarily, it was possession of a very large country house, secluded from the common gaze by a park and woods, and which cost many thousands of pounds and years of effort to create, and several thousand pounds a year to maintain. Secondly, it was ownership of a sufficient concentration of land to sustain a powerful political influence in county elections and, not infrequently, in borough ones also. And thirdly, it was command of sufficient income not only to maintain a vast country mansion, but also to own or rent a large house in London where, during the 'season', the great owner could entertain on a lavish scale as well as patronise the luxury trades of the capital, the tailors, dressmakers and milliners, the goldsmiths and silversmiths, the furniture-makers, coach-makers and harness-makers, the architects, portrait painters, and many others. This implied a minimum disposable income of at least some £10,000 a year in the later eighteenth century, perhaps twice as much at the end of the following century. Translated into

land rents, this meant a minimum of some 10,000 to 20,000 acres, depending on the situation of the estates and their value.

Of course, as we have seen, some great landowners had their farmland rentals heavily supplemented by the ground rents of urban property, and in a number of cases the latter might well outweigh the former in contributing to the total income of the estate. Similarly, there were owners with relatively unimportant agricultural estates but whose incomes came mainly from minerals, ironworks or canals and, in the nineteenth century, from railways. The Earls of Dudley depended largely on their mines and ironworks in the Black Country; the Leveson-Gower family basked for a period in the golden inheritance of the revenues of the Bridgewater Canal; the Marquess of Bute busily built docks at Cardiff and Barry for the shipping of the lucrative product of his Glamorgan coal mines; while in the 1850s the Duke of Cleveland was no doubt more than a little gladdened to receive a steady £14,000 a year from his lead and coal mines.[6] Other lesser families had aspired to enter the ranks of landowners by means of the professions and banking, trade, engineering, brewing and, not least, cotton. Another source of income, though usually a minor one, consisted of investments in the Funds (government stock and other safe stocks in the Bank of England and old-established trading companies); and some families extended in the nineteenth century into a wider range of shares – railway shares both at home and abroad, brewery shares, public utilities and the like. Such diversification proved wise when agricultural rents tumbled in the 1880s, not to recover for many years to come. Other owners held land abroad, in America and the West Indies; and a few became personally involved in the development of their ironworks, chemical works or shipyards, as did Earl Fitzwilliam in Yorkshire, and the seventh and eighth Dukes of Devonshire in Barrow-in-Furness.

Already in the later seventeenth century the total incomes of the greatest of great landowners very comfortably exceeded £10,000 a year, and in the early eighteenth century at least seven peers could boast of enjoying revenues of over £20,000 or even more than £30,000.[7] Subsequently, incomes of this kind became more commonplace as farm rents rose substantially in the thirty years after 1760, and then doubled during the Napoleonic Wars. Royalties from industrial ventures and profits of commercial woodlands also mounted at the same time, while in the nineteenth century increased returns from industrial investment and dividends on railway shares more than made up for the dwindling profits of the majority of canals. Urban property, also, yielded much higher revenues as the towns

expanded and the first 99-year leases fell in, so that in the instance of the Duke of Bedford his London estate contributed £162,000 (as much as 61 per cent of his total revenue) by 1895. Landed incomes exceeding £100,000 a year could be claimed by sixteen other noblemen in 1883, with three of them, the Dukes of Westminster, Buccleuch and Bedford, enjoying figures comfortably in excess of £200,000. Although, as we have noted, income tended to go with rank, this was not always so by any means: six commoners were among the twenty-one landowning millionaires of the nineteenth century, and three of the titled fifteen were not peers but baronets.[8]

There was, however, an important difference between gross and net income, though this could not be ascribed to the burden of taxation. Direct taxation was, in fact, very low in the nineteenth century, with the income tax, re-introduced in 1842 at a mere 7d in the pound (less than 3 per cent), seldom exceeding that figure for the remainder of the century. Even the Boer War raised the rate to only 1s 3d, and the furore over Lloyd George's 1909 Budget raged over a proposed standard rate of 1s 2d and a new 'super-tax' of 6d in the pound (a total of 8 per cent) on incomes above £5,000.[9] Estates necessarily had to be administered and maintained, but landowners' expenditure on their agents and repairs made only a tiny dent in their revenues, although some substantial sums were laid out on mid-nineteenth-century improvements such as subsoil drainage and new farm buildings.

Usually the most burdensome drain on a large income was provision for relations, especially dowries for daughters and jointures for widows, which were specified in family settlements. Very large sums might also be required for a new or re-modelled country house, and to feed a taste for sport and gambling. Accumulated debts arising from these causes, and from an excess of zeal in engaging in elections, crippled some recipients of apparently ample incomes. Some, indeed, were obliged to live quite frugally on the residue of income that was left after meeting interest charges. Not a few owners strained a princely income by costly building schemes. Lavish country houses in the latest style, and with all the *bravura* needed to impress the plutocracy, did not come cheap. William Beckford's ill-starred Fonthill Abbey was thought to have run away with some £400,000, the Marquess of Ailesbury's Tottenham House perhaps £250,000, and the reconstruction of Alnwick Castle for the Duke of Northumberland some £320,000.[10] These were exceptional examples, but the magnificence deemed necessary to accompany a lustrous title was rarely inexpensive.

LANDLORD AND TENANT

Apart from a home farm situated near the mansion, the farmlands of an estate, and usually any mines or works there might be, were in the hands of tenants. Large concerns, whether agricultural or industrial, were let for terms of years under carefully regulated leases, the legally enforceable agreement being designed to protect the property against damage by a careless or fraudulent tenant. Small farms, on the other hand, and sometimes even some large ones, were more casually let on verbal agreements. These, though needing only six months' notice to terminate, were nevertheless rarely insecure, and some tenants' families held the same farm for several generations. Tenants, large and small, were expected to farm reasonably well, at least up to the standard of the district, which however might not be very high. They were expected to keep the premises in repair (often with the help of materials from the estate) and, unless given special permission, to eschew those actions which were regarded as breaches of trust, such as subletting the land, residing away from the farmhouse, ploughing up valuable permanent pasture, cutting down mature trees, and selling manure off the farm. On a small estate the owner himself might come round on occasion to see that all was well, or perhaps if he resided at a distance he would send an estate agent from a nearby town. A large estate required full-time management by a professional land agent working from a central office, and who could call on the help of surveyors and lawyers when required. Outlying portions of the estate, however, might see much less regular inspection, with perhaps a local farmer, country attorney or estate agent holding a rent day every six months, and calling from time to time to see what repairs or improvements might be warranted.

The landlord-tenant system was an arrangement of inter-dependence. The landlord needed tenants to provide the working capital and to take the risks involved in farming or in operating a mine or works; he preferred to be a *rentier*, to sit back and enjoy the rents and royalties without having to trouble his head with the daily routine of management. The tenant, on the other hand, liked to rent rather than own, because then the fixed capital – the land and buildings – were provided by the landlord, leaving him free to devote all his own funds to operating as extensive a concern as his resources would allow. In bad times, too, when prices fell, or severe weather or other natural disasters caused heavy losses, the tenant could look to the landlord for relief in the form of an abated rent or some new injection of fixed capital to make the business more viable. So long as

all went reasonably well there was little fear of disturbance or ejection for the period of the lease, and landlords seldom troubled tenants on annual agreements provided they kept their end of the bargain. There might be occasions, however, when tenants would be expected to fall in with major schemes of improvement initiated by the landlord. Thus large-scale enclosures of open fields and commons would make the tenants liable to disturbance costs when they might be obliged to farm quite different land in another part of the parish, and perhaps move to a different farmhouse also. When subsoil drainage was in vogue in the middle decades of the nineteenth century the tenants were often expected to bear a large part of the heavy cost involved, being required perhaps to provide the labour for digging the trenches and laying the pipes or tiles supplied by the estate.

Tenants were subordinate, too, in a more general sense. The agent who kept an eye on the farming (and whose advice the tenant was sometimes bound by his agreement to take), would also come round at election times to inform the tenant which candidate to favour. Through ownership of some freehold property or other title many estate tenants possessed the right to vote, and the landlord expected them to vote as he desired; though sometimes only one of the tenant's two votes was required, the other being left to the tenant's own inclination. Not all landowners were greatly interested in politics or closely concerned with elections, but they were often bound by kinship or loyalty to a candidate or his sponsor, and accordingly promised delivery of their tenants' votes. Possibly, in return, some gifts of political favours or patronage were expected, just as the tenants expected favours from their landlord in return for their votes. Such favours to tenants might be of a direct monetary kind, such as a low rent for the farm; or they might be of an indirect communal kind, where the landlord used his influence to secure some local advantage, such as a turnpike Bill or a measure for river improvement. An interesting example of the communal variety occurred in the later eighteenth century concerning Sir Joseph Banks, the celebrated botanist who had sailed with Captain Cook to the South Seas. Sir Joseph's estates lay on the Lincolnshire coast, and he was asked by his tenants to petition the Admiralty for naval protection, they having suffered losses through the depredations of 'smuggling pyratical Vessels'. Sir Joseph asked for a cutter of eight to ten guns to be sent to cruise between Wainfleet and Saltfleet Haven in order to deter the plunderers.[11]

Some landlords expected as much conformity in matters religious as in matters political. Numbers even imitated Sir Roger de Coverley

(as did Rider Haggard's father) in counting the numbers at church of a Sunday and sending to enquire of any who were absent.[12] Some owners, indeed, would not accept as tenants men who were not devoted to the Church of England; nor those not of their own persuasion if the owners happened to be Roman Catholic or Nonconformist. Attendance at church was expected as a matter of course, unless the roads were impassable in winter or there was a great press of urgent business, as at harvest. In addition, tenants were expected to live in a respectable manner and do nothing which might cast a slur on the estate and its owner. A farmer who proved to be an habitual drunkard might first be given a warning, and then if his misbehaviour persisted, be told to quit. A farmer's penchant for gambling, for pursuing illicit liaisons with ladies of easy virtue, or for supporting such vulgar entertainments as cock-fighting and steeple-chasing, might well earn the same penalty. In financial matters, on the other hand, landlords were often surprisingly tolerant. They accepted repeated excuses for failure to pay rents on time, or to pay only in part, and their agents would report a 'good collection' if only a small minority did not pay in full on rent day. However, arrears of rent were regarded as reflecting on the estate and its management, and unless times were exceptionally hard defaulting tenants would eventually be called on to make good the arrears or suffer a distraint on their property.

One reason for the landlord's reluctant acceptance of rent arrears was the trouble and difficulty involved in replacing discharged tenants, together with the associated risk that the farm might lie untenanted for a period, resulting in even greater loss. Sporting landlords were the more lenient since their tenants had to put up with crops ravaged by game, and fences and hedges broken down by the hunt. True, their rents often reflected these disadvantages, and tenants were sometimes kept complaisant by cash payments for damage or by invitations to join in the sport. Probably it was the case that, just as independent-minded farmers would avoid an estate where the landlord insisted on religious conformity, so those who objected to the depredations of sporting landlords would not accept their tenancies. Whether sportsmen or no, landlords liked to be popular in what they thought of as their 'own country', to prefer, as Arthur Young complained, an 'extra-low bow and scrape' when they rode by, to an additional 5s per acre per annum. Some of the larger owners thought it incumbent on men in their position in society to not appear greedy by renting their lands to the hilt, and accordingly kept their rents low, acting, as Young said, 'through a false magnificence' and a 'false pride'; or

perhaps to secure greater influence and power for their agents in fostering the landowners' local interests.[13] And this often had a widespread effect, for as we have seen, in the matter of rents lesser owners took their cue from the greater ones, particularly when it came to giving tenants abatements in bad times.

THE SOCIAL MOBILITY OF LAND

The tendency for the landlords of a district to act in uniformity owed much to respect for the leading proprietor and acceptance of his judgement, just as lesser owners were tied to greater ones through bonds of a political nature, through a desire for patronage and, not least, through kinship. Many local families were inter-related by marriage, and where they were not, there still existed other common interests – those of securing the rights and privileges that went with landownership, of improving the local means of transport, the condition of the roads and canals, the efficiency of railways and, of course, of maintaining law and order. Just as landlords came together to hunt and shoot, so they joined in measures to check the depredations of robbers and footpads. They formed associations to prosecute poachers and other offenders, just as they joined together to promote an enclosure Bill, or perhaps to oppose a railway Bill that seemed likely to damage their estates. They met and caroused on social occasions such as a coming of age, a wedding or a funeral, or at the annual county ball or a victory dinner in wartime. They met also, more soberly, as Militia Commissioners, Commissioners of Sewers and justices in quarter sessions. Beyond enforcing law and order they had a common concern in the administration of the Poor Law, in the maintenance of country roads and bridges, and in closing alehouses that were suspected as being houses of call for poachers or smugglers, highwaymen and robbers of horses and sheep.

For a lead in many of these matters they looked to the most active and influential landowner of the neighbourhood, whether a prominent commoner or the bearer of an illustrious title. The great house might have a widely pervasive authority where its owner chose to exercise it. Lesser men sought the magnate's opinion on political questions, his advice on local issues, his wisdom on racehorses, the breeding of hounds or more mundane agricultural matters – though for the last the advice of his agent might be better founded. The modest country gentleman felt himself distinctly honoured if asked on occasion to dine at the great house, and even more honoured if the

lord and his great friends should deign to call on him at home. There was an acute awareness, not only of greater wealth and over-riding power, but also of social rank and status.

This, however, did not go so far as to make for a universal toadying to superiors. Many of the gentry were justly proud of their own lineage, which might indeed go further back in time than that of the great lord. They had their own little local spheres of influence, their own estates where they were the masters, their own part of the county where, as justices, their word was law, their own circles of friends and their own sports and entertainments. The social relations between the different ranks of landowners were a nice balance of dependence and independence, of polite deference and proud self-respect. The old-fashioned country squire had no pretensions to pomp or luxury which he could not afford. He kept careful accounts of all his expenditure, and like Nicholas Blundell, a small Lancashire owner of the early eighteenth century, had his ordinary suits run up at home from his own home-made cloth, and was not above doing odd jobs round the house, such as repairing furniture or hanging pictures. In a not untypical phrase one such gentleman once told Lord Berkeley and some other important visitors that as 'a plain country squire' he would make them welcome and afford them 'the best reception . . . I am able', but 'without ceremony'.[14]

It was from this pride in family, in lineage, in long residence in a particular spot that flowed the spring of hostility towards newcomers. Particularly was this so in regions more remote from the burgeoning centres of trade and industry which spawned many of the *nouveaux-riches*. A common concern with traditional rights and local issues, a closeness and mutual exclusiveness, and the presentation of a united front to the outside world were marked characteristics of the provincial gentry. Even the Kentish squires, within 50 miles of the capital, prided themselves on never taking their brides from outside the county, and although the gentry of Wales were much poorer – some of them living on only £100 or £200, or even less in the early eighteenth century – they had enormous pride in their lineage, 'As long as a Welsh pedigree' was a not unmeaningful encomium derived from the 'parchment squires' of the Principality.

It was difficult indeed for newcomers to establish themselves among the greater landowners because of the huge capital investment required to buy or build a country house and its estate. And even when the money was there, such properties rarely came on the market in one block. Wealthy newcomers therefore sometimes decided to build an estate from scratch, gradually buying out small freeholders

in the chosen district until there was a sufficient acreage put together to justify creating the mansion and its park. Others made a more substantial start by buying a small gentry house and estate as the nucleus of a greater empire. Most of the newcomers brought their wealth from trade, and some of the great merchants who acquired estates near the turn of the eighteenth century included Sir Stephen Fox, Sir John Banks, Sir Francis Chapman, once Lord Mayor of London, and Thomas Vyner. They were later joined by successful West Indian planters, while Indian nabobs such as Thomas Pitt and Robert Clive laid the foundations of new noble families, the latter spending more than £200,000 on acquiring property in Shropshire. A profitable practice in the law produced the means for some new families to put down roots in Northamptonshire, Northumberland and Hertfordshire, and banking enabled Henry Hoare, of Hoare's bank in London, to build his famous Stourhead estate. In a somewhat exceptional instance, the lucrative post of Paymaster of the Forces made it possible for James Brydges to rebuild his wife's home of Cannons – the 'most magnificent house in England' according to Defoe – and to become first Duke of Chandos and lose a fortune in the South Sea speculation, all in a space of only fifteen years.[15] The nineteenth century provided less rich pickings in the colonies or government, though most of the more prominent newcomers still came from trade, supplemented more often now by industrialists such as Armstrong, the armaments manufacturer, Lever, the soap magnate, and Wills, tobacco manufacturer. Railway contracting enabled Brassey to buy Lord Westmorland's antiquated house, Apthorpe, while the expansion of retailing brought to the fore such parvenus as Lipton, the grocer, and Boot of 'Boots the Chemist'.[16]

Not all the newly rich, by any means, yearned for the respectability of landed property. Many preferred to keep their capital in business, where it could produce a far higher return than the inconsiderable $2\frac{1}{2}$–3 per cent net that land would yield. They formed commercial and industrial dynasties, as wealthy and powerful in their own sphere as landowners were in theirs. However, they were not infrequently related to land, even perhaps to the aristocracy, through marriage: for landowners' heirs were not above seeking out a handsomely-dowried bride, even if of scandalously unaristocratic origins. Such injections of commercial or industrial wealth thus obtained were not infrequently instrumental in rescuing a proud estate from sinking in debt, and on occasion might be the means of hoisting a rather modest family to a level of greater distinction.

But where a merchant, lawyer or banker founded his own landed

family it might take two or three generations for the newcomers to be fully accepted into county society. Old-established families, rich in ancestral portraits if not otherwise, looked down on wealth that still smelled of the counting-house or factory office, even though their own origins might easily be traced to a background just as vulgar. Even country-house servants snobbishly preferred to serve those who were 'real gentry', and despised colleagues who succumbed to the tempting lucre of ill-bred upstarts. The newcomers might set higher standards of ostentation, elegance and comfort; but in other respects they were obliged to conform to the habits and manners of county society, to adopt an enthusiasm for country pursuits, and accept the outlook of the old country houses.

However, there were parts of the country, especially round expanding ports and manufacturing centres like Bristol, Liverpool, Newcastle and Hull, where the newcomers were thick on the ground and might well be dominant. Especially was this so in the country districts surrounding London. Here City merchants, bankers, financiers, con-tractors and professional men moved out of the smoky environs of Ludgate and Cheapside to establish homes in the rural quiet of nearby Middlesex, Hertfordshire, Essex or Surrey. Early in the eighteenth century Defoe noted that the then villages of Leytonstone, Walthamstow, Wanstead, West Ham and Plaistow were peppered with 'handsome large houses', built by men who could afford to keep two establishments, one in town and one in the country, or who had entirely retired to the villages 'for the pleasure and health of the latter part of their days'. Middlesex, reported Defoe, was made 'rich, pleasant, and populous' by the neighbourhood of London, and Uxbridge, in particular, showed an 'abundance of noble seats of gentlemen and persons of quality'. The district lying between Kingston in Surrey and Greenwich to the east was also resplendent with the 'magnificent country seats' of 'innumerable wealthy city families'.[17]

Even in those extensive areas not much invaded by wealthy men of business there was a large turnover of the existing gentry families. In part this was due to demographic reasons, to a failure of male heirs – when the property, and usually the family name also, consequently dropped from view. Owing to a high mortality rate among male babies, and also to losses of young adult males through disease and riding accidents, or on the battlefields of the numerous eighteenth-century wars, estates often came into the hands of heiresses, and so were usually passed on to the husbands' families. Other families disappeared through the failure of the heir to marry; or because

of unwise speculation or heavy accumulations of debt. Although it was possible in some cases for the estate to be vested temporarily in trustees, who might retrieve the situation by paying off the most onerous liabilities and imposing a regime of strict economy on the owner, yet still there might have to be sales of land; and trustees or no, there were instances where the whole estate had to go to satisfy the creditors. Sometimes, indeed, the bankrupts were obliged to flee the country and live on the Continent to escape from debt – Boulogne was a favourite resort of such exiles as being near to home, though few dared to return. A notorious example was the nineteenth-century sporting squire George Osbaldeston – though he was never reduced to quite the Boulogne level. Osbaldeston had an insatiable passion for the turf, and admitted to losing nearly £200,000 in betting and keeping racehorses. By the 1840s his rentals were almost entirely absorbed by the interest charges on his debts, and in the end he was obliged to sell up for £190,000, leaving him just enough, after settling with his creditors, to live modestly in a country villa, his evening wagers at the Portland Club limited to a guinea an evening.[18]

If Osbaldeston was exceptional, there were always numbers of lesser men who ruined themselves by unbridled expenditure, who declined and disappeared along with those families brought to extinction by the accidents of birth, marriage and death. Although land was permanent, its ownership was often much less so. Thus, when Defoe mentioned the names of several ancient families still in possession in the neighbourhood of Maidstone in Kent, he was obliged to add the sad note that there were also 'some good families extinct and gone, whose names however remain in memory'.[19]

SPORT AND THE LAND

As old families disappeared – to remain only in memory, in Defoe's phrase – there were others rising and becoming more prominent, and often anxious to add to their estates. Both old-established families and new ones were interested in acquisitions which would help expand a park, or round out some existing portion of the estate and perhaps pave the way for an eventual enclosure. Some purchases might be made solely for political ends, to gain greater influence and voting power in a certain town or district. And there were questions of prestige and self-importance: many owners had in mind the pleasing objective of being able to look out of their windows and gaze on no one's land but their own. With the general exception of the

greatest estates, the constant rise and decline of the majority of families kept the land market active. The occupying freeholders, too, were also in the market in a smaller way and for much the same reasons. With them, however, other factors which might be influential included the farming climate, whether prosperous or discouraging: the combination of farming with some other trade or craft, until it might seem best to concentrate on the one or the other; the division of property among heirs, when the smaller parcels might be sold; and, in the nineteenth century especially, the attraction of a career in the cities or the beckoning vision of vast new lands in America or in Australia and New Zealand.

Although land was often changing hands, and gentry families rising and declining, there was nevertheless a remarkable conformity in the attitudes of owners – not so much in politics, of course, where rivals frequently reviled and cheated each other, but certainly in matters which most closely affected landowners as landowners. Among these was the fostering of the sports most generally followed by the country élite.

In the eighteenth century the squirearchy supported a wide range of sporting activities, not only those most obviously connected with the countryside, like riding, racing, hunting, beagling, shooting and cricket, but also ones more associated with London and town life generally: sword-play, prize-fighting and cock-fighting. Some amusements, such as cudgels, football, skittles, cock-throwing, and bear- and bull-baiting, were rather too closely associated with riotous public holidays, plebeian village fairs and the alehouse to offer much attraction to the superior members of the community, and indeed a number of these, together with cock-fighting, were eventually prohibited as the movement to protect animals from cruelty got under way. Some landowners were sufficiently enthusiastic to promote their own cricket teams, made up from their grooms, gardeners and gamekeepers; boxing had its share of devotees, their interest accentuated by the chance of a successful wager; and a few eccentrics went in for the Cornish variety of wrestling, like Sir Thomas Parkyns, who, although remote from the origins of the sport – having his home at Bunny, near Nottingham – still practised with young men from the village on his hearth-rug, and even wrote a treatise entitled *The Cornish Hug*.[20]

Race meetings were widely held on holidays near county towns and attracted large crowds, though only the well-heeled could afford to go in for the training of racehorses or the promotion of races by the offering of prizes. Newmarket early became the established centre

of the sport, and by the later eighteenth century meetings were held there over a period of three months. Wealthy landlords built stables in the area, but the expenses were large and could create a serious drain on even a substantial income. Lord Grosvenor, for instance, was spending as much as £7,000 a year on his Newmarket activities in the 1770s, at a period when his annual income of £20,000 was largely swallowed up by unavoidable outgoings and by interest on his accumulated debts of over £150,000.[21]

Hunting and shooting were also sports closely associated with the landed élite, and became increasingly popular as time went by. Both were expensive. A pack of hounds could change hands for up to £2,000, and with the additional expenses of hunt servants and the protection of the coverts, the outgoings could rise to as much as £6,000 a year. It is not surprising, therefore, that from as early as the middle of the eighteenth century subscriptions were introduced, the members paying collectively some £500 a year for a hunt that went out only one day a week, £1,000 if it went out two days, and so on. Even then, Masters of Foxhounds could still be heavily out of pocket, for there were many associated expenses: most serious the loss arising from the low rents usually charged to tenants of a sporting landlord, but also the compensation paid for damage to the farms, and the burden of a great deal of entertaining. In return, the Master of Foxhounds of a renowned hunt enjoyed prestige and popularity, and the hunt itself provided some welcome colour and excitement to enliven a dull country winter; but the estate suffered, the owner's income was reduced, and his tenants chafed under the requirements of helping to protect foxes and of boarding hound puppies for replenishing the pack.

Shooting involved a considerable outlay on keepers and maintaining unprofitable woodlands as preserves, while tenants complained of plundered seed-beds and meagre crops, and had to be quietened by giving them 'good bargains' for their farms. Shooting was more aristocratic and exclusive than hunting, and this made it valuable for owners who wanted to ingratiate themselves with powerful friends. As a consequence it was less popular with the community, though villagers readily turned out to act as beaters for a modest reward. But you could not have game preserves without having poachers also. The deliberate fostering of game birds offered a challenge to an adventurous village lad, and the addition of a partridge or pheasant to a meagre cottage larder was not to be despised. Some men were notorious as habitual poachers but were difficult to catch, while organised gangs of poachers, often emanating from nearby industrial

towns, were attracted by the profits which large-scale poaching produced. The gangs left their bags at certain inns on the highway, there to be picked up by the drivers and guards of stage-coaches who were an essential link between the poachers and the fashionable poulterers. The illicit trade continued after the coaches were displaced by railways, the venue now changed to an out-of-the-way station on a line to London or some other large town.

Because of the Game Laws, occupiers of less than some 200–300 acres were prohibited from taking deer, pheasants, partridges, hares and rabbits. Moreover, as the enclosure of commons and wastes gathered momentum, rising to a peak in the years after 1790, extensive areas of former heaths, moors, fens and marshes become fenced-in private property and were no longer available for ordinary villagers to enjoy a little sport and help themselves to a wildfowl, a rabbit or hare.

The Game Laws, it is true, were widely disregarded. 'The more laws, the more evasion,' expostulated the conservative John Byng. 'Go where you will, everyone is a sporter, alias poacher; every market place is overrun by greyhounds and pointers.'[22] The reaction of the sporting landlords to such disrespect was to appoint more gamekeepers and to stiffen the law. In the later eighteenth century there was a general trend towards more stringent penalties for theft of all kinds of property. A larger number of criminal charges were made capital offences, and the justices administered the law with greater harshness. One magistrate boasted when sentencing two men convicted of robbing a farmer, that he would execute the law 'with such severity as shall enable any gentleman to hang his watch by the highway with the full confidence of finding it there on his return another day.' But as the penalties were made more fearsome, so it became more difficult to get juries to convict, and it was common practice to value stolen goods at less than a shilling so that the charge should not be a capital one. Transportation, seen as more humane, was also often substituted for the death penalty.

The Game Laws mounted in severity along with the measures concerned with other kinds of property. A Parliament of landowners passed a new law in 1770 that made persons convicted of taking game at night subject to from three to six months' imprisonment, and from six to twelve months and a public whipping for a second offence. In 1800 imprisonment with hard labour could be imposed by a single justice, sitting on his own, perhaps in his own house. Further, legislation attempted to curb poaching by imposing even more severe penalties. Yet the poaching continued. The poor, both

urban and rural, clung to the view that the fencing in of immemorial open spaces was injust, and the claim to owning wild creatures as private property both iniquitous and absurd. 'God sent the land,' it was held, and sent too the wild beings which inhabited it for the benefit of all.[23]

Labourers who were made unemployed once the harvest was over preferred the risk of imprisonment to the choice of regimented, monotonous and laborious days in the workhouse. Sometimes they joined large gangs, such as the one organised by Frederick Gowing, Suffolk's most notorious poacher. Gowing provided snares, nets and air guns, and set the rules: not to go armed with bludgeons, and only to work in small parties. Even the appearance of county police forces in the 1840s and 1850s made little difference, for the police were generally unwilling to be cast in the role of supplementary gamekeepers paid for from the public purse.[24]

And just as poaching continued to vex landlords, so the game preserves remained to annoy their tenants. The souring of relations between landlords and farmers formed a dangerous crack in the armour of the landed interest which could be exploited by its radical opponents.[25] It was not until 1881 that the law permitted tenants to destroy hares and rabbits on farms without the landowner's permission, although long before that some farmers had enjoyed limited shooting rights granted by their landlords, and others had frequently taken matters into their own hands. There were not many farmers, it was said, who could not produce from their pantry a hare, or two or three brace of birds; and some turned a blind eye towards poachers who paid them off with a brace to send to a friend in town. Despite the hostility of the farmers, shooting remained fashionable and even increased in popularity. Shooting gave the sporting owner an excellent reason for remaining in residence in the autumn, and when from the 1870s agricultural depression depleted rentals, shooting came to the rescue; owners were often happy to let out their box and rights to wealthy *aficionados* from the cities – who were prepared to pay very well for the privilege.

REFORM AND THE LAND

The controversy over game tended to bring the landowners together in its defence – although not all owners were keen sportsmen, and some were provoked to outright hostility by the liberties with their property that hunting and shooting squires seemed to think they

were free to take. The issue of free trade versus protection, which came to a head in the 1840s, was, however, much more divisive. The division owed something to geographical factors, for owners of estates in western pastoral districts had little direct interest in the price of corn; while owners in arable areas, on the other hand, in parts of Northumberland, the Vale of York, Lincolnshire, much of East Anglia and east Kent were very much aware that their tenants' well-being, and therefore their own rents, depended on corn being profitable. Large numbers of owners, however, as we have noted, were not greatly influenced by such economic considerations. In the case of large owners, their estates were often widely scattered and consisted of both arable properties and pasture ones. Even quite small estates, too, might have a mixture of farms, and some owners were more concerned with other farm products, the prices of hops or fruit, for example, or those of oak and coppice wood.

In any event, the politics of free trade tended to over-ride any worries about the future course of corn prices. Some owners took the view that protection formed such an essential prop of the landed interest that to allow it to be knocked away would mean the inevitable collapse of land and the triumph of industry. Others adopted a wider, more national view, which held that free trade was beneficial to the country as a whole since it was coming more and more to depend on the products of industry for employment and trade. Moreover, they believed that protection was not vital to the prosperity of efficient arable farming, and that enlightened farmers holding well-provided farms and employing the latest ideas of 'high farming' could still prosper if prices were to fall once protection was removed. It was for this reason that the pill of free trade came to be sweetened by the provision of cheap government loans for under-drainage and farm improvement. Landowners of the first persuasion were truly conservative, fearing change and desiring to maintain the *status quo*; the second were more progressive, arguing that the landed interest had to make concessions if it were to continue as a major political force in a more industrialised and more urbanised society where the price of food was a major concern – a recognition of the changing place of land in the mid-nineteenth-century economy.[26]

That place was slowly but inexorably changed by the rising tide of democracy. Although after 1883 it was difficult for landowners to exert undue pressure on their tenants, the 1867 reform had left the boroughs and the countryside with different electorates. In the boroughs householders had the vote and there was a fair degree of democracy; in the countryside the paucity in many areas of small

independent property-holders meant that the territorial magnates continued to hold sway. A further reform Bill to end this anomaly and bring the countryside into line with the boroughs was launched in 1884. The new measure was held up by reactionary peers in the Lords, and an agitation grew concerning the unrepresentative nature of the upper House. 'Peers against the people' was one cry, 'Mend them or end them' another. The veteran reformer John Bright, one of the leading spirits of the Anti-Corn Law League of forty years before, suggested the solution that was eventually to be adopted in 1911: for the Lords to have a right only to suspend a Bill, not an absolute veto.[27] In 1884 the Lords were persuaded to give way, and the new Act effectively ended the landowners' political control of the countryside. The total electorate was raised from about 2.6 million to some 4.4 million (about two-thirds of the adult male population). Seventy-nine towns of less than 15,000 population ceased to be parliamentary seats, and thirty-six of less than 50,000 lost one of their two Members. Only the larger boroughs now returned more than one Member, and the rest of the country, both rural and urban, was divided into single-member constituencies. The old historic counties and boroughs ceased to be the basis of the Commons, and 'the individual for the first time became the unit, numerical equality ("one vote, one value") the master principle'.[28] Although less than one-third of all adults now had the vote, the basis for the election of the Commons was for the first time established on modern democratic lines.

This left the problem of the Lords. It seemed that an upper house, whose members represented no one but themselves, and in which the seats were hereditary, could not long survive unscathed. In fact it went on, unchanged, for a further twenty-seven years – until another rearguard struggle by conservative peers brought about the abolition of its right of veto, the compromise that Bright had suggested, the concession which so far has allowed it to continue down to the present. The occasion was the reformist Budget put forward by the Liberal Chancellor, Lloyd George, in 1909. Many new ideas first appeared in this Budget, including the allocation of funds to finance road improvements, to provide a national system of labour exchanges ('job centres' in modern parlance), and the intriguing but still-born suggestion of a Development Commission to develop country life and natural resources. A small allowance for children, to be set against income tax, was also introduced. But it was the new taxes that raised the uproar. Income tax was to go up from 1s to 1s 2d in the pound, higher than it had ever been in peacetime, and a new super-tax of 6d in the pound (2.5 per cent) was to be levied on all incomes above

£5,000 (on the amount by which such incomes exceeded £3,000). To the present generation, long inured to rates of taxation which in the recent past have been as high as 13s or more in the pound, and are currently still at rates equivalent to 5s and 8s, such figures seem paltry indeed; the more so, when it is remembered that many unskilled workers with families were being paid only some £50 a year at the time of Lloyd George's budget. But the new taxes in that Budget, though really very low, created furious opposition from those who saw them as the thin but threatening edge of a socialist wedge, while Tariff Reformers feared that the increased revenue they would bring in would undermine their case.[29]

More frightening to the big landowners was another new proposal of 1909 – the Land Value Duties. These involved a tax of 20 per cent on the increase in value realised whenever land changed hands (the 'unearned increment'), and also a duty of ¹/₂d in the pound (0.21 per cent) on the capital value of undeveloped land and minerals. These new ideas owed much to the arguments of Henry George, an American economist, and to complaints in Britain of the difficulty of persuading large owners to sell land, even though it was lying idle. The proposal – never to be brought fully into effect – involved making a complete valuation of all the land of Great Britain, and to this the landowners violently objected; and the more they objected the more the public believed that they objected for sinister reasons.[30] Lloyd George's attacks, ridiculing the peers as the protagonists of monopoly and privilege, aggravated the rancour.

The Lords rushed headlong to defeat. The Budget was thrown out of the upper House by a huge majority – an event unknown for over 250 years. Two general elections were fought over the issue of the Lords' right of veto, and in 1911, after the new monarch, George V, had agreed to create, if necessary, sufficient new peers to ensure the passage of the constitutional reform through the upper House, the Parliament Bill became law. Under it, 'money Bills' could become law without the consent of the Lords; other Bills could be held up by the Lords for only two years; and the maximum duration of Parliament was reduced from seven years to five. The Lords continued, shorn of their former powers, but otherwise unreformed; they might well have gone on entirely unscathed but for their unreasonable rejection of what was in fact a very modest budgetary reform.[31]

While in two years of unwise obstinacy the Lords had themselves brought about their own *débâcle*, the lesser landowners had long before seen the onset of a gradual erosion of their local power and influence.

The initial change was the shift of responsibility from the justices and amateur parish officials to elected boards of ratepayers and paid officials, beginning with the New Poor Law of 1834, when elected Boards of Guardians were created to manage poor relief in unions of parishes. The justices, it is true, sat on the new Boards *ex officio* and served as chairmen, and minor landowners rubbed shoulders round the table with large farmers. The last were often as narrow-minded and penny-pinching as the most reactionary of owners might desire, so that few issues of principle arose; though where a more progressive landowner was elected, he might (like Rider Haggard, the author) resign his seat in protest against the niggardly cruel treatment of helpless paupers. Nevertheless, democracy had begun to make a substantial dent in the traditional control of landowners. Subsequent changes extended the more democratic elected body into other spheres, with the appearance of Police Watch Committees and School Boards. Ultimately, in 1888, came the County Councils. This reform was the logical corollary of the extension of the parliamentary franchise to rural householders in 1884: those who had the right to vote for a Member of Parliament must surely have the right to vote for their local rulers also.

The new County Councils took over from the justices their former administrative powers, notably those over highways and bridges, leaving them only their old judicial and licensing functions. True, landowners were often to be found among the new County Councillors, though this was not so everywhere. Six years later, in 1894, second and third tiers of elected local councils were introduced, in the form of Urban and Rural District Councils, and Parish Councils. The whole of English local government was now based upon direct popular election. Landowners found that not only had they been superseded by the new democratic District Councils but that they were often brought into direct conflict with them. Where an owner wanted to build cottages on his own land he had to modify his plans in line with the building by-laws imposed by the District Council; if he owned old, dilapidated cottages the Council's Medical Officer might compel him to close the premises, or even pull them down in the interests of public health. Fewer conflicts arose over Parish Councils because their powers were miniscule. Early enthusiasm for them evaporated once it was realised how little could be done with a spending power limited to the product of a 3d rate, or in extreme cases a 6d one. As a result, parish elections were soon submerged in apathy, and parish affairs continued to be run by a close oligarchy of squire, parson and large farmer.

The decline of landowners' influence in the countryside was not due solely to new legislation, however. Another factor was an increase in absenteeism. There had always been some owners who rarely visited their estates, preferring to spend their lives in London or on a round of the fashionable watering-places, like Bath, Scarborough, Brighton or Harrogate; or abroad, at Paris, Baden-Baden, Spa or Boulogne. The diverse attractions of London society made the country seem terribly dull, and with greater ease of travel in the later nineteenth century some owners took to extensive journeying abroad, spending less and less time at home. This tendency was increased by the fearful discomfort of many old-fashioned country houses and the cost of keeping them habitable as expenses rose while income from rents dwindled with the fall in agricultural prices. The decaying country house, with its neglected estate, dissatisfied tenants, and tumbledown cottages presented an enduring reproach which absentee owners shrank from encountering.

A further factor was the breaking away of the farmers from the traditional tutelage of the landlords. In the agricultural depression which set in after the disastrous harvest of 1879, farmers came increasingly to realise that, unlike in former bad times, the landowners could now do little to help them. The Corn Laws were gone, and any prospect of a return to protection seemed certain to founder on the rock of the urban demand for cheap food. Landlords met the depression, as ever, by abating rents, and a number spent some money on the farms to help the tenants survive. But, in general, survival depended on the farmers themselves – changing their farming methods, perhaps their farming entirely, to meet the new trends in the market. Often enough, the old tenants were too wedded to their customary ways to move with the times, and they gave up, to be replaced by new men from Scotland or the West Country, men who abandoned the old labour-intensive arable husbandry and put the land down to grass and roots for economical forms of dairying. The changes in occupiers, the greater independence of the new tenants, went far to weaken the traditional bond between the estate and its farmers.

Government, it is true, provided the farmers with some palliatives: a Board of Agriculture was established in 1889, later to be promoted to a Ministry; the unpopular malt tax was repealed, grants were made to reduce the burden of local rates, and measures adopted to stamp out disease among livestock and to protect farmers against adulterated feeding-stuffs, and against the sale of spurious butter and cheese; the Ground Game Act permitted tenants freely to destroy rabbits and

hares, the primary liability for payment of the tithe rent-charge was transferred from occupiers to owners, and a railway and canal Act attempted to end the unequal rates charged on the carriage of home and foreign produce – long a farmers' grievance; and, furthermore, the law of distress was modified. These changes were all desirable, and helpful, so far as they went, but did nothing to remedy the farmers' main problem, the rise of foreign competition and the unprofitable levels of prices, especially grain prices.

But landowners, too, had increasingly come to face economic and political truths. They adopted the maxim: 'If you can't beat 'em, join 'em.' This they did by gradually moving away from land, investing more in non-agricultural assets, and by selling farms to the tenants, thus converting a low and uncertain return from rents into a better and more certain one from interest on mortgages. The change in investments can be seen in the widening range of stocks purchased by the second Earl of Leicester, especially after 1870. By 1891 he had various sums tucked away in the shares of breweries such as Guinness, Allsop and Trumans, and in banks such as the National Provincial; but most of all in railways, including the Great Western, the London and North Western, and the Midland, as well as, among others, the Madras Railway, the Sind, Delta and Punjab Railway, the Canadian Pacific, the Pennsylvania, and the Buenos Aires Great Southern.[32] Landowners were also increasingly accepting seats on the boards of industrial and commercial companies, adding an aristocratic cachet to a perhaps otherwise undistinguished list of directors. Sometimes, indeed, they were inveigled in doing this kind of thing for fraudulent purposes, as Trollope described in his *The Way We Live Now*. Landowners, like farming itself, were adjusting to economic change, and if the old glory of the country house was fading, never to be restored, its owners were seeking survival in the new environment of the democratic industrial state.

NOTES

1. **F. M. L. Thompson**, *English Landed Society in the Nineteenth Century*, Routledge & Kegan Paul, 1963, pp. 267–8.
2. **J. V. Beckett**, *The Aristocracy in England 1660–1914*, Basil Blackwell, 1986, Appendix, pp. 482–95.
3. Thompson, *English Landed Society*, pp. 32, 114–15.
4. **J. H. Clapham**, *Economic History of Modern Britain*, II, Cambridge University Press, 1952, pp. 260–1.
5. Thompson, *English Landed Society*, p. 218; **G. E. Mingay**, *English Landed Society in the Eighteenth Century*, Routledge & Kegan Paul, 1963, p. 67.

6. Thompson, *English Landed Society*, p. 266.
7. Beckett, *The Aristocracy in England*, p. 288.
8. *Ibid.*, pp. 290–2.
9. **S. Dowell**, *A History of Taxation and Taxes in England*, III, Longmans Green, 1884, pp. 121–2; Clapham, *Economic History*, III, 1938, pp. 402–4.
10. Thompson, *English Landed Society*, pp. 89, 92.
11. Lincolnshire Record Office, Hill MSS. 22/2/2/14.
12. **H. Rider Haggard**, *The Days of My Life*, Longmans Green, 1926, p. 19.
13. **Arthur Young**, *Northern Tour*, IV, London, 1770, p. 496; **Arthur Young**, *Observations on the Present State of the Waste Lands of Great Britain*, London, 1773, p. 41.
14. **M. Blundell** (ed.), *Blundell's Diary and Letter Book 1702–28*, Liverpool University Press, 1952, pp. 59–60, 123–4.
15. Beckett, *The Aristocracy in England*, pp. 66–70; Mingay, *English Landed Society*, pp. 72–6.
16. Thompson, *English Landed Society*, p. 302.
17. **Daniel Defoe**, *A Tour through England and Wales*, Everyman edn, Dent, 1928; I, pp. 6, 169; II, p. 13.
18. **E. D. Cuming** (ed.), *Squire Osbaldeston: his Autobiography*, Lane, 1926, pp. 3, 10, 278, 281, 301, 312.
19. Defoe, *A Tour*, I, p. 115.
20. Mingay, *English Landed Society*, p. 153.
21. Mingay, *English Landed Society in the Eighteenth Century*, p. 151.
22. **C. Bruyn Andrews** (ed.), *The Torrington Diaries*, Eyre & Spottiswoode, 1954, pp. 184, 300.
23. **G. E. Mingay**, *The Gentry*, Longman, 1976, pp. 131–3, 180–1.
24. **John E. Archer**, 'Poachers abroad', in **G. E. Mingay** (ed.), *The Unquiet Countryside*, Routledge, 1989, pp. 59, 62.
25. Mingay, *The Gentry*, p. 133.
26. See **G. Kitson Clark**, 'The Repeal of the Corn Laws and the politics of the forties', *Economic History Review*, 2nd ser., **IV**, 1951–52, pp. 10–12; **David Spring**, 'Earl Fitzwilliam and the Corn Laws', *American Historical Review*, **LIIX**, 1953–54, p. 291.
27. **R. C. K. Ensor**, *England 1870–1914*, Clarendon Press, 1936, p. 88.
28. *Ibid.*
29. *Ibid.*, pp. 413–15.
30. *Ibid.*, p. 414.
31. *Ibid.*, pp. 430–1.
32. **Susanna Wade Martins**, *A Great Estate at Work: the Holkham Estate and its Inhabitants in the Nineteenth Century*, Cambridge University Press, 1980, pp. 267–9.

CHAPTER SEVEN

Down on the Farm

FREEHOLDERS AND TENANTS

If one were to believe the propaganda put about by the Anti-Corn League in the 1840s, then English farmers would be envisaged as some species of bucolic dunces, blinkered rustics who blindly followed the political road marked out for them by their landlords, and servilely gave up their independence in exchange for an easy rent and a few flattering attentions. Propaganda invariably exaggerates, however, and this instance was no exception. Intact, a high proportion of the cultivated land of England and Wales was held by what an earlier age called 'capital farmers', men of considerable means and intelligence, men capable of stocking and managing valuable concerns which ran to hundreds, even thousands, of acres. The Census of 1851 showed that in total there were almost a quarter of a million farmers and graziers in England and Wales, and while a good majority of these had holdings of less than 100 acres – the kind of holding that very often the farmer and his family could manage by themselves – there were also a great many larger farms. It is certainly true that informed observers of the farming scene tended to indict the small farmer as ignorant, conservative, and backward in his ideas, and to look for improved kinds of farming to come from only the larger men, men who were better educated, who travelled, who supported farming societies, attended shows and compared notes with fellow-enthusiasts. There was probably some justification for this view, and even if it was not entirely valid, there were still significant numbers of farmers of all kinds who were unlikely to fit the League's unflattering description.

It should be noticed that, despite their numbers, small farmers of less than 100 acres held between them only a little over a fifth of

the total farmland; that is to say that nearly four-fifths was held in larger units. In fact, judged by acreage, it was the medium-sized farm of between 100 and 300 acres that was the typical farm unit which, with nearly 45 per cent of the total farmland, dominated the mid-nineteenth-century countryside. Such farms were generally too large for a farmer to manage alone unless he were blessed with an unusually large crop of able sons and daughters; indeed, units as large as 200–300 acres required a regular labour force of between three and ten men (assisted by boys and women workers), according to the extent to which the fields consisted of grass or arable. The 1851 Census also revealed that there were as many as 4,300 farms of between 500 and 999 acres, and 771 of over 1,000 acres, covering together nearly 4m acres, or almost a sixth of the total farmland.[1] These large units were considerable enterprises, and although the farmer might be only a tenant rather than the owner, his own capital employed in the business would amount to some thousands of pounds, while he would need to be capable of managing (probably with the help of a bailiff or foreman) a labour force which in the case of the 1,000-acre arable unit would run to as many as forty or fifty hands. And even beyond this, there were numbers of successful big farmers who, with the help of grown-up sons and bailiffs, ran several large farms spread over a neighbourhood, involving a total tenant capital of perhaps £20,000 or £30,000 or more.

Clearly, the very big tenant-farmer was a capitalist in his own right, and consequently he commanded a fair degree of independence and respect from his landlord. Indeed, when such a man was thinking of giving up a farm, it was the landlord who, in alarm, sent his agent to ask if he would not reconsider – supposing his rent were to be reduced a little or money spent on new barns. Landlords knew by experience that farmers of large capital and appropriate experience were not to be found every day, and they feared the prospect of putting a large concern into unknown and possibly unsatisfactory hands, or in the last resort having to divide the acreage into smaller units. Hence when a large farm did fall vacant the landlord would enquire into a prospective tenant's experience and command of resources, and would seek references from the man's previous landlords. On the other hand, it is true that even the wealthy tenants who held big farms under an eminent landowner would expect to have to meet his wishes in regard to voting at elections, to defer to his interest in sport, and to respect the usual social conventions and maintain the reputation of the estate.

Of course, those farmers who were freeholders, owning their land in their own right, could be entirely independent in such matters as

how they voted and how they lived. But many of them, in practice, felt the consequences of having a much larger proprietor as their neighbour. Although in principle they were entirely free agents, they might still find it worth their while to defer to the large owner's preferences in politics, sport and religion. This arose in part from the traditional deference of ordinary country people to the old-established and important families of the district. But further, in more material terms, the large owner often commanded influence and patronage as well as wealth, and it might be wise to be on good terms with him rather than the opposite. The large owner might, for instance, be prepared to pull strings in order to help the freeholder avoid nomination to an onerous and unpopular parish office, such as that of overseer of the poor, or constable, or surveyor of the highways. He might also help find openings for the freeholder's younger sons to enter professional careers, in the Church perhaps, or in the government service. The majority of freeholders were not in a large way of business and commanded little influence even in their own neighbourhood, so that any assistance in overcoming the recurrent problems of life was well worth the gift of a vote or a complaisant attitude towards any damage wrought by game or the hunt.

At all events, freeholders were usually thin on the ground. Nationally they were in a clear minority of all farmers, being greatly out-numbered by tenants, though there were certainly areas of the country where they were strong, as for example in parts of the north-west of England and the North Riding, north Wiltshire, Essex and Kent, and in more limited areas like the Isle of Axholme in Lincolnshire. It has been estimated that only between about a seventh and a tenth or so of the cultivated acreage was in the hands of freeholders at the end of the eighteenth century, and it appears that this proportion did not change appreciably in the following hundred years. The first official statistics, beginning in 1887, indicate that over the period 1887–91, some 18 per cent of occupiers were owners, with 14 per cent owning all the land they were farming, and another 4 per cent owning only a part of it and renting the remainder. In terms of acreage, some 15 per cent of the farmland was owned by the occupiers, confirming that freeholders were generally farming on a smaller scale than tenants.[2] However, it is probable that the 4 per cent of freeholder-farmers who owned only part of their land consisted of men who were often in a fair way of business, frequently renting much more land than they owned themselves.

Whether it made good economic sense for farmers to own their land, rather than rent it, is doubtful. Owners enjoyed security, of

course, and land was a uniquely enduring and valuable asset which could be bequeathed to one's heirs, and could be mortgaged or sold if it became necessary to raise money. From the security aspect, however, it was true that the majority of tenants enjoyed *de facto* security of tenure, even when holding the farm on merely an annual verbal agreement, for landlords rarely disturbed satisfactory tenants. Freeholders had no rent to pay, but this saving was usually a minor one. Rents varied with the situation and quality of the land, but generally the sum to be paid annually ran at only between about a twentieth and a thirtieth of the value of the land. That is to say, in relation to the capital value of the land, rent represented a return of only some 3–5 per cent. Capital invested in stocking rented land, on the other hand, produced a return of about 10–20 per cent in the profits that could be earned in reasonably prosperous times. Hence, £1,000 laid out in buying land yielded the farmer a saving of only about £30–50 a year, while the same sum used to work rented land produced a net return up to three times or more as great, if however at considerably higher risk.

It is not surprising, therefore, that the majority of English farmers were content to be tenants, and preferred to expend their profits in stocking an expanded rented acreage to sinking them into the purchase of land. In the eighteenth and nineteenth centuries it was uncommon for farmers to buy land, though there are certainly some examples of their doing so. The large farmers of the Lincolnshire Wolds (or uplands), for example, bought land in the nearby coastal marshes for fattening purposes, and a few went in for whole 'lordships' of 1,000 or 1,500 acres, representing an investment of probably as much as £20–35,0000. It is estimated that in 1873 some sixteen Lincolnshire farmers each owned over 1,000 acres. Significantly, however, these rich farmers frequently let out the land they owned while continuing to farm by renting somebody else's land.[3]

Successful farmers of large means, such as these Lincolnshire ones, were thus able to enjoy both the security and income derived from an investment in land, and the profits to be made from farming rented land. At least, this was so until economic conditions changed. Earlier, at the end of the Napoleonic Wars in 1815, numbers of large farmers in various parts of the country had been caught unawares by the sharp fall in agricultural prices and a painful restriction of bank credit. They had taken advantage of the high prices during the Wars to extend their operations very substantially, and then found themselves over-stretched when the wartime boom collapsed and the banks called in their loans. Similarly, the long-term decline in grain prices which set

in from the mid-1870s forced many farmers to draw in their horns and rely on what cash reserves they had. In time, some found that despite a fall in rents they had come to the end of their resources and could continue no longer. The more elderly retired; the younger thought, perhaps, of emigrating to America or the Antipodes. The tenants who replaced them were men of new ideas, with the necessary initiative and capital for transforming the whole nature of farming, turning derelict arable into pasture and concentrating on dairying, selling 'railway milk' to meet the expanding demand of the large towns. On the undrained and run-down Essex clays the newcomers were often Scots who came south attracted by the bargain-basement rents and proximity to the great London market. In some cases they brought their own herds of Ayrshires with them, and by farming with strict economy, using little hired labour, they could make land pay that had bankrupted their arable predecessors.

In eastern England, where arable predominated, rents were very slow to recover from the depression of the last quarter of the nineteenth century. The landowners, finding their incomes sadly reduced, and attracted perhaps by the higher and more stable returns that could be obtained from mortgages, equities and government stocks, began to think of selling land. Often they sold only a part of the estate, but in some instances they eventually sold most or all of the land, and sold or rented the house too. The land market became more active as increased quantities of land were put up for sale, especially in the years during and just after the First World War. When selling, landowners frequently made it a practice to give the tenants an opportunity of buying their farms, and numbers decided to do so, helped by mortgages from banks or from the landowner himself. It is perhaps a little surprising that they should want to change their status from that of tenant to freeholder – particularly when it seems they had rarely wanted to do so previously – and to do so at a time when rents in arable districts had fallen to very low levels. But now land was also much cheaper, and moreover they were being offered the land that they were familiar with, the very land they were farming. In effect, the farmer-purchasers exchanged a low rent for a mortgage to be paid at a fixed rate of interest, often resulting in an increase in their outgoings.

No doubt they were tempted by the prospect of securing the future of their families on the farm at the cost of a long-term but relatively low outlay, and probably they were optimistic that the low prices for crops would not last for ever and markets would soon recover to more profitable levels. This expectation, however,

took a long time to be realised, for apart from the brief burst of prosperity in the higher prices obtained during and just after the First World War – when many farmers set out on buying their land – farming generally remained unprofitable even after the worst of the late nineteenth-century depression was over, with little long-term improvement seen over the bulk of the years between 1900 and the outbreak of the Second World War in 1939. Nevertheless, after some decline in the years before 1914, the shift from tenancy to ownership moved sharply upwards, so that by 1921, when the brief years of post-war prosperity ended, the share of the farmland in the hands of owners had risen to 20 per cent, compared with only 11 per cent in 1914. By 1950 the figure had increased much further, to over 41 per cent.[4] The era after 1914 saw a transformation in the farming structure of the country, with freeholders owning a share of the land that was probably as high as, or higher than it had been at any previous time in English history.

SMALL FARMS AND LARGE

Farms varied so greatly, both in size and in type, that it is difficult to generalise about farmers' incomes and living standards. A large, if uncertain, income could be obtained from quite small acreages used for specialised purposes, such as hop-growing, market-gardening, poultry or fruit, and less so perhaps from dairying; but very often the income had to be supplemented by some other business, especially one which helped fill up the blank winter months, such as innkeeping, milling, carrying, or retailing of coal and wood. In this way small-holders and little farmers could obtain a year-round income sufficient for a family to live on. Even a somewhat larger enterprise, such as mixed corn and pasture farms of between some 30 and 100 acres, might return a net income of only about £100 a year; though much less than this with the smaller businesses, yielding barely enough to support a family and maintain the farming stock. However, a large part of the family's food would come directly from the farm, and as with the smallholders, some members of the family might practice a trade or craft which brought in additional income.

In the eighteenth century these farmhouse and cottage crafts included spinning and weaving, metal-working, cutlery, and the making of items from wood such as poles, barrels, tubs, stools, chairs and ladders. Eventually the rise of factory production or competing

imports brought about the decline of many part-time country occupations, but others developed, especially for the womenfolk. Handmade lace, gloves and items of clothing, straw-plait, buttons, baskets, nets, cordage, and many other such little crafts could be found down to near the end of the nineteenth century. Nevertheless, it was true, as contemporaries remarked, that many of the smallest farmers and their families worked as hard as or harder than the landless labourers, and lived little better. Indeed, the unpretentious nature of many old farmhouses is shown by their often being converted to labourer's tenements or cottages when no longer required for a farm.

At the other end of the scale were the great capitalistic farmers whose land ran to several hundred acres or much more. Some of the big freeholders commanded very large acreages indeed when they had the capital to rent land additional to that owned. In the Cliff district of Lincolnshire in 1842, for example, John Dudding of Saxby added 1,000 acres of land rented from Lord Monson to the 500 he owned himself, while another substantial freeholder, Francis Iles, owning 320 acres, rented two other farms on the Wolds totalling 1,287 acres. Lord Monson's outstanding tenant, however, was a Richard Dawson, who occupied the whole 2,500 acres of Withcall parish and another 700 acres besides. Farmers such as these were able to live in style, and on the Yarborough estate in the same county, the farmhouses, surrounded by their lawns and woods, were said to be quite comparable to the homes of the gentry.

The affluence enjoyed by big farmers in prosperous times was derived from the sheer scale of the farming operations and the lowness of the rents, the latter constituting in effect a valuable subsidy financed by the landowner. A taste for hunting and shooting was cheaply indulged when feed was obtained direct from the farm and the breeding of hunters went hand in hand with the breeding of farm horses, surplus stock being profitably disposed of at horse fairs – locally, at the famous Horncastle horse fair. A luxurious life-style did not absorb all the profits of good years, and it is significant that two farmers helped establish a Lincoln oil and cake mill in 1840, while three of the directors of a Grimsby firm of oil-cake manufacturers were Wolds farmers. Some of these farming magnates retired with great fortunes: one who farmed 865 acres under the Earl of Yarborough was said to have made £80,000, and another, a Quaker and something of a miser, left the great sum of half a million pounds at his death in 1834.[5]

The detailed accounts of a Lincolnshire Wolds farmer, William Scorer of Burwell, showed an exceptionally high profit averaging

over £600 a year in the middle 1850s, a figure which was arrived at after including in his costs all his living and miscellaneous expenses, even down to furniture, watch repairs, chimney-sweeping and rat-catching. His household was not a small one, since it included his wife and five children, three maids and four farm servants living in – and this on a farm of some 600 acres, for which he paid only £650 a year in rent. Of course his income varied considerably from year to year, depending on the yields he obtained for his various crops, the numbers of livestock to be disposed of, and the movement of prices. In 1842–48 he averaged a yield of 32 bushels an acre for his wheat, and obtained a return of nearly £9 per acre from this crop alone. In addition to the profits produced by his other livestock, sheep produced nearly £600 a year in 1859–62, increasing to well over £1,000 a year in 1863–64. His wages bill for 1849–55 averaged over £450 a year, and the importance of his shepherd was indicated by a relatively high annual wage of about £35, together with extra payments in kind. His wagoner received £25, and was allowed 30 stones of pork as well as unlimited potatoes; but a housemaid and kitchenmaid were paid much less, a mere £5 and £6 10s respectively (with their keep), and both were expected to help in the fields when required.[6] Perhaps this carefully calculating and successful farmer was a hard master who expected a lot from his work-people.

Large-scale capitalist farming was a feature also of the famous Holkham estate in Norfolk. Some of the tenants here were in a very large way of business: approximately twenty-five of a total of some 150 tenants held more than one farm, and six sometimes occupied as many as three farms, worked perhaps by different members of the family. The farms were also marked by long periods of occupation: in the period between 1790 and 1900 thirty-one farms were held by the same families for over fifty years; sixty-nine tenants held their farms for over thirty years. Most of the Holkham tenants were local men, and there was a certain amount of inter-marriage between the families. The average size of farm was large, with twenty-eight farms exceeding 500 acres in 1850, while six of those on the light soils ran to over 1,000 acres. In 1816 a dozen or so of the tenants were regarded by Francis Blaikie, Lord Leicester's agent, as very progressive, commanding enough capital to farm at a high standard and on a large scale, while the majority were described as 'industrious', 'persevering' or 'deserving'. A later comment by William Keary, the agent in 1851, indicated that nineteen of the farms were in good hands, but another fourteen were 'badly managed', and six 'fairly farmed'. Despite its fame,

it is evident that farming efficiency on the Holkham estate varied considerably.[7]

Another account of 1843 described the Holkham tenants as very superior farmers, employing a great deal of capital. They were 'generous, independent, hospitable, free, intelligent and very many have carried on intellectual pursuits and acquirements far beyond the race of farmers in former times'. The development of the livestock side of the farming after the 1850s was a sensible diversification which helped the Holkham tenants survive the falls in grain prices in the later 1870s. The falls in prices marked the onset of a prolonged period of difficult conditions, and already in the 1880s some Holkham farmers had fallen behind with their rents. In 1881 it was said of one farmer that he had decided to vacate his farm 'before he has lost all he has got', while another had given up, having already 'lost all he has got'. By the 1890s the Holkham farms were difficult to let, a situation unknown for many years previously, and for the first time they had to be advertised – significantly, in Scotland. Although large reductions in rents were made of between 42 and 56 per cent, these proved insufficient to retain tenants: as many as twenty-eight farms were vacated between 1880 and 1896, six in 1895–96 alone. Rider Haggard, who farmed not far away on the Norfolk-Suffolk border, noted the effects of failure on the attraction of farming as a career: it cost less, he said, to put a man into a profession – £1,000 – while £3,000 was needed to farm, 'which he stood a good chance of losing'; it was remarkable that nearly all the holders of small official posts in the district were 'farmers' sons or broken down farmers'.[8]

In the good years before the depression, the bigger Holkham farmers were able to live well. They generally kept between two and four servants, with sometimes a groom or housekeeper as well, and were well provided for travelling, keeping a brougham and a luggage cart, together with a dog cart and often a couple of gigs also. They would ask the agent to make new additions to the farmhouses to make them better adapted to a more gracious style of living, and the popular bay windows became incongruous excrescences on the plain Georgian façades. In many of the villages on the estate it was the one or two large tenant-farmers who took on the role of local squire. They looked to the state of the roads and bridges, the repair of the church, and the setting up of schools and charitable funds. Although sufficiently eminent and influential with the estate to undertake these initiatives, they were not, however, considered distinguished enough to become magistrates: no Holkham tenant appeared on the nineteenth-century justices Bench.[9]

Holkham fostered men of great distinction in farming circles, nevertheless. One such was John Hudson, who was tenant of Lodge Farm, Castle Acre, for forty-seven years from 1822 to 1869. He and his father managed neighbouring farms totalling some 1,500 acres, paying together a rent of £1,238. Hudson took on land described at the time as 'poor' and 'foul', and by dint of heavy expenditures on oil cake and manures transformed it, raising output by a third. He increased the numbers of sheep and bullocks carried by more than five-fold, and almost doubled the yield of barley. His stock and implements represented an investment of some £4–5,000, and his reputation was such that on the establishment of the Royal Agricultural Society in 1843 he became a founding Council member. John Hudson's son, however, experienced more difficult times. From 1881 he frequently had difficulty in finding the rent, and even after it was greatly reduced in 1890 he was still often in arrears.[10]

This was a far cry from the prosperity of mid-century, when one of the Overman family of Holkham tenants, Robert Overman, was said to have left the very handsome sum of £10,000 to each of his ten children, and John Hastings, another of the larger tenants, himself built a double cottage for the poor, endowed with 6 acres of land, to house 'two married couples or four widows not under the age of 60 years'. It was Hastings' grandson, another John Hastings, who in his family bore the brunt of the depression years. Several times he gave notice and was persuaded to stay only by a drastic reduction in rent and the loan from the estate of £500 at 5 per cent. Even so, further rent reductions and some expenditure by the estate on repairs and improvements were necessary to continue to keep him in occupation. This story again reveals how the combination of low prices and adverse weather conditions ate into the tenants' resources, and it was only by huge reductions in the rents – in Hastings' case by 60 per cent – and perhaps some diversification away from traditional farming, that the land could be kept tenanted at all. When John Hastings died in 1907 and his widow finally left the farm, she must have reflected on the changes that had come about since old John Hastings' death in 1869. No longer was it possible for the large farmers to live in style and bequeath great sums to their heirs, and no longer was it possible for even this most famous of estates to contemplate expenditure of the kind that had been lavished on new buildings when rents were paid in full and regularly, and when the farming outlook seemed set fair.[11]

In Lincolnshire it was the same tale of pride brought low. There it is thought that it was the tenants of the more generous landlords

who were best able to weather the storm, absorbing part of their losses through big rent reductions. Those who survived included some well-established and successful graziers, but also new men who 'skinned' the land, taking on scattered holdings at low rents, or buying out smallholders, combining the holdings into acreages totalling 1,000, 2,000 or even 3,000 acres. The larger owner-occupiers were among the hardest hit, especially those who had bought land with the aid of big mortgages when times were more prosperous. In the depression they found themselves saddled with heavy interest charges on land that had sunk catastrophically in value, and which could have been rented for much less than the interest payments.[12]

In some instances it was a case of rags to riches and back to rags again within three or four generations. Before the Wolds had been enclosed and ploughed up during the scarcities of the Napoleonic Wars, the farmers of that district had known hard times, with 'but two pot-days in the week . . . and seldom any bread but what was made from barley and oatmeal'. Subsequently, wartime prosperity and the farming changes enabled large uplands farmers to make fortunes and live in houses described as 'fit for the occupation of a large genteel family'. William Marris, who farmed at Great Limber, had in 1851 a household consisting of his wife and seven children, six domestic servants (including a governess and two nursemaids), and six indoor farm servants. In total he employed on his holding of 1,050 acres a labour force of forty. One of his brothers was another Yarborough tenant, another became a solicitor, and his two sisters married well. The son of a niece married the dowager Lady Yarborough in 1881.[13]

THE MIDDLING FARM

Large farmers such as those just discussed were exceptional outside certain districts, and over the whole country the majority of farms, as we have seen, were of less than 300 acres, many of them under 100 acres. The evidence of estate archives, however, indicates that tenanted farms were slowly tending to get larger. Thus, on the Duke of Kingston's Nottinghamshire estates in the eighteenth century, the numbers of tenants holding less than 100 acres were diminishing, while those above that figure were gradually increasing. Similarly, on the Leveson-Gower Midland estates of Trentham, Lilleshall and Stittenham the share of the land held by tenants of between 20 and 200 acres fell substantially over the long period between 1714–20 and

1829–33, from about 75 per cent of the total to just over 31 per cent; and in the same period farms of over 200 acres increased from under 19 per cent of the total land area to over 59 per cent. In consequence, the average size of farms on these estates rose from just under 83 acres to 147 acres.[14]

The rise in farm size was not connected with enclosure, for the figures from the Kingston estates refer to parishes still in open fields, while those from the Leveson-Gower properties concern lands that were already enclosed at the beginning of the period. Rather, the causes appear to lie with difficult conditions in farming over the first half of the eighteenth century, and particularly in the second quarter of the century, and also with the management policies of the owners' agents. It was a common-sense practice to take land away from less efficient farmers and add it to the holdings of more enterprising and successful ones. Further, estate outgoings would be reduced if in the long run a small increase in the number of good-sized farms replaced a numerous body of small ones, not least in the costs of management and the expenditure on farmhouses and farm buildings. Over a lengthy period the expansion in the ranks of farms run by effective full-time farmers, rather than by men who held them in conjunction with some other occupation, or by farmers who lacked capital, or were elderly or idle, meant that the overall standard of farming improved.

These middling farmers of 200 or 300 acres were probably not the sort described by Hardy in his *Mayor of Casterbridge* as carrying 'ruffled cheque books in their pockets which regulated at the bank hard by a balance of never less than four figures'. Their resources were generally more meagre, though they might still be of some note in their own 'little world of leggings, switches and sample-bags'; and in appearance they fitted his description of

> men of extensive stomachs, sloping like mountain sides; men whose heads in walking swayed as the trees in November gales; who in conversing varied their attitudes much, lowering themselves by spreading their knees, and thrusting their hands into the pockets of remote inner jackets.

The more prosperous of them lived in houses with impressive, but seldom opened, drawing rooms and dining parlours, preferring for daily life the more informal 'house' or kitchen, where of an evening the farmer dozed in his armchair by a great log fire while his wife plied her needle by the feeble glimmer of one small candle. The ceiling was hung with smoked bacon and hams, and the fare at table

was plain indeed but rich in quantity – Rider Haggard had a tenant who regularly breakfasted at 5 o'clock off a pound and a half of cold pork.[15] At dinner the repast was washed down with a bottle of good port, and a hogshead of it, at least, waited in reserve in the cellar. Maids were in attendance, for there was much work to be done about the farmhouse, and domestic labour was cheap. The prudent farmer, thought Arthur Young, should never go in for costly pastimes which distracted from his business: his stable held a good nag for him to ride on, but 'not good enough for hunting, a recreation too common, as it is apt to lead into a dissipated, idle, drinking and expensive life'.[16]

The farmer was no recluse, however. He visited the markets and compared notes with other farmers at the 'market ordinary'. He enjoyed an occasional tipple with congenial companions, as did John Carrington, farmer and local collector of taxes, of Bacon's Farm, Bramfield, in Hertfordshire. One evening in the spring of 1805 when Carrington came home merry with wine and content with all the world, his good humour was shattered by finding 'one of my Cows hanging on an arme of Cherritree in upper Orchard, Dead, Busted in the Clover, and another all but dead, Saved by pricking' (that is, by piercing the body to allow the gases generated by the too rich fodder to escape). Carrington was never too engrossed with his own affairs to be unaware of what was going on around him, and in the severe weather of January 1809, for instance, he made a special journey to Bramfield with a load and a half of faggots, for which he paid 60s, in order 'to Give the poor families wood and some Relieff in the Sharp frost and Snow'.[17] A later farmer, Richard Cobbold of Wortham, Suffolk, told of the ties of mutual esteem which bound farmers to their long-serving workpeople. There was, for instance, James Fuller, 'a fine old Labourer . . . very highly respected by every master who employed him. He used to delight in talking of the Harvests he had known, of the Squires he had worked for.' And there was another 'faithful old servant' whose 'master put up a Stone in the Churchyard and at whose funeral four tenant farmers out of respect to his memory followed his corpse to the grave'.[18]

The many years spent working together in field and barn also induced the conscientious farmer to have regard for his men when age and physical limitations made them unable to perform a normal day's work. Elderly hands were kept on to do a bit of gardening or potter round the barn – the more so since the aged poor showed a profound horror of the workhouse. Indeed, some old people who had to give up their farm cottages refused to accept the bleak charity of the public institution, preferring to sleep where they could, in

an outhouse, cowhouse or stable. Similarly, the employment of the workforce during periods of bad weather depended on the attitude of the farmer. When the ground was too wet to be worked, or was covered with snow, kind-hearted masters found odd jobs for the men round the farmyard, although on a majority of farms, probably, the hands were laid off without pay when normal work could not be done.

The middling kind of farmer was sometimes noted for possessing some unusual skill which caused him to be called in by other farmers when needed. He might, for example, be particularly knowledgeable about the right manures to be used on different soils or the prevention of blights on the crops, or he might be clever in designing water meadows or under-drainage systems. Together with such other likely authorities as the farrier, shepherd or butcher, he might also claim some skill in treating sickness among livestock. Farmers still resorted to amateurs long after the founding of the Royal Veterinary College in 1844, and some farmers followed outlandish prescriptions recommended in old farming manuals. William Ellis of Little Gaddesden, not far from Hemel Hempstead, was one agricultural writer who specialised in advocating home-made treatments, and in the mid-eighteenth century his books enjoyed a certain vogue. Ellis's treatment for a cow 'blown up' by clover was a quart of buttermilk, a drench of urine with salt, and a small dose of tar or a red herring. That for one with a 'gargetty' or inflamed bag was a dose of pepper, turmeric and fenugreek boiled in ale or, more simply, a mere rubbing of the bag with stinging nettles. 'For a cow that pisses blood' he advocated a piece of toast covered with tar. Alternatively, 'a frog put down a cow's throat, and she immediately drove into water, will directly piss clear. It's a present cure.'[19]

Before the railway age, when supplies of guano and superphosphate could be delivered to the nearest railway station, farmers were dependent on their own supplies of farmyard manure and whatever additional materials could be obtained cheaply near at hand. The cost of sending a cart on a day's journey – perhaps some 15 or 20 miles there and back – was high, so proximity of supplies was all important. Those farmers situated within a few miles of a large town could utilise the cart sent to market with produce to bring back on the return journey a load of 'town muck' or nightsoil mixed with the sweepings of streets and stables. The sale of London muck was an extensive business: it was carried out to the farms by wagons and canal barges, loaded into empty colliers as a return cargo for Newcastle and the Northumberland farmers, and was even dried and packed into

barrels for export to the colonies. The eventual coming in of main drainage in towns, and the competition of other manures, cleaner to handle, greatly reduced the trade but did not bring it entirely to an end. As late as 1898, as Rider Haggard recalled, he spread his land with fifty loads of refuse from the undrained town of Bungay, very near his Ditchingham estate. It cost about 2s a load, and the carting as much again, and was effective as well as cheap: 'This compost, disagreeable as it is in many ways and mixed with troublesome stuff, such as old tins and broken glass, is the best manure which I have ever used.'[20]

Towns were the source of a wide variety of manures: soot, which could be bought in London for 6d a bushel, ashes from barracks and other institutions, and the waste products of breweries, malthouses and slaughterhouses, including hoofs, hair, pigs' trotters and horn shavings. Cartloads of old rags, hats and shoes were brought down to the farms, to be cut up by the old folk at the rate of 6d a hundredweight. Near the coast seaweed was raked up after a storm, and carted off to be burnt or composted, or ploughed in raw. The countryside itself yielded lime, chalk and marl, the last used to give body to thin, sandy soils, as well as ditch and pond earths, old thatch, and urine, which was used to soak wood ashes in and also as a seed dressing. Some small farmers used their carts in quiet seasons to fetch manures from the canal or town for other farmers in the neighbourhood. The amounts needed were huge in relation to the quantity of a single load, and a large farmer would use hundreds of loads to dress a single field, though with some manures like chalk or marl this might be done only every so many years.

The larger farmers, together with the more important tradesmen and craftsmen, were selected to serve in a variety of unpaid parish offices, as churchwardens, surveyor of the highways, and constable. The churchwardens had responsibility for the maintenance of the church, including not only repairs, major and minor, but also such routine matters as the laundering of the surplice and communion cloth. They might serve also as overseers of the poor, ascertaining the settlement of claimants, dispensing relief and regulating a poorhouse or workhouse. They had also a more general duty of helping distressed wayfarers and those who passed through the village with authentic claims to charity. The churchwardens of Little Gaddesden, for instance, paid out various sums to help maimed soldiers, ship-wrecked sailors, foreign merchants, gypsies, and sundry persons who had suffered loss by flood or fire, by robbery, or by the depredations of the rebels of 1715. In this long procession of supplicants were featured also '3 turkey slaves, 2 outlandish men, 2 tongueless slaves,

a man y^t had his tongue cut out by the Turks'. It was a more pleasant duty, no doubt, to meet the expenses of the bellringers at the annual fifth of November bonfire, or to pay for drink on the occasions of Marlborough's famous victories (although the battle of Ramillies became anglicised as that of Ram Hill). Other miscellaneous responsibilities included providing refreshment when the parish bounds were beaten, and rewarding those who destroyed such vermin as foxes, polecats and hedgehogs. The churchwardens cared also for the necessitous sick, and a surgeon was engaged at an annual fee to attend on the ill of the parish, the agreement excluding, however, broken bones and smallpox.[21]

From 1555 until the passing of the General Highway Act of 1835 the repair of parish roads depended on 'statute labour', the compulsory six days' work which was required of parishioners, and in the case of wealthy ratepayers the provision of horses and carts or the money composition which many preferred to pay in lieu. The surveyor of the highways was responsible for levying a highway rate to meet the cost of materials and other expenses, and his unpopularity was augmented by accusations levelled against him of undue partiality in his choice of repairs and his general lack of skill in the business. Often enough he merely ordered a few cartloads of stone or gravel and had them tipped into the worst potholes; frequently only the crown of the road was kept in reasonable condition and free of obstacles. The office of constable was also one to be avoided if at all possible, for it involved tiresome absences on escort duty as well as dangerous confrontations with neighbours engaged in drunken brawling, to say nothing of well-armed footpads and gangs of robbers.

County posts, which at least had the advantage of carrying a low salary, included those of Tax Assessor and Collector, and Chief Constable. At Bramfield in Hertfordshire farmer John Carrington held both of these offices, as well as those of overseer of the poor and surveyor of the highways. In his role as tax collector, Carrington had to make numerous visits to extract in person payment of the land tax and window tax, as well as other imposts known as the assessed taxes, which during the financial pressures of the Napoleonic era expanded to include duties on every kind of luxury, including horses, carriages, servants, armorial bearings, dogs, watches and even candles. To this problematic range of exactions was added in 1799 the income tax, a new and radical departure, which, with its prying into individuals' financial circumstances, was greatly detested. And as Chief Constable, Carrington supervised the work of the seven parish constables for whom he was responsible, decided what presentments

should be made to quarter sessions, and attending the sittings of the courts. In between times – and one wonders how he got his farming done – he attended the statute fairs and travelled round the bakers' establishments to check the weight of the quartern loaves, bread being then very dear and the fraudulent practices of bakers a byword since the Middle Ages. It was no doubt a well-known thing in the neighbourhood that he frequently travelled with considerable sums of cash on his person, and this may have been the cause of his being robbed on his way home one Saturday evening in August 1806. Two Irishmen stopped his horse, 'clapped a pistol to my head and demanded my money and they blow my brains out if I made a noise'. Frightened as he must have been, Carrington kept his wits about him and gave them his purse with only some halfpence in it, which they took along with his knife and handkerchief, omitting to search for the little pocket in the lining of his waistcoat which held nearly £20.[22]

Few of the smaller farmers could hope to aspire to the local importance of a man of affairs like John Carrington. Rather, they were of the kind described by a contemporary, William Marshall, as 'plain, frugal, painstaking, close and unintelligible'. Arthur Young, Marshall's rival, scorned them as the 'Goths and Vandals of open fields', men who shielded 'a dark ignorance under the covert of wise suspicions; a sullen reserve lest landlords should be rendered too knowing; and false information given under the hope it might deceive'. In pursuing his enquiries into farming conditions, Young met farmers who replied with 'accounts too improbable to credit; whether from ignorance or an intention to deceive, I know not'. He found that 'a profusion of expense was often necessary to gain the ends I had in view: I was forced to make more than one honest farmer half drunk, before I could gain sober, unprejudiced intelligence.'[23]

Young, it is true, was biased against small men, from whom, he believed, little or nothing was to be expected in the way of enlarged ideas for making farming more efficient. But he was not the only observer who believed them to be hugely ignorant, suspiciously conservative, and massively complacent, following unthinkingly an unvaried, time-honoured routine. The small farmers on the Surrey clays were clearly much the same half-a-century after Young's time, as Caird noted: 'in intelligence and education they are extremely deficient; many of them, as we were told, being scarcely able to sign their own names'. They farmed without any plan, deciding the next crop of a particular field 'according to the opinion of one or two neighbours, at their weekly consultations in the alehouse on market-days!'[24]

Their failings arose in part, no doubt, from their poverty and lack of capital, and their having to do much of the work on the farm themselves, leaving little time for thinking about anything but how to pay for the last delivery of seed or meet the wheelwright's bill for repairs to the wagon. In a highly class-conscious society their very appearance marked them out for contempt, their 'suits which were historical records of their wearers' deeds, sun-scorchings, and daily struggles for many years past'.[25] But, with luck, little farmers of this sort often went on for generations. Failure, when it came, was not always the consequences of low prices, bad seasons or undue mortality among the livestock. Rather, failure often came gradually, through a combination of misfortune, unwise speculations, and personal failings such as drunkenness or idleness. But often the most sober, prudent and hard-working of small men came to grief through some factor beyond their control: ill-health, perhaps, or a crippling accident. Accidents were very numerous, and included dangerous kicks and trampling by beasts, falls from ladders and haystacks, deep cuts from sickles and reap-hooks, fingers caught in unguarded barn machinery, and bones crushed by overturning carts. Even the walk home at night, befuddled, from the alehouse might end in a fall into a pit or a stream. In consequence, small farms were often carried on by wives alone, and even by widows.

There were, on the other hand, certain periods of particular difficulty which saw unusually high numbers of failures, and of tenants 'run away' to escape arrears of rent they could never hope to pay off. A long spell of low grain prices, as in the second quarter of the eighteenth century, could be fatal to arable farmers who lacked the means of diversifying their farming, while in the middle decades of the eighteenth century, and again more briefly in the 1860s, major outbreaks of 'cattle plague' (rinderpest) played havoc among those who relied on dairying and fattening. Over-confident expansion in periods of prosperity, especially the unprecedented run of high prices for both grain and livestock products which marked the period of the Napoleonic Wars, involved farmers in accumulating debts in order to increase their acreage and improve their farm stock and equipment. The subsequent depression, when prices fell sharply near the end of the Wars, damaged farmers large and small. And there were other more short-lived depressions; for livestock specialists, particularly, in the early 1820s and again in 1827–30, and for grain producers in the years shortly after the Repeal of the Corn Laws, in 1849–52.

Much depended on the severity of the price fall, its length and the flexibility of the farming. Those men farming poorly drained

claylands, and generally in a small way of business, were more likely to be affected by poor seasons and low prices because their costs of cultivation were high and their soils offered little scope for shifting into alternative crops or to grass. By contrast, farmers who combined varying proportions of arable with livestock on superior soils were in a much better position, since they could more easily change the emphasis of their farming to meet market trends. However, even this flexibility was of little advantage in the last quarter of the nineteenth century when mixed farming systems retreated as the arable element became increasingly uneconomic. And though pasture farmers suffered less in this period, many of them felt the competition of cheap imported livestock, wool and dairy produce, and eventually that of frozen or chilled meat.

Availability of credit was invaluable in riding out short-lived price falls and bad seasons, and here the willingness of many landlords to abate rents and accept some arrears helped many farmers. Unfortunately, relatively little research has been done on other sources of credit, and it is unclear just how many farmers relied on bank loans, though we know that numbers of the larger ones had come to do so by the time of the Napoleonic Wars. It seems likely that small men continued to depend on personal loans from relations and friends in the neighbourhood, as they had been doing since at least the early eighteenth century. However, during a prolonged period of difficulty this kind of credit must have been difficult to obtain, if it did not dry up completely. Few farmers would have been in a position to lend, while other potential lenders might be put off by rumours that certain men were about to break and were so suspect as to be unworthy of credit.

THE FARMERS' PROBLEMS

The great majority of farmers, as we have seen, were tenants, and on many estates the connection between them and their landlords was not a close one. Generally, they would deal not with the owner, but with the owner's land steward or agent, or in the case of a detached part of an estate the local attorney, farmer, or professional estate agent who was commissioned to supervise the property and collect the rents. Except perhaps with trusted tenants of long standing, the relationship between agent and tenant was often a somewhat uneasy one. The agent was there to see that the rent was paid regularly, that the farming was of an acceptable standard, and that nothing

was being done to damage the value of the land and buildings. The tenant, for his part, knew that not only his farming was under inspection but also his private life, for many owners would not put up with tenants who were drunkards or who otherwise breached moral conventions. The tenant was aware also that reports of the sporting activities he indulged in, the character of his family, and even his treatment of his workpeople were among the matters that would reach the landowner's ears. And if he was a small farmer, one in some difficulty in making ends meet, a more than usually close eye would be kept on him to see that he was not quietly disposing of his stock and equipment in order to forestall a distraint for rent arrears.

But tenants had their grievances, too. The agent's office was not infrequently besieged by tenants who came to ask for urgent repairs or improvements to be made, or to complain of the depredations of gypsies, canal boatmen, vagrants or gangs of robbers, or yet to warn of the dangers of flooding from a nearby river or the sea. Requests for repairs or improvements were often brushed aside, or met by an offer of some timber and bricks from the estate, leaving the tenant to do the work himself. Where the owner was a persistent absentee who spent much of his time in London or abroad, an over-cautious agent would refuse to consider any repairs in case the owner might subsequently refuse to sanction the expenditure. If this was the situation, the estate gradually deteriorated and might eventually decline to the condition where the tenants had to erect props to support the buildings, or even had to live elsewhere because the farmhouse had become ruinous and unsafe. In his country-wide survey of 1850–51 James Caird noted 'buildings of such a character that every gale of wind brings something down which the farmer must repair, and of so combustible a nature that among ill-disposed people he lives in continual dread of midnight conflagration'. Farmers, he complained, were expected to farm to modern standards with accommodation suited to a past century, leading to waste of fodder and manure, and preventing efficient management of stock.[26] And, on the other side, it must be said that some tenants were extremely difficult to deal with, failing to heed advice, or to turn up on rent days, and meeting the agent's reproaches with abusive language and threatening behaviour.

Leases were an uncommon cause of friction between agents and tenants, if only because leases themselves were uncommon, except for big farms. The majority of farms, and especially the smaller ones, were let on annual agreements, with only a general understanding that the tenant was expected to conform to certain rules, to farm up to the standard of the district, for example, and to reside in the farmhouse,

not to sublet, not to remove manure from the premises, and to seek permission before felling large trees or ploughing up permanent pasture. Leases, more usual for large and valuable properties, were by the nineteenth century commonly for terms of years, perhaps for seven years or longer, and renewable by mutual agreement. The rules, understood in the case of the smaller farms, were here set out in a legally binding agreement, and there might be additional conventions concerning the husbandry and the maintenance of the fertility of the soil, perhaps prescribing the marling or manuring of the land at certain intervals and stating the number of white (or grain) crops that could be taken over a period of years. Husbandry covenants were usually not very specific, because efficient farmers did not wish to be bound by a fixed regime which hindered the shifting of the emphasis of the farming to meet changing market trends.

The nature of the leases was influenced to a large extent by the practice of the estate and the views of its agent, but also by the characteristics of the soils.[27] Some agents came to use a standard form of lease, which might be a printed document requiring only the name of the farm, the tenant, the number of years for which it was current, and the rent to be filled in. It was frequently the situation, however, that a lease had to be specially drawn in order to meet a particular set of circumstances – where, for example, the farm had been badly run down by the previous tenant, or where it consisted of land freshly enclosed from the waste, which had to be cleared of weeds, stones and scrub, and manured and ploughed repeatedly before it was ready to bear a crop. In such instances the lease might be for a lengthy term of years, and might specify a low rent in the early years when the tenant would have to expend large sums in getting the land into good condition, and a higher rent subsequently when it was fully productive.

Except for those estates which had large farms or where leases were standard practice, the use of the long lease was generally unusual. One reason for this was that both owner and tenant had become wary of agreeing to a fixed rent for a lengthy period when the future movement of prices was uncertain. The exceptionally long run of extraordinary seasons and prolonged period of severely fluctuating but generally high prices of the Napoleonic Wars made for a distrust of the long lease. Landowners found that when prices were rising the rent was quickly outdated and the tenant gained greatly at his expense; on the other hand, when prices fell tenants asked for abatements or threw up the farms. Those farmers who had taken on a long lease in the good years and then experienced the collapse of wartime prosperity after 1813 found themselves encumbered by

commitments which suddenly became excessively burdensome as the farming climate changed. Another cause of tenants refusing to be bound by a long lease was the fear, particularly among the older occupiers, that they might not live to see it out, with the consequence that responsibility for keeping on the farm would fall on the wife and family. The average expectation of life was much lower than it was to become in the present century, and indeed the early death or incapacity of the farmer was a major factor in the turnover of occupiers.

However, lack of leases did not necessarily imply insecurity, for landowners rarely disturbed satisfactory tenants. It may be, as experts like Caird complained, that farmers who had no lease were discouraged from investing heavily in their farming, but in many parts of the country a system of 'tenant right' had grown up which helped to compensate for this.[28] Under tenant right the 'unexhausted improvements' left behind when a tenant quitted a farm (such as land that had been recently limed or manured, or freshly sown with a crop) were valued by an independent assessor and paid for by the incoming tenant. The main objections to this was the risk of fraud and the financial burden placed on the new occupier, although there was the offsetting advantage that it obviated the risk of the farm being run down by a tenant coming to the end of his period of occupation.

In the first half of the nineteenth century a more serious form of insecurity than any uncertainty of tenure was that of damage caused by 'ill-disposed people', as Caird put it. In this period outbreaks of arson and machine-breaking and, less frequently, maiming of animals and attacks on the person of farmers, were widely experienced, but more especially in East Anglia and southern England where wages were low and under-employment was rife. Serious outbreaks of rioting, often accompanied by arson and machine-breaking, occurred in 1816, 1822 and 1830–31, though the extent and nature of the disturbances varied on each occasion. The Swing riots of 1830–31 were by far the most serious and widespread of these disturbances, and even after these riots ended numerous incidents of arson and animal-maiming continued through the 1830s and 1840s. These incidents, though fairly widespread, tended to be concentrated in East Anglia, and especially in Norfolk and Suffolk. The years after 1834 also saw widespread attacks on the hated workhouses, newly built following the reform of the Poor Law, while in south-western Wales the grievances of tenant-farmers and labourers fuelled the Rebecca riots of the early 1840s, in which toll gates and farm property were put to the torch.[29] Between the more serious outbreaks there flowed an undercurrent of unrest, which even in the quieter years expressed itself

in sporadic attacks on unpopular individuals and their property.

Large numbers of farmers in the affected regions suffered heavily in this period from destroyed or damaged threshing machines, livestock killed or injured, and barns and haystacks reduced to ashes. Some 400 threshing machines were destroyed in the Swing riots of 1830–31, ninety-seven in Wiltshire alone, though arson was a cause of much more serious losses and was widespread over a much longer period. There were at least 250 fires on the property of farmers, clergymen and Poor Law guardians in Norfolk and Suffolk in the fifteen months between October 1843 and December 1844, and villages in Bedfordshire and Cambridgeshire 'were literally put to the torch'. The large water-powered threshing machine cost about £500, but the smaller horse-driven machines more commonly destroyed by the Swing rioters in the southern counties were of much less value, while the burning down of farm buildings could result in losses running into the thousands of pounds.[30] It is uncertain how far farmers' losses were covered by insurance, but no doubt it became difficult for farmers in the worst-affected areas to obtain insurance at all in the 1830s and 1840s. In the Swing riots about a third of the incidents of arson occurred on the property of landlords and justices, tradesmen, parsons, and Poor Law overseers, though many of these were in fact farmers, or ran a farm as a secondary source of income. Losses not covered by insurance, and these may have been the majority, must have been very serious, even for those who had other sources of income; while for those who were primarily farmers the loss of buildings and stores of hay in the years of low prices, when many of the attacks occurred, must often have been sufficiently damaging to tip the victims over the line between solvency and insolvency.

More serious still perhaps in the long run was the constant dread of an attack, a fear which must have haunted many of those who saw their neighbours' property lighting up the night sky, never knowing whether they were destined to be the next victims. Harsh employers, and heavy-handed justices or overseers, lived not only in fear of material loss but also personal danger. Those who ventured out on dark nights had always been obliged to be wary of footpads and gangs of robbers, but in these years they never knew whether some abruptly dismissed labourer or rejected claimant for relief was not waiting an opportunity to wreak personal vengeance. Even to keep indoors at night was not an absolute guarantee of safety, for it was not unknown for the farmhouse itself to be set ablaze or for a gun to be fired through a window, with possibly fatal effects. The breakdown of community spirit, of good relations between masters and men, the

difficult problems of labour surplus, unemployment, the containment of the costs of relief – all added to the strains imposed on rural society by political change and economic difficulties.

It is true, nevertheless, that no victims' lives were lost in the succession of major riots, although the authorities extracted a heavy penalty from those arrested for the offences. After Swing as many as 252 men were sentenced to death, of whom nineteen were executed, while more than 500 were sentenced to transportation and hundreds more sent to gaol. This severe retribution failed to pacify the country-side, for the underlying grievances of inadequate wages, under-employment and harsh conditions for relief continued to fester. Unrest continued in a more concealed, clandestine way, breaking out in certain years into a sudden swell of incidents. Eventually, after mid-century, there was a gradual return to more peaceable relations. Some of those most aggrieved had been removed in the aftermath of Swing, others voluntarily migrated from the villages and continued to do so in later years. Those who remained were slowly influenced by an improvement in the availability of work and the gradual advance of wages. Poaching, robbery and theft continued much as ever, but the more violent forms of protest were laid aside. Even so, as late as the 1860s fearful farmers sat up at night with a gun to protect their barns, and might still find sand poured into the bearings of their machines or iron spikes planted in the fields to wreck the cultivator or reaper.

THE ONSET OF DEPRESSION

The farmers emerged from the trials of the post-1815 decades into the welcome prosperity of the mid-Victorian boom years. Much of the third quarter of the century saw rising prices for livestock products, and only a small fall in the average price of wheat. Then, after 1878, depression struck. The disastrously wet year of 1879 saw an average price for wheat of 43s 10d the quarter, very low in view of the destruction of much of the home harvest. In the years between 1854 and 1878 wheat had averaged nearly 54s; in the following thirty-six years down to 1914 only 32s; in the worst years between 1893 and 1906 only a little over 27s. Barley fell also, but not so badly: in some years it fetched nearly as much as wheat, in 1894 more than wheat. Oats, too, held up relatively well, though in 1895–96 it was below 15s, when in 1874–75 it had been over 28s.

With an expanding home market and despite increased imports, prices of meat held up well in the long-run, although there were

considerable price falls in the 1880s and 1890s. Over the period 1870–1913 prices even rose slightly, and the total value of UK meat production also rose a little. However, much of the improving home market for dairy produce, that concerned with butter and cheese, was captured by imports, and British dairy farmers turned increasingly to meeting only the demand for liquid milk, in which there was no foreign competition. In 1860 sales of liquid milk represented only about a quarter of total milk production, but by 1914 they had risen to some 70 per cent, with home-produced butter and cheese accounting for only some 25 per cent between them. Wool, by now only a minor product in British farming, was badly affected by imported supplies, so that in the years 1897–1902 prices were about a half, or even only a third, of those ruling in the 1860s and 1870s.

The major immediate consequence of the rise in imports was the decline in the importance of grain. In 1867–69 grain accounted for over 35 per cent of the total value of UK farm output; by 1911–13 only a little over 25 per cent (when, indeed, it was nearly overtaken by milk at almost 24 per cent).[31] The grain acreage in Britain fell by over 2.7 million acres between 1871 and 1914, over 20 per cent, while permanent grass rose by over 5.1 million acres or over 41 per cent. It was the traditional story of 'down corn, up horn' with a vengeance, and it was the farmers who relied on grain for the major part of their income who suffered the most. The depression brought with it clear evidence of a long-term change in the national position of agriculture. As an occupation, it was once the main source of employment for the whole country, but it proceeded rapidly on a long decline first to the status of a large but shrinking element of the economy, and eventually to that of a mere appendage of the industry state. But this aspect of the farmers' story requires a fuller discussion, reserved to a later chapter of this volume.

NOTES

.1. **J. H. Clapham**, *An Economic History of Modern Britain*, II, Cambridge University Press, 1932, p. 264.
2. *A Century of Agricultural Statistics: Great Britain 1866–1966*, HMSO, 1968, p. 24.
3. **R. J. Olney**, *Rural Society and County Government in Nineteenth-century Lincolnshire*, Lincoln, History of Lincolnshire Committee, 1979, pp. 58–9.
4. *Century of Agricultural Statistics*, p. 25.
5. **T. W. Beastall**, *The Agricultural Revolution in Lincolnshire*, Lincoln, History of Lincolnshire Committee, 1978, pp. 181, 183–4.

6. *Ibid.*, pp. 202–5.
7. **Susanna Wade Martins**, *A Great Estate at Work: the Holkham Estate and its Inhabitants in the Nineteenth Century*, Cambridge University Press, 1980, pp. 106–9.
8. *Ibid.*, pp. 110–11, 113.
9. *Ibid.*, pp. 113–14.
10. *Ibid.*, pp. 114–17.
11. *Ibid.*, pp. 117–25.
12. Olney, *Rural Society*, p. 180.
13. *Ibid.*, pp. 55–6, 58.
14. **G. E. Mingay**, 'The size of farms in the eighteenth century', *Economic History Review*, 2nd ser., **XIV**, 3, 1962, p. 481; **J. R. Wordie**, 'Social change on the Leveson-Gower estates, 1714–1832', *Economic History Review*, **XXVII**, 4, 1974, p. 596.
15. **H. Rider Haggard**, *A Farmer's Year, being his Commonplace Book for 1898,* Longmans, Green, 1906, p. 56.
16. **Arthur Young**, *Annals of Agriculture*, I, Bury St Edmunds, 1784, p. 84.
17. **W. Branch Johnson** (ed.), *'Memorandums for . . .': the Carrington Diary*, London, Phillimore, 1973, pp. 115, 167.
18. **Ronald Fletcher** (ed.), *The Biography of a Victorian Village: Richard Cobbold's Account of Wortham, Suffolk, 1860*, Batsford, 1977, pp. 134, 140.
19. **Vicars Bell**, *To Meet Mr Ellis; Little Gaddesden in the Eighteenth Century*, Faber, 1956, pp. 96, 120–1.
20. Haggard, *A Farmer's Year*, p. 47.
21. Bell, *To Meet Mr Ellis*, pp. 120–1.
22. Branch Johnson, *Carrington Diary*, pp. 14–15.
23. **William Marshall,** *Review of Reports to the Board of Agriculture*, I, York, 1818, p. 231; Arthur Young, *General View of the Agriculture of Oxfordshire, 1809*, pp. 35–6; **Arthur Young**, *Northern Tour*, W. Nicholl, 1770, I, preface.
24. **J. Caird**, *English Agriculture 1850–51*, London, 1852, reprinted Cass, 1968, pp. 122, 124.
25. **Thomas Hardy**, *The Mayor of Casterbridge*, 1886, ch. 22.
26. **Peter Roebuck** (ed.), *Constable of Everingham Estate Correspondence 1726–43*, Yorkshire Archaeological Society, 1976, p. 143; Caird, *English Agriculture*, pp. 490–1.
27. **J. V. Beckett**, 'Landownership and estate management', in **G. E. Mingay**, ed., *The Agrarian History of England and Wales VI 1750–1850*, Cambridge University Press, 1989, pp. 611–18.
28. Caird, *English Agriculture*, pp. 503–9.
29. See **John E. Archer**, 'Under cover of night: arson and animal maiming', and **David Jones**, 'Rural crime and protest in the Victorian era', in **G. E. Mingay**, (ed.), *The Unquiet Countryside*, Routledge, 1989, pp. 65–79, 111–24.
30. See Jones, 'Rural crime and protest', p. 120; **G. E. Mingay**, 'Rural war: the life and times of Captain Swing', in Mingay, *Unquiet Countryside*, pp. 47–8.
31. **R. Perren**, *The Meat Trade in Britain, 1840–1914*, Routledge & Kegan Paul, 1978, p. 7.

CHAPTER EIGHT

The Other Villagers

THE ESSENTIAL SERVICES

Too often, the agricultural industry is seen, even by some historians, as involving only three elements – the unholy trinity of landowner, farmer and farmworker. In practice, of course, their joint exploitation of the land required the support of many other country-dwellers: a wide variety of professional men, large numbers of tradesmen and craftsmen, and many others.

The owner of the large estate necessarily required much expert advice. He relied for the day-to-day management of his affairs on a land steward or agent, who in turn depended on his assistant agents and clerks and the specialised knowledge of lawyers, surveyors, valuers, auctioneers, builders, and rent collectors, to say nothing of dealers in timber and under-wood, and men prepared to undertake the operation of brickworks, lime-kilns, coal mines and ironworks.

The farmer, for his part, could hardly work his land efficiently without the help of the village craftsmen who made and repaired his implements – subsequently reinforced, if not supplanted, by the factories which turned out implements, steam engines and machinery designed for farm use. In the course of the year the farmer had to deal with such specialist characters as seed merchants, suppliers of fertilisers, drovers, auctioneers of livestock and horse breeders; after harvest he was in the hands of corn and hop factors, maltsters, millers, and dealers in fruit who inspected orchards and bought the fruit while still on the trees. The farmer's horses needed to be shod by the blacksmith, their harness made and repaired by a saddler or harness-maker, and their ailments treated by a farrier. His carts and wagons, together with his own trap or carriage, were supplied by

specialist manufacturers and kept in repair by local wheelwrights, while carpenters and joiners were needed to make and repair gates, barn doors, the fittings in the stables, cowsheds and dairy, and the furniture in the farmhouse. Further, the farmer, especially if he were in a large way of business, might well be operating with the assistance of a bank loan; and if he were involved in negotiating a mortgage or a new lease, or engaged in some dispute over boundaries or rights of way, might have to call on the country attorney and surveyor. And when he or his family were ill, the doctor's carriage was seen at his front door (though in the case of medical advice being needed by the squire it might more likely be stationed at the back, by the servants' entrance).

The farmworker seldom needed, or could afford, to call on the services of professional men, even those of the doctor, unless the practitioner were one of those who ran a village sick club by annual subscription or was paid from the poor rates. His wife, like more superior housewives, perforce relied on the untrained village midwife; but otherwise she and her family generally put their faith in traditional homely treatments, and even occult remedies of an outlandish nature, rather than in the licensed mysteries of the doctor – who himself was quite likely to be qualified only by experience and reputation. To the farmworker, the clergyman was a somewhat remote and august personage, not frequently encountered should the man prefer the chapel to the church. The vicar or rector might be more familiar to his children attending the church school, though the parson might be so conscientious as to make a point of visiting the cottages in which he knew there was sickness or a bereavement; and in addition he might endeavour to interest the farmworker's wife in a coal or clothing club run by his good lady. Generally, the cottagers who bothered with religion at all felt much more at home with the chapel minister, a man whose education, background and speech more closely resembled theirs.

On days of leisure the cottager and his family resorted to local fairs and markets whenever opportunity offered, and for their food and clothing and household necessities they patronised the village shopkeepers and the numerous itinerant pedlars, packmen and cheap-jacks – to the extent of their straitened resources. The need for economy made it less likely they would call upon the village tailor, seamstress or cobbler, nor would these worthies visit the cottage as they would journey out to the larger farmhouses and mansions to take orders and measurements. The cottagers ran up and repaired their own clothes, or depended on the second-hand garments discarded by

the more well-to-do; and in a numerous family the younger children inherited the clothes of older brothers and sisters who had grown out of them. Sometimes, indeed, the young boys had to be dressed in girls' clothing, and the girls in that of their older brothers. The family's boots and shoes, too, were obtained from the cheapest store of a nearby country town, or from passing bagmen and itinerant shoemakers, and were kept in repair by dint of some amateur home cobbling. However, the services of a baker's van were becoming more necessary as home baking went out of use, the cottage oven now being more often cold than in the past – perhaps because of the cost of fuel, or where the wife was fully engaged in the fields or in some domestic industry like glove-making or lace-making. Neighbours helped in sickness, and housewives exchanged their eggs or honey for another's jam or pies. A visit to the attorney's office, to see about a will or an apprenticeship for one of the sòns, or some matter affecting the cottage – and a small minority of farmworkers did own their cottage – was a rare occasion, much dreaded in anticipation and long remembered afterwards; and until well into the nineteenth century a call at the post office might be almost as infrequent. This last was one of the more striking contrasts with the habits of the squire, whose affairs required constant resort to the lawyer, and who set aside part of every day for dealing with correspondence, carefully writing out his important letters from the corrected drafts which he kept for reference in his copy-letter book.

THE RISE OF PROFESSIONS

Many villages were too small or too near to a town to possess a full range of professional services, commercial facilities and crafts. There was always a clergyman, of course, though in very small places he was often an absentee. The resident clergyman, however, was usually the most respected person after the squire, especially if he were related to that gentleman or came from another family of note. In terms of income, however, he was very likely to be inferior, perhaps by a considerable degree, to the lawyer. The country attorney, as he was first called, was already well established in the eighteenth century. By the end of that century the legal profession nationally may have numbered some 5,000 or so, and from 1729 entry to it had been regulated by legislation. Subsequently, provincial societies of lawyers came into being which developed reinforcement of this

monopoly, and also regulated fees. Quite naturally, the mortgaging and conveyancing of land early formed the staples of the attorney's business, and from this base many lawyers offered their services as managers of landed property and as surveyors.[1]

However, the attorney was called upon to advise and act on a wide range of matters pertaining to land, not merely mortgages and conveyances, but also family settlements and wills, taxes, rates and tithes, the drawing up of leases and agreements relating to farms, mills, mines and industrial works developed on estates, and in addition rights of way and the construction and operation of river improvements, turnpikes and canals – to say nothing of processes for debt and distraints on defaulting tenants. Numbers of country attorneys, especially in the Midlands where extensive areas of open fields had survived, were involved in preparing Bills of enclosure for submission to Parliament, and in getting the necessary written and witnessed consents, and the other documents associated with these Bills. An enclosure also called for correspondence with firms of London lawyers, who were more directly concerned with the passage of the Bill through the legislature.

The wealthy owners of the more important estates generally preferred to use London rather than provincial lawyers, leading experts who often acted as their financial consultants as well as legal advisers. Such landowners might therefore have little contact with the local members of the profession, especially where their land steward or agent was himself a lawyer. Some metropolitan lawyers, indeed, specialised in handling the affairs of great landlords, and like Mr Tulkinghorn in Dickens' *Bleak House*, were respected for their sagacity and caution, and not least for their tight-lipped reticence on the subject of the family's private business. Like Mr Tulkinghorn, too, these guardians of powerful interests were prepared to travel down to the country mansion when needed for a consultation, and might go so often as to have a room specially set aside for their use there.

Lesser owners, however, rarely visited the capital, nor could they afford an expert of Mr Tulkinghorn's eminence. For them a local man was both more convenient to hand and substantially cheaper. Thus the country lawyer's chambers, like Mr Tulkinghorn's, exhibited an array of antiquated deed boxes and dusty files – bearing names less illustrious than might be found in the keeping of his London counterpart, but nevertheless ones of considerable local importance. With the railway age the practice of the country lawyer, now known as 'solicitor', widened significantly. If he were in a district affected by the expansion of industry, then that side of his business increased to

the point where he spent much more of his time in discussion with directors of companies than in meetings with landlords and farmers. Even in areas that remained more purely agricultural, the country solicitor came to be more and more concerned with the business of insurance companies and the affairs of newly established public utilities for the supply of water, gas and eventually electricity, and from 1894 with those of the new Rural District Councils and Parish Councils. Again, he might often be seen in his official capacity at the sessions of the County Court or pleading for a client before the Bench of magistrates. At election times his office bustled as the makeshift headquarters of one of the contending parties, and between elections he was immersed in the all-important work of registering electors.

With all these new kinds of business, and also with the growing numbers and wealth of the middle class who valued his services, the country solicitor could do very well. His style of living soon came to surpass that of the parson, for though the rectory might sometimes be an impressive edifice, standing in extensive grounds, the rector's income increasingly failed to match the grandeur of his establishment. Towards the close of the nineteenth century, the parson, indeed, might be obliged to resort to a bicycle, while the lawyer visited important clients in his own carriage; and the parson's lady spent much of her time in pondering how to make her husband's stipend stretch to cover all the outgoings of the parsonage, the children's education, servants, clothing and food. The lawyer's home might be more modest in size, but it was in good repair, and was often marked by some little display of opulence hinting at ample wealth in reserve. He, furthermore, was in a position to accumulate profitable assets, for in his business dealings there were frequently opportunities for investing in mortgages and stocks and shares, and not least, perhaps, in choice parcels of land. Not all members of his branch of the profession did so well, of course. There were those whose indiscretions and looseness of tongue had lost them the confidence of the more valuable clients; those whose extravagance or excessive taste for the bottle, or for other men's wives, had brought them low; those whose incapacity for work and neglect of their clients' interests had reduced them to a meagre subsistence on the scraps rejected by more assiduous colleagues. The law, then as now, required hard-working men of wisdom and probity, and not all its practitioners could measure up to the necessary standards, even those stranded in a rural backwater.

Country doctors, like country lawyers, were generally not the brightest stars of their profession, even if there were some notable

exceptions like Edward Jenner, the discoverer of vaccination against smallpox, and William Budd, another West Country practitioner, who observed that a local outbreak of typhoid could be traced to a contaminated well.[2] Country doctors were commonly less well qualified than their urban colleagues – indeed, often not formally qualified at all. They came from diverse and often modest origins, and some frequently had some difficulty in finding the several hundred pounds required in the early nineteenth century for the purchase of a country practice. Even so, the practice was sometimes so limited that the doctor was obliged to carry it on in conjunction with some other source of income, perhaps that from a farm; while there were many parishes which lacked a doctor at all, medical treatment of sorts being provided by a parson, the squire's lady, or even a farrier – or indeed anyone who kept a stock of drugs and professed a little specialised knowledge.

Accordingly, the doctor's income was often substantially less than that of a successful country lawyer or a well-beneficed parson, and was generally of the order of a few hundred pounds a year. Much depended on the nature of a confined district – and few doctors were prepared to travel more than 6 or 7 miles from home without charging an additional fee. If that district included a thriving country town with a large and well-to-do middle class and prosperous tradesmen and craftsmen, then the doctor certainly would not starve. If, in addition, the farmers were in a big way of business, this would be helpful too. A few gentry families, with their relations and servants, added a bonus, while the onerous and unpleasant duty of acting as part-time medical officer to a Poor Law union might bring in anything from £50 to £250 a year, though more commonly about £150 or £200.[3] Subsequently, an appointment as Medical Officer of Health to a sanitary authority became a useful perquisite, if with the drawback of involving its holder in local politics. Problems arose where there was no town of importance, where the villages were small, the farming was on only a petty scale, and no Poor Law or public health post was available. Everywhere bad debts were a drawback – with many patients, even the wealthier ones, long deferring settlement of their bills, and the poorer ones frequently offering payment in kind, in the form of poultry, eggs, a basket of fruit or a sack of potatoes.

Many of the poorer country-dwellers rarely resorted to a doctor, fearing the size of his bill, and preferring to put their faith in homely remedies and the advice of neighbours. In the later nineteenth century doctors sometimes tried to bring these people into the practice by organising annual subscriptions for suitable families, schemes which

covered elementary treatment and basic drugs. These became the more widespread since the friendly societies offering medical benefits had rarely succeeded in spreading their membership beyond the larger towns. Country doctors had to be physically tough, prepared to turn out in rainstorms, snow and ice to visit distant farmhouses accessible only by muddy tracks, and they had to be unafraid of carrying out an emergency operation in the grime of the back kitchen or even in a barn or the farmyard itself. Perhaps this was why country doctoring, like country schoolteaching, was a haven of the unqualified, and why numbers of the qualified practitioners consisted of retired or half-pay navy and army surgeons, long accustomed to hardship and primitive conditions.[4]

The profession of surveyor developed in the eighteenth century as the importance of having truly accurate measurements of land became increasingly recognised. A significant turning point came with the parliamentary enclosures of the later part of the century, when it was the regular practice of the commissioners to order a complete survey of the lands to be enclosed as an essential preliminary to the re-allocation of the various owners' property. Interestingly, some of the commissioners who featured in the later Acts were described as 'surveyor' rather than by the earlier term 'gent'. However, the development of surveying as a recognised profession came much later, as the Land Surveyor's Club, founded in London in 1834, led to the subsequent establishment of the Institution of Surveyors in 1868.[5]

A key element in this was the growth of firms of specialist estate agents in the capital and elsewhere, of which an early and well-known example was that of Nathaniel Kent, whose business was established in London in the closing decades of the eighteenth century. By the 1830s such firms had become widespread, meeting the needs of those proprietors whose estates were too small or too scattered to merit the care of a full-time agent, but who needed a responsible man on the spot. The local agent, in return for a fee, would take care of such tiresome but essential matters as the letting of farms and collection of rents and tithes, supervision of repairs to buildings, and the valuation of property and timber destined for sale. Necessarily such agents required surveying skills, while through their handling of large sums of money they often developed an interest in local banks, as did, for example, the Oxley Parker family of estate agents at Chelmsford. The building of canals, and later railways, much increased the demand for the surveying and valuation of land, as did the introduction of a uniform method of assessing and collecting tithes following the

Tithe Commutation Act of 1836. In the first six months of 1838 Christopher Comyns Parker, of the Oxley Parker family, attended no fewer than eight-seven tithe commutation meetings in forty-six different parishes.[6]

The management of a large estate, however, with its many thousands of acres and hundreds of tenants, was a major task which required full-time attention. Such estates were often widely scattered across the country, so that although there was a degree of central control exercised through an agent's office in London or at the principal mansion, local agents still had to be used for the more distant properties, to collect rents and arrange lettings and repairs. These local men were often substantial farmers who could provide security for the sums they were handling, and who understood the farming of the area. However, the practical difficulties of supervising the local rent collectors, who were often dilatory, and sometimes incompetent or dishonest, proved a major weakness in the management of the large owner's property. Local rent collectors were, in particular, liable to be unacceptably slow in making up their accounts and remitting their balances, and where the tenants fell into arrears and claimed a rent reduction they were only too likely to side with them.

Another weakness was the possible incompetence of the main agent himself. In the eighteenth century it was usual to employ lawyers in this position, though it was often argued that a lawyer might have little understanding of farming and might be reluctant to make arduous journeys to visit the more distant properties. Later, although lawyers remained numerous, it gradually became more common to have men with a practical background in surveying and farming, and indeed the tenancy of a farm at a favourable rent was often one of the valuable perquisites offered to the agent as a supplement to the salary. Some of the leading agents of the nineteenth century were highly respected for their detailed knowledge of soils, crops, fertilisers and livestock, as well as cognate matters such as the design of farm buildings and installation of under-drainage. These were men such as Francis Blaikie, agent to the celebrated Coke of Norfolk, and H. W. Keary, a later agent of the Holkham estates, John Grey of Dilston, agent of the Greenwich Hospital estates, Christopher Haedy, chief agent in the mid-nineteenth century to the Duke of Bedford, and Herbert Smith, the agent to Lord Lansdowne and Lord Crewe, and author of a treatise on *The Principles of Landed Estate Management*. Most extraordinary was Rowland Prothero, later Lord Ernle, who in 1899 was appointed Chief Agent to the Bedford estates and subsequently became the first Minister of Agriculture; it was his

responsibility suddenly to expand the production of food in order to meet the acute shortages of the First World War.

But there were many agents of much less note, men of little or no training, and lacking in experience and technical knowledge – relations of the proprietor perhaps, or retired army officers, or other rank amateurs. The nature of the work appealed to men who liked the outdoors and country sport, for frequently the agent was asked to help make up a shooting party, even if he were seldom invited to dine with his employer. The perquisites, too, could be attractive, often including a house rent-free or a farm at a low rent, and a variety of allowances to cover travelling and entertaining, while an office staff was provided to cope with day-to-day business. Some agents found their work not so demanding as to exclude generous leisure time: Kersey Cooper, agent to the Duke of Grafton, managed an estate of 14,000 acres, the Duke's home farm and his mansion, and 1,300 acres of his own, but still found time to visit the weekly markets and ride with the Suffolk hounds; while Prothero, who had a literary background, wrote his celebrated *English Farming Past and Present* while managing the Bedford estates.[7]

The salary offered a leading agent varied from a fairly respectable few hundred pounds in the eighteenth century to substantially higher figures in the following century. Christopher Haedy's salary in the mid-nineteenth century of £1,800, together with a London house, was remarkably high, although the Bedford estates were of course exceptionally large and valuable; probably a sum often substantially below £1,000, or up to a little over that figure, was more typical at that time. Even so, the salary and perquisites were sometimes insufficient to discourage some dishonest agents from engaging in illicit transactions. By its nature estate management offered many opportunities for defrauding the owner; for example, by deferring the payment of receipts into the bank and making short-term private use of the cash, and by colluding with unscrupulous builders to submit fictitious accounts for work on the farms that was never carried out. Such practices were difficult to detect unless the landowner made it his business to check his accounts frequently and to inspect his properties in person, and many owners were too immersed in sport, politics or London society to find time for such chores. Perhaps the worst example of long-term fraud was that perpetrated by Robert Short Waters, agent to the seventh Earl of Shaftesbury, who for ten years took advantage of the Earl's customary absence from his Dorset estates to falsify accounts or even keep no accounts at all, living as it was said 'at a rate of £2000 a year with an income of £500'.

Nevertheless, with the exception of men of the Waters stamp, land agents as a whole did much to safeguard their employers' interests, working hard to improve their estates and augment the revenues. They often played a part in increasing the tenants' efficiency as farmers, and encouraged landowners to invest in important key advances such as enclosure and under-drainage. Where they may be criticised is for their sometimes advising their employers to adopt unbusinesslike attitudes towards the setting of rents and acceptance of arrears; and in the later nineteenth century persuading them to invest more heavily in such costly improvements as drainage and new buildings at a time when free trade was making the long-term prospects of agriculture at the best uncertain, and at the worst disastrous.[8]

Land agents, attorneys, brokers and many others sometimes acted as auctioneers when there were lands or goods to be sold quickly, especially those of bankrupts and emigrants. The emergence of the specialised auctioneer, however, came about only in the middle eighteenth century. Auctioneers often combined their professional calling with some other type of business, such as dealing in furniture, or in gold and silver and jewellery; and indeed a large proportion of the goods sold by auction consisted of urban property, furniture and fittings, together with horses, carriages and miscellaneous goods. Only gradually did sales of land become a major element of the auctioneer's business, to be supplemented subsequently in the nineteenth century by sales of farm stock and equipment.[9] Some auctioneers came to specialise in sales of livestock, regularly appearing at the markets and at annual sales of pedigree stock. Their detailed knowledge of the individual families of a breed of cattle was of prime importance in conducting the sale and the setting of reserve prices, and earned the respect of the leading breeders of the day.

OCCUPATIONAL VARIETY

A wide variety of tradesmen and craftsmen were able to find a living in the country towns and larger villages. Sometimes this was a very good living indeed, but on the other hand it might be so thin that it had to be combined with some other occupation. Thus the keeping of an inn was often combined with a little farming or with some craft, such as that of carpentry or joinery, or with the business of a country carrier. The local carrier whose weekly routes were confined to one or two market days at nearby towns filled in his time by dealing in

coal or wood, or by keeping a shop. As is shown by inventories made at the time of death, country blacksmiths, carpenters, weavers and others often engaged in some farming, and quite frequently the value of their farm implements and livestock greatly exceeded that of their craft tools and stock in trade.[10]

Even professional people, especially those living in remote areas, often had insufficient business to fill their time and went in for farming to supplement their fees. Many parsons farmed, of course, rather than let out their glebe lands; and where enclosure had resulted in the extinction of tithes they had in lieu a large allotment of land to utilise. Even so superior a parson as Sidney Smith of Foston-le-Clay was a part-time farmer, as was the Revd Mr Huxtable of Sutton Waldron in Dorset. Huxtable was a well-known farming innovator, celebrated in particular for his belief in the advantages of housing cattle and keeping them warm, a practice which he held to promote fattening and save fodder. The floors of his cattle-houses were so designed as to allow the dung to be easily collected, and the liquid manure was run off to the fields by an irrigation system.[11] Another farming innovator was the Revd S. Smith of Lois Weedon, near Towcester, who followed in the steps of the famous Jethro Tull by growing wheat without the benefit of manure or fertilisers. He planted his wheat in narrow strips separated by equal strips of hand-dug fallow, alternating the wheat and fallow strips each year.

Country parsons might be obliged to farm (or take up teaching) by the meagre stipends attached to many livings, but frequently their ploughs were matched by those of the attorney, doctor, land agent, surveyor and other part-time farmers. Many of these needed land to augment a professional income, and numbers of tradesmen and craftsmen found themselves in the same position, especially in the smaller communities. Research by J. A. Chartres and G. L. Turnbull has shown that in Norfolk in 1836 a village's population had to reach some 500 or so before a blacksmith, wheelwright or saddler was likely to be found there. A community of under 400, however, might well support a public house, a part-time business, no doubt – and one of between 400 and 500 a shopkeeper and grocer. Nevertheless, some forty years later in the North Riding of Yorkshire, the minimum population needed to support a blacksmith or wheelwright (again presumably part-time) was only about 350, while even one of some 300 might have its own publican and shopkeeper; communities of between 370 and 500 could house a butcher and a grocer.[12]

Many craftsmen and shopkeepers, however, like the saddlers and bakers and confectioners, were to be found only in larger villages or

country towns, where indeed the customer frequently had a choice of several to meet his needs. The large village of Binbrook, 8 miles north-east of Market Rasen in Lincolnshire, boasted a population in 1851 of some 1,300, making it almost the equivalent of a small market town of the time. Despite its proximity to Market Rasen, and also to Louth, a much bigger market centre, Binbrook was home to a remarkable number of craftsmen, 109 in all. They included as many as fourteen wheelwrights and thirteen blacksmiths, eighteen dressmakers, fifteen shoemakers and thirteen tailors, as well as ten builders or bricklayers and ten joiners and carpenters. These were not all separate businesses, of course, for a number of the craftsmen were masters employing journeymen and apprentices. Nevertheless, it seems that most of Binbrook's inhabitants and those of neighbouring parishes preferred to take their custom there rather than travel through poor roads the eight or nine miles to Market Rasen or Louth.

Binbrook also provided the services of two doctors and a solicitor, a land surveyor (who also kept the post office and acted as assistant overseer of the poor) and, remarkably, an architect. Four carriers offered a service to Louth, two to both Market Rasen and Grimsby, and one to Caistor. The village possessed no brewer or maltster, though there were innkeepers and a substantial total of thirty-one tradesmen, including seven millers and five butchers. The three leading drapers and grocers each employed one shop assistant and one female servant residing in their households.[13]

Let us take as another example, Ashwell, a Hertfordshire village lying 4 miles north of Baldock, and having in 1851 a slightly larger population than Binbrook, a total of 1,425. Ten years earlier the Census had revealed a small army of craftsmen and tradesmen catering for the inhabitants of Ashwell and its neighbourhood: fourteen carpenters, nine bricklayers, nine wheelwrights, five blacksmiths, seven shoemakers, four millers, two bakers, six publicans, four tailors, three thatchers, three saddlers, two carriers, three grocers and a brewer, a baker, a ropemaker, a painter and glazier, and even an old-established family of rat-catchers. Each of the major occupations could boast from three to five master craftsmen; and including the labourers and apprentices, nearly a hundred men, about a quarter of the adult males of the village, were wholly employed in crafts and trades. And this in a village which nineteenth-century directories described as 'wholly engaged in agricultural pursuits'.[14]

Some large villages owed much of their importance to a strategic position on a main road. By the early nineteenth century Welwyn, on the Great North Road in Hertfordshire, saw numerous coaches

running through it on their way to destinations in the Midlands as well as to the more distant York, Scarborough, Shields, Hartlepool, Penrith, Appleby, Berwick and Edinburgh. The White Hart inn, at the entrance to the village, was early enlarged to cater for the needs of travellers, with new stabling added, together with a brewhouse, a small farmyard and kitchen garden; and its accommodation came to include seven best bedrooms, eight lesser ones and seven garrets, while its dining room extended to an impressive 28 feet by 20 feet, and the inn could boast of its three parlours, a bar room, and even a pulley for lowering the luggage from the coach roof.

In 1851, with a population of 1,557, Welwyn still retained, however, a strong reminder of its more agricultural past, since its eight farmers employed between them sixty-six men and eight boys, while another fifty-three farmworkers were also listed in the Census. Two blacksmiths, a wheelwright, a miller, a saddler and harness-maker, a lime burner and a cattle dealer supplied essential services for the farmers, and they were supplemented by, among others, three shoemakers, three carpenters, three grocers, two butchers, two bakers, two tailors, two linen drapers, two coal merchants, a greengrocer, brickmaker, gunmaker, ropemaker, and a dealer in hay and straw. Two doctors, a surgeon and a veterinary surgeon provided a substantial medical presence, while there was also an Inspector of Police. The existence of a well-to-do middle-class element was betokened by the listing of a small army of 113 female servants (including housekeepers, cooks, housemaids and laundresses), as many as eleven butlers, footmen and gentlemen's servants, and seven farm bailiffs, park-keepers and gamekeepers, seventeen gentlemen's gardeners, twenty-eight grooms, coachmen and ostlers, thirteen charwomen, and twenty-four dressmakers, milliners, needlewomen and bonnet makers. The venerable rector, a gentleman of ninety-five, evidently lived in some style, for his establishment included a butler, two footmen, a coachman, a groom, cook, and two housemaids and three ladies' maids – one a French girl of nineteen years.[15]

Villages such as Welwyn were likely to experience some noticeable changes when the railways arrived, though if they were sufficiently near to the capital they soon came to be the homes of clerks and businessmen, who used the new, faster means of transport to work in London and still live in the country. At Ashtead, a village lying between Leatherhead and Epsom in Surrey, there were resident in 1861, among others, a clerk to the Bank of England, another to the Royal Exchange Assurance Company, and a Senior Calendar Keeper at the Court of Probate Commons. This was only two years after

the railway had opened, though possibly there was already some not inconsiderable commuting to London by coach.

Ashtead also had its farmers, five of them, and eighty-one agricultural labourers, as well as eleven carters, eight carpenters, five bakers, four wheelwrights, three blacksmiths, three shoemakers and two shopkeepers, in addition to innkeepers and the usual array of domestic servants. Nearby Leatherhead and Epsom, larger places, must have been considerably affected by the opening of the local railway line. Even in 1823 Leatherhead had as many as eight coach services linking it with London, as well as frequent wagon and van services, while on one day in May 1848, on the eve of the opening of the railway, Epsom had seven coaches pass through the town bound for the capital, and another seven travelling the other way. Already in 1851 the railways had made an impact, with fewer coaches, wagons and vans passing on the route through Epsom, Ashtead and Leatherhead.[16]

The occupational structure of country places was greatly influenced of course by the presence of an important trade or handicraft. The small market town of Redbourn, midway between St Albans and the hat-making centre of Luton in Bedfordshire, contained 2,085 souls in 1851. Indeed, it had nearly doubled in size since the first Census was taken in 1801, but almost a fifth of its 1851 population – 351 women and 50 men – were engaged in plaiting straw. It was an occupation that was learned when very young, and it is not surprising to find that twenty-one of the straw-plaiters were under the age of seven, and forty-eight were between seven and ten. In addition, there were eleven straw-cutters and three male straw-dyers, while seventeen male and three female plait-dealers handled the selling of the straw and the purchase of the plait for the making of bonnets. A bonnet manufacturer, a 'trimming weaver', and ninety women bonnet-sewers made up the total of 527 people employed in connection with the straw-plaiting trade in Redbourn, a quarter of the town's population.

The straw-plaiting, indeed, gave work to far more people than farming, since the twenty-seven farmers employed only 300 farm-workers between them. However, the building trades were well represented in the town, and there was also a substantial leather trade, with a fellmonger and currier, shoemakers and cordwainers. Despite the extent of these workaday trades, there were as many as six male and nineteen female residents of independent means, a middle-class element which helped employ the numerous housekeepers, governesses, housemaids, laundresses, gardeners, gamekeepers, grooms

and other domestics. The shopkeepers, too, were correspondingly more varied than in the typical small market town, with three poulterers, a fishmonger and a confectioner, as well as the usual butchers, bakers and grocers. And apart from the customary complement of dressmakers and milliners, there were the less usual well-digger, a chair-turner, two blind-makers, a chandler, a watch-finisher, an umbrella-maker and a hairdresser-barber. A midwife and six nurses were listed, as well as a surgeon, a chemist and two cowleaches, not forgetting, lastly, a schoolmaster and three schoolmistresses.[17]

A smaller community, Aldbourne, lying between Hungerford in Berkshire and Swindon in Wiltshire, also possessed some straw-plaiting, although on a much lesser scale than at Redbourn. More numerous than the straw-plaiters were those engaged in the craft of willow-weaving, as many as 133 of the total population of 1,602 listed in the Census of 1851. Some of the willow-weavers made baskets, others bonnets, and William Pizzie, listed in an 1841 directory as a 'Willow Bonnet Maker', himself employed no fewer than ninety-two girls and four boys. Willow-weaving was light and clean work, for the strands of willow used were even finer than straw, and girls would not become domestic servants or work on the farms when, in the trade's heyday, they could earn as much as 11s a week – more perhaps than their fathers earned on the land. A small chair-making business was also growing up, and hurdles, used for penning sheep, were made by woodmen in the copses.

Agriculture, however, was pre-eminent in Aldbourne, with seventeen farmers employing a total of 362 hands, including a dozen or so married women. Seventeen of the men employed were shepherds, outnumbering the ten ploughmen and boys, and thus testifying to the domination of sheep in the district. But the farmers also employed fifteen carters, and so gave work to the four blacksmiths and the saddle-maker, harness-maker and horse-collar maker. Three shoemakers, a shoebinder, and four cordwainers, the last possibly specialising in lighter shoes for the women, provided the village with its footwear; and eight tailors plied their needles, probably on the stout fustian cloth which at one time the village itself had produced in some quantity. Aldbourne, it seems, was not marked by a numerous class of well-to-do residents, for there were only twenty-one domestic servants, four charwomen and two laundresses, while the shopkeepers included only one butcher in addition to an itinerant dealer in meat. No doctor had found it worth his while to establish a practice there, and the two midwives seem to have constituted the sole medical resources of this large village. There were,

however, four schoolteachers with more than a hundred scholars, so education had succeeded in taking a fair hold.[18]

NINETEENTH-CENTURY CHANGES

As the century wore on, the competition of cheap factory-made goods and increasingly accessible town shops wrought their effects on village commercial life. Some craftsmen, like the thatchers, were hit by the greater use of alternative roofing materials, particularly slates, while village women and girls in parts of southern England found their straw plait, bone lace and cottage-made gloves affected by changes in fashion, cheaper imported substitutes, or by a move into factory production. The villagers who made baskets and a wide variety of other articles from cane, rushes and willows similarly found their living slowly falling away. On the other hand, some of the largest and most widespread crafts actually expanded, especially those connected with horses and horse-drawn vehicles. The numbers of horses in use were increasing, since the railways catered primarily for long-distance transport and hardly affected local country movement; indeed, the railways needed horse-drawn vans and wagons for the delivery of goods carried by rail, and farmers and country manufacturers needed horses, of course, to carry their produce to the railway stations as well as to nearby markets.

Thus, in the half-century after 1851 the numbers of rural black-smiths increased by over 42,000 or nearly 45 per cent; saddlers, and whip and harness-makers, by nearly 14,000 or over 80 per cent; while wheelwrights, at nearly 29,000 in 1901, became slightly more numerous. Shoemakers also saw a small increase, but this craft was influenced by the large-scale manufacture of boots and shoes on a putting-out basis, in which numbers of village shoemakers, as well as town ones, were involved in some parts of the production process. Rural carpenters and joiners rose by as many as 114,000, or nearly 73 per cent, reflecting the expansion of building activity in the later Victorian countryside; while coopers, after seeing their craft expand considerably between 1851 and 1871, subsequently experienced a decline, so that by 1901 their numbers, at nearly 16,000, were back to the 1851 level. Cooperage was influenced, like many other crafts, first by the growth of the population, but subsequently more by the concentration of those trades using barrels, casks and tubs in the towns. Millwrights shrank by 2,300, representing a fall of 30 per cent, the consequence of the changed location of milling to large-scale

plants in the ports, rail centres and larger country towns as a rising proportion of the country's grain was imported. Finally, farriers and veterinary surgeons declined by over a half as their occupation became professionalised and they moved to take advantage of a larger clientele in urban centres.[19]

These various influences were reinforced over the four decades before 1914 by the malaise in farming and the movement of younger people off the land. The decline of earnings in cottage crafts like straw-plaiting, lace-making, basket-making, and the manufacture of buttons, nets, string and much else had some effect in encouraging girls to move to towns to find work in the various clothing trades, in town shops, and, especially, in domestic service. In one respect parents were not sorry to see daughters go, for their departure relieved over-crowding in cramped cottages and eased the problem of finding separate bedrooms when the girls got too old to sleep with their young brothers. Moreover, a daughter might be able occasionally to send home a few shillings from her earnings, a great help to a mother trying to bring up a young family on a labourer's wage.

As migration proceeded, a falling-off in custom hit village shops, the more so where a town was sufficiently near to encourage a Saturday shopping expedition. Except for building workers and those concerned in one way or another with horses, village crafts and trades generally declined. Professional men, too, moved to towns to enjoy a more lucrative practice, and the old bustle and coming and going which enlivened the larger villages gradually gave way to rustic somnolence. However, as we have noted, those country towns and villages with railway stations, or within easy carriage distance of a major city, were being revitalised by the arrival of middle-class families seeking relief from the noise, dirt and disease of town life and looking for the opportunity of building a house in its own grounds, perhaps one with a croquet lawn, a tennis court and a paddock for a pony.

The experience of individual country towns clearly depended on a variety of factors, including, especially, location, access to railway routes, the importance of a local specialisation, and the competition of rival market centres. The continuing prosperity of the market – which in some towns might be especially concerned with dealings in cattle and sheep, or horses, cheese, or other provisions – was crucial, as was also the extent of the business in its Corn Exchange, if one existed. A lively market brought in the carriers and the farmers' wagons as well as local people, and the inns did well with their dining rooms and farmers' 'ordinary'. Market day might perhaps be

185

accompanied by a meeting of a local agricultural society or farmers' club, and people visited the shops, bought their newspapers and dropped in to the circulating library.

Most market towns, however, depended heavily on providing for the regular needs of the resident population as well as those of the inhabitants of neighbouring villages, and generally commerce was of much greater importance than any industrial activities. Nevertheless, there were exceptions, and some county towns grew rich on the profits of some specialised industry, as witness textiles in Norwich, boots and shoes at Northampton, and hosiery and lace at Nottingham and Leicester. Not a few towns housed the barracks of the county regiment, and an exceptional proliferation of inns catered for the perennial thirst of the soldiers. As we have seen, the towns often had a substantial number of residents of independent means, people whose presence was important to the better shopkeepers and to the ranks of domestic and outdoor servants who depended on it. The assize towns, in particular, had a busy social life on the occasions when the courts were sitting. Then the gentry of the neighbourhood came in to attend the court, to transact county and private business, to visit their lawyers and bankers, and to spend leisure hours at the tailors and dressmakers and milliners as an essential preliminary to the races, the balls and dinners which accompanied the arrival of the Judge.

At the opening of the Victorian era the typical market town had a population of only between 1,000 and some 3–4,000. Except for their weekly or twice-weekly markets, and their shops, many of the smaller ones were indistinguishable from large villages. In the western part of Sussex, the smaller market towns cited by Dr Chalklin – Petworth, Arundel, Midhurst and Steyning – had populations varying from just under 1,500 (Steyning) to a little over 3,300 (Petworth). These, however, were the numbers for the parish, and those for the town alone would have been considerably less. Larger towns serving as regional centres had parish numbers of several thousand, Horsham over 5,750, and Chichester 8,500. The possibilities of growth for a small town were frequently limited by the existence of larger rivals within a short distance; thus the development of Midhurst (1,536) was confined by its situation, since it was within 10 miles of the much bigger Chichester, and only 6 miles from Petworth, while Petersfield and Haslemere, important towns across the Hampshire border, were only 8 miles away in different directions.[20]

Generally, as the local population fell away or grew only slowly in the later nineteenth century, urban growth became concentrated in a few of the larger and best-situated towns. There the existing

middle-class residents moved out to the outskirts, leaving the centre to become more and more taken up by shops, hotels, and the consulting rooms and offices of professional men. The Rural District Council, water companies, gas companies and eventually electricity companies, established their headquarters there, public libraries appeared, new theatres, often catering for the music hall vogue, replaced ones that had disappeared, and in time a 'picture house' or cinema opened its door. But it was the growth of commerce and industry which underpinned the expansion of the town and created much of the new employment available there. Ironfounders, undertaking commissions from farmers, builders and contractors, became commonplace, and sometimes developed into specialised engineering firms, concentrating perhaps on agricultural implements and machinery. In Essex the ironfounder William Bentall designed his own 'Goldhanger plough', which he marketed through agents whose districts spread beyond the confines of the county. Many a country town, especially in eastern arable districts, had its own manufacturer of steam engines, cultivators, reapers or threshing machines, finding a local market against the competition of the big national firms like Ruston of Lincoln or Garrards of Leiston.[21]

Lincolnshire was one of the agricultural counties which saw employment in the towns increased by the growth of engineering, not least in the county capital. Older businesses changed, too. Almost every country town there had its malting, but new large maltings, built by firms of brewers and located by railway lines, saw concentration of the trade in fewer and more strategic centres as many small town breweries and public houses were bought up and amalgamated into one business. But there were many other activities, some quite old – like those of the boot and shoe makers, seedsmen and soap-boilers – others quite new. The latter included makers of cigarettes and cigars, and of clay pipes – though this declined – steam laundries, manufacturers of jams, sauces, feather mattresses and organs, and builders of carriages and boats; and there were makers of bicycles, and even of motor cars.[22]

By the 1880s the more important country towns offered an extremely wide range of services to a large and varied community. Let us take the example of Canterbury, which boasted not only its great cathedral, but also extensive shopping facilities and, indeed, served as the major market town of east Kent. Canterbury's population, just 15,000 in 1841, had grown by nearly a third to reach 21,704 in 1881. No doubt the numerous visitors to the town, as well as the presence of army barracks, help account for the 162 public houses which drove

their trade in 1882 – a proportion of one for every 134 inhabitants. Six newspapers provided information of current events for the city, and of course circulated in the neighbouring villages. A miscellany of small industries provided a part of the city's employment, notably breweries, maltings, tanneries, soap and candle works, brickfields, whiting works, lime-kilns, coach lofts, a tobacco pipe workshop, ironfoundries, a linen-weaving and worsted manufactory, and rope walks.

The city housed forty-eight boot and shoe makers, twenty-seven tailors and the same number of dressmakers, fourteen milliners and five hatters, together with twenty builders and no fewer than nineteen schools, but those were dwarfed by the fifty-five bakers, thirty-five grocers, thirty-three butchers, twenty-four greengrocers, and sixty other miscellaneous shops. The craftsmen domiciled in the parish included thirteen engineers, twelve blacksmiths, twelve cabinet-makers, ten carpenters and five painters, together with twelve watchmakers and four clockmakers, eleven printers, eight coach-builders, seven upholsterers, four carvers and gilders, four picture-frame makers, three taxidermists and two organ builders. There were dealers of all descriptions – dealers in coal, in china and glass, in fodder, eggs, gravel, horses, leather, linen and hopsack, manure, potatoes, rags, seeds, sewing machines, timber, toys, wardrobes, wool, and wines and spirits – not forgetting two pawnbrokers. Some of the more specialised requirements of the community were met by a bicycle agent, bill posters, bookbinders, ginger beer and mineral water manufacturers, chimney sweeps, confectioners, corset makers, furniture brokers and removers, gun makers, hairdressers, ironmongers, livery stables, music sellers, nurserymen, outfitters, photographers, five 'professors of music and dancing', stationers, tobacconists, and eight undertakers.

The ranks of the professional men were extensive, and included three accountants, ten insurance agents, three appraisers, three architects, nine auctioneers and two auditors. The legal profession was represented by no fewer than eighteen solicitors, and medicine by twelve surgeons, five physicians, two dentists, an optician and a chiropodist, and as many as eleven chemists. Four veterinary surgeons also were in practice. Dealings in land and house property were assisted by ten estate agents, five land agents and seven surveyors. There were several less commonplace occupations; six artists, for example, three fly proprietors, a 'jobmaster' (someone who let out horses and carriage by the job), two 'licensed horse letters', two station masters, a solitary perfumer, and as a touch of the antique, a town crier. The parish

also housed as many as eighteen farmers. The church dignitaries and professional people of Canterbury, together with residents of independent means, kept a substantial number of domestic servants: 161 in all were listed in the 1871 Census. The highest number of servants in one household was six, the Archdeacon of Maidstone keeping a manservant and a footman, a cook, a lady's maid, a housemaid and a kitchen maid.

In the later nineteenth century Canterbury also offered a wealth of leisure activities. There were concerts and recitals, theatrical performances, exhibitions, flower shows, railway excursions – for example, to Epsom races and to Ostend and Brussels – sailing, shooting and cricket week. The clubs and societies included, among others, a Rose Society, an Ornithological and Rabbit Society, a Swimming Club which met in the open-air bath opened in 1876, a Dancing and Grecian Exercises Club, a Natural History Society, the Kent Archaeological Society, the East Kent Gun Club, an Archery Club, and not least perhaps, the Canterbury Harmonic Union.[23]

FAIRS AND MARKETS

As some market centres grew in commercial importance the country fair declined. Well-established weekly markets in the larger country towns survived, especially where they were primarily concerned with livestock, and they continued despite the complaints of the shopkeepers and those residents who disliked the noise, dirt and congestion which they occasioned. Some of the annual country fairs had once been famous institutions, renowned for the extent of their trade in some particular livestock or commodities. Thus the Weyhill fair near Andover was a great one for sheep, St Faith's, near Norwich, was celebrated for its dealings in cattle, and that at Horncastle in Lincolnshire widely known for its trade in horses. In Kent at the beginning of the nineteenth century the old-established fairs were said to be so numerous that hardly any place of note could be found without one. Several autumnal sheep-fairs were held in east Kent, and a new wool-fair, proposed by Sir Edward Knatchbull in 1792, was established at Ashford and was reported as 'very numerously and respectably attended'. 'Considerable' fairs for the sale of fat and lean cattle were also held at Maidstone, Ashford, and other places in the weald of Kent.[24]

Gradually, however, the weekly markets in livestock took over much of the trade and the great regional fairs declined. The statute

or hiring fairs persisted longer, and were still widely used even in the later nineteenth century for the hiring of farmworkers. Men seeking new places gathered in the town on the day of the fair and offered themselves for employment, while masters seeking new hands also went to that meeting place.

Apart from the hiring fairs, many of the small country fairs had early come to lose much of their commercial function and continued largely as annual occasions for sport and merrymaking. In the eighteenth century almost every town, and even villages of importance, had their own fairs or 'revels' – a term indicative of their character – events which sometimes continued for several days and attracted people from miles round. In 1792 the number of fairs held in May, the most popular month for them, totalled some 220, and in October, the next most popular month, still as many as 160.[25] But already by this date the lesser fairs were disappearing. Some fell victims to unfavourable trends in the changing patterns of marketing and transport; others aroused the hostility of the justices, who frowned on the drunkenness and licentiousness which accompanied them. So the justices, in the interests of sobriety and morality (as well as of maintaining good order and restraining the burden of poor relief), issued orders of prohibition, and institutions which had long provided a welcome break in the monotony of the country year vanished. The prohibition might even extend to the casual visits of strolling players and musicians, keepers of performing animals, giants, dwarfs and miscellaneous curiosities, fortune-tellers, and other mountebanks of doubtful honesty. Fairs, like markets, were objected to by shopkeepers, although certainly they brought people and their money into the town. Their numbers gradually declined, though even as late as 1888 they remained numerous, when some 170 were held in the May of that year and 150 in the October.[26]

Fairs became increasingly a town event, but villages still resounded occasionally to the cries of travelling showmen and bands of travelling actors, dancers and musicians, who performed in farmyards and barns as well as in town assembly rooms. Some country towns retained their theatres, and they also developed popular concerts and penny readings; they had their annual parades of friendly societies and their sporting events, and were visited by travelling circuses. The prohibition of cruel sports in 1835 sounded the knell of many of the old brutal pastimes, but there remained the compensation of village football and cricket, the bowling greens attached to many country inns, fishing, and not least perhaps, a little risky poaching. Labourers were hired as beaters when the great house had a shooting

party, and there was the colour and excitement of the hunt, which the village lads followed on foot. But village feasts, which were given by the squire to mark his marriage or birthday, became a thing of the past, particularly when in the later nineteenth century the squire often became an absentee, living in London or on the Continent and only rarely visiting his estate. Even the harvest home, with its singing and carousing, was made obsolete by those farmers who successfully persuaded their men to accept a cash payment in its place. The much-treasured perquisite of beer or cider issued daily by the farmer was at length made illegal, even though it often continued in a clandestine manner. Many farmers, even those who were not themselves strict teetotallers, were glad to see its going, for the furnishing of large quantities of drink had become troublesome and expensive. In these ways Victorian sobriety, and the temperance movement that was gathering strength in the towns, made their presence felt in the countryside.

Country housewives could not often find the time nor the means to do their shopping in a country town, even though a greater variety of goods could be found there, and cheaper ones too. Five miles of muddy lanes were as much of a deterrent as fifty would have been. The great majority of villages never had a railway station, and even in those which had, the station might be a mile or more away from the cottages, and the fares an obstacle for women trying to manage on their husband's income of 12 or 14s a week. Very often, however, the tradesmen came to them. The vans of travelling bakers, grocers, butchers and fishmongers made their regular circuits round the villages, and bagmen came by with lengths of cloth and cheap clothing, and a variety of tawdry finery for the women and toys for the children. Sometimes these hawkers were independent dealers, in other instances agents of a shop in a nearby town. Higglers passed with their eggs, chickens, fruit and other provisions, tinkers called at the cottage door to repair pots and pans, knife-grinders set their wheels going in the lane, and cheapjacks set out their displays of crockery and miscellaneous hardware on a convenient bank. There were vendors of patent medicines and doubtful pills and cure-alls, and those who sold tracts, accounts of a notorious murder perhaps, or pirated versions of Dickens' latest novel.

But as time went by all these familiar characters got fewer. By the end of the nineteenth century the countryside was slowly moving towards a sharper division between town and country, towards the later twentieth-century villages that were frequently bereft of any craftsmen, or even any shop, where housewives were obliged to

make their purchases in a nearby town, and most people found their amusements in a standardised or town-orientated form. There were of course still some country towns that retained their vitality, revived by the arrival of modern light industry and made prosperous by the commercial needs of the families of commuters. In the village, for the most part, only the pub, if not yet converted into a fashionable steak-house for the entertainment of car-borne visitors, remained as an institution to which the ordinary country-dweller could relate, where he could find local company to his liking, the one remnant of the more independent, close-knit community of the past.

NOTES

1. See **J. A. Chartres** in **G. E. Mingay** (ed.), *The Agrarian History of England and Wales, VI 1750–1850*, Cambridge University Press, 1989, pp. 454–8.
2. **G. E. Mingay**, *A Social History of the English Countryside*, Routledge, 1990, pp. 75, 77.
3. *Ibid.*, pp. 80–2.
4. *Ibid.*, pp. 64–6, 82–3, 85.
5. Chartres, *Agrarian History*, p. 452.
6. *Ibid.*, pp. 452–3.
7. **F. M. L. Thompson,** *English Landed Society in the Nineteenth Century*, Routledge & Kegan Paul, 1963, pp. 161–3; **David Spring**, *The English Landed Estate in the Nineteenth Century: its Administration*, Johns Hopkins Press, 1963, p. 133; **Lord Ernle**, *Whipping Law to Westminster: the Reminiscences of Lord Ernle*, John Murray, 1938, pp. 203–5.
8. See **G. E. Mingay**, *Rural Life in Victorian England*, revised edn, Alan Sutton, Stroud, Gloucs., 1990, ch. 6.
9. Chartres, *Agrarian History*, pp. 448–51.
10. **Dennis Clarke** and **Anthony Stoyel**, *Otford in Kent: a History*, Otford, 1975, p. 160.
11. **Ted Ward**, 'Archdeacon Anthony Huxtable (1808–1883) - radical parson, scientist and scientific farmer', *Proceedings of the Dorset Natural History and Archaeological Society*, vol. 101 for 1979, pp. 7–25.
12. **J. A. Chartres**, 'Country tradesmen', and **J. A. Chartres** and **G. L. Turnbull**, 'Country craftsmen', in **G. E. Mingay** (ed.), *The Victorian Countryside*, I, Routledge & Kegan Paul, 1981, pp. 304, 321–2.
13. **R. J. Olney** (ed.), *Labouring Life in the Lincolnshire Wolds: a Study of Binbrook in the Mid-19th Century*, Society for Lincolnshire History and Archaeology, Sleaford, Lincs, 1975, pp. 8, 12–13, 15–16.
14. **B. J. Davey**, *Ashwell 1830–1914: the Decline of a Village Community*, Leicester University Press, 1980, p. 15.
15. **W. Branch Johnson**, *Welwyn Briefly: Two Thousand Years in Outline of a Hertfordshire Village*, Welwyn, 1960, pp. 56–7, 64–5.
16. **Alan A. Jackson** (ed.), *Ashtead: a Village Transformed*, Leatherhead and District Local History Society, Leatherhead, 1977, pp. 92–3, 198–200.

17. Redbourn Workers' Educational Association, *The Story of Redbourn*, Redbourn, Herts., 1962, pp. 48–51.
18. **Ida Gaudy**, *The Heart of a Village*, Moonraker Press, Bradford-on-Avon, Wilts, 1975, pp. 44–8, 80–2.
19. Chartres and Turnbull, 'Country craftsmen', p. 316.
20. **C. W. Chalklin**, 'Country towns', in Mingay, *Victorian Countryside.*, p. 276.
21. **John Booker**, *Essex and the Industrial Revolution*, Essex County Council, Chelmsford, 1974, pp. 29, 31.
22. **Neil R. Wright**, *Lincolnshire Towns and Industry 1700–1914*, Society for Lincolnshire History and Archaeology, Lincoln, 1982, pp. 212–16, 221–2.
23. **J. Whyman**, (ed.), Kent History Group Research Project, *Living in Victorian Canterbury, 1851–1901*, University of Kent, Canterbury, 1979, pp. 18, 21, 25, 29–34, 50, 102–16.
24. **John Boys**, *General View of the Agriculture of Kent*, 2nd edn, London, 1805, p. 202.
25. Chartres, 'Country tradesmen', p. 306.
26. *Ibid.*, p. 306.

CHAPTER NINE

The Decline of Agriculture

THE AGE OF MACHINERY

The farmers, as we have seen, remained a significant element even in those villages which had become hives of industrial and commercial activity. Over England and Wales as a whole the number of farmers remained constant at some 249,000 in the Censuses of 1851, 1861 and 1871; there was a fall to just under 224,000 in the Census of 1881, and the figure declined slightly over the next twenty years. The Census of 1911 returned the number as 208,761. In 1851 the 16,671 farmers who returned acreages of 300 acres or more formed only a small proportion of the total number of farmers but they occupied a third of the total farmland (excluding holdings of under 5 acres). The holdings figures for 1885, although not exactly comparable, indicate that the situation had not changed very much since 1851. It was particularly these 16,000-plus farmers with holdings of over 300 acres, together with a substantial proportion of the much larger numbers holding smaller acreages, who took a close interest in the innovations of the period.

This was not so evident in pastoral districts, for rearing, fattening and dairying were not so easily susceptible to technical advances, although even here breed societies were refining the favoured strains of cattle, sheep and horses, and the making of butter and cheese and curing of bacon were in course of removal from the farm dairy to specialist factories which could produce a cheaper and more consistent product. The laborious work of milking, however, proved resistant to inventors' ideas, and it was long before a satisfactory milking machine was devised, and even longer – till well after the Second World War, in fact – before the majority of the country's herds were milked by machine.

The rise of mechanisation, indeed, was concentrated on arable farming, and it was no accident that the majority of agricultural engineering works were established in the eastern counties where arable predominated over pasture. The new factories, like Ransomes of Ipswich and Garretts of Leiston, made a wide variety of farm equipment, from ploughs, harrows and cultivators to drills, reapers, threshers and hay-tedders, and the age-old dependence of farmers on the skills of the local blacksmith declined. Many blacksmiths still had plenty of work shoeing horses and making and repairing small metal tools, but numbers met the advent of factory-made machinery by becoming agents for the large firms, providing spare parts and undertaking repairs. Some even developed lines of their own and became manufacturers themselves on a small scale. The diversity of farming conditions and the idiosyncracies of many farmers in preferring traditional local designs gave plenty of scope for manufacturers large and small. In 1840 Ransomes produced as many as eighty-six different designs of ploughs to suit local markets, and hundreds more were developed by small producers in various parts of the country. Each year brought new designs of implements and machines, as well as improved models of older ones. At the Royal Agricultural Society's Show of 1853 as many as 2,000 were displayed, while only nine years earlier the number had been under a thousand, and at the very first Show in 1839 only twenty-three.[1]

This upsurge of machinery for the cultivation, harvesting and processing of crops was really a by-product of the Industrial Revolution. Cheap iron was readily available, large-scale methods of production could be adapted by agricultural engineering firms, and these, together with competition between rival firms, kept prices down. About the middle of the century ploughs could be bought for £4 or £5, harrows at about the same figure, horse-rakes and horse-hoes began at a few pounds more, and drills were priced at between £20 and £50.[2] In the late 1850s portable threshing machines worked by four horses could be bought for as little as £45 or £50, although by this date large threshing machines powered by steam engines, which farmers could hire from contractors, were making the horse-powered models obsolete.[3] Cultivation by means of steam engines was in vogue among enthusiasts, but here the cost and the cumbrous nature of the rigs made this more of a curiosity than a system for general use.

The market for the new machinery came mainly from the larger farmers who had the capital to invest in it and who could see the advantages that it offered. The best of the factory-made equipment was more efficient in operation than traditional tools, and, with

standardised parts available, the machines could be easily repaired. Machinery made it possible to cultivate the soil more thoroughly, and in association with the new fertilisers of the period – bone-meal, guano and superphosphate – helped in seeking higher yields. The reaper speeded up harvesting – particularly so the later models which incorporated a self-binder – and so made it possible to catch the best of the weather, while machine-threshing enabled the farmer to get his corn quickly to market when prices were high.

The saving of labour was probably less of a consideration, since labour was cheap and generally plentiful, despite the gradual movement of labour off the land. And compared with the revolutionary machinery applied to textile production, the farm machinery was not spectacularly labour-saving, as Philip Pusey, the farming squire of Pusey in Berkshire and editor of the Royal Agricultural Society's journal, recognised.[4] Farmers often used machines to cultivate at higher standards than before; even though the field machinery involved a substitution of relatively expensive horsepower for cheap manpower – and of course horses had to be led, fed and tended. Much labour was needed to convert small irregular fields to broader stretches suitable for machines, and this work involved the grubbing up and straightening of hedges and shaws, felling of timber and removal of obstacles. The up-to-date barn machinery, such as winnowing machines, chaff cutters and turnip slicers, was increasingly powered by stationary steam engines on the more advanced farms, but steam engines had to be supplied with fuel and water, and many hands were needed to feed the machines and remove the produce. Overall there was, no doubt, some reduction in labour needs, but the statistics of the labour force show only a gradual decline in numbers, and the decline was probably influenced less by machinery than by the variety of forces inducing workers to give up farm labour as an occupation, to move into other jobs in the countryside or in towns, or to emigrate.

The great innovation of the third quarter of the century was effective under-drainage of wet lands, and this work was certainly labour-intensive, involving the making of many thousands of pipes and tiles on the farm, carting them to the fields, the digging of the trenches at regular intervals across the lands to be drained, and the covering over of the newly laid drains. A large part of the claylands of the Midlands was drained in this manner, though no doubt a great deal of the work was done by contractors, whose men, however, probably included numbers of former farmworkers. Under-drainage was seen as the great fundamental improvement of the period, one

which enabled farmers to diversify their cultivation, make the best use of machinery and of expensive manures, and provide the conditions for maximising production of both crops and livestock.

HIGH FARMING

The adoption by many farmers of 'high farming' methods – designed to produce heavier crops through drainage, new fertilisers and higher standards of cultivation, the adoption of superior breeds of livestock, and the integration of arable and pasture to diversify output and take advantage of market trends – necessarily involved substantial investment. All the elements of high farming, drainage, machinery, new fertilisers, prize stock, improved farm buildings, were costly, and added together meant a very considerable investment on the part of landlords, who usually paid part or all of the costs of drainage and buildings, and of farmers, who bought the machines, fertilisers and stock. Although individual machines might be cheap, the acquisition of a range of machines to meet all the varied needs of arable farming entailed in total a considerable outlay by farmers, as also did the grading up of herds and flocks with better breeds. The use of the machinery involved a heavy investment in horses and often a stationary steam engine in the barn, while under-drainage, though normally only a once-off investment, was expensive at a cost of several pounds per acre. The heavy outlay on under-drainage was often shared between landlord and tenant, but where the landlord participated, or footed the whole of the bill, there was usually an increase in the rent, perhaps a rise equivalent to 5 per cent of the total investment.

By the 1870s, therefore, many landlords and farmers had put large sums into the improvement and mechanisation of the farms, often taking out loans to do so. Their assumption, of course, was that the investment would pay off in increased rents and higher returns from produce over a long period of years. For those who spent money on under-drainage in the 1840s and 1850s, when cheap machines for making the pipes and tiles had become readily available, the assumption proved justified; but for those who were slow to take up the improvement, leaving it until the 1860s or 1870s, it proved not to be. For in the 1870s came the beginning of a long-term fall in the prices of agricultural products, especially those of most concern to arable farmers – wheat and, to a lesser extent, barley and wool.

Despite the Repeal of the Corn Laws and the gradually rising tide of foreign competition, farming was generally prosperous over the third quarter of the nineteenth century. The population was growing rapidly, was becoming more urbanised, and improvements in living standards were reflected especially in the growing demand for meat and dairy products. Between the 1850s and 1870s the price of beef rose on average by 31 per cent, and that of mutton by 27 per cent; cheese was much affected by the competition of Irish and Danish imports but still rose by 13 per cent, while milk, in which there was little or no competition, rose by as much as 36 per cent. Cereals were affected by swelling imports but still largely held their own, with barley rising 10 per cent, and wheat falling by only 7 per cent.[5]

With wheat falling against the general trend of rising agricultural prices, the markets were thus undoubtedly moving in favour of pasture and against arable, as generally they had been since the 1820s. The leading agricultural expert of the day, James Caird, was not slow to point this out, noting at mid-century that 'in the manufacturing districts where wages are good, the use of butcher's meat and cheese is enormously on the increase', while even the humble farmworker 'does now occasionally indulge himself in a meat dinner'. 'Every intelligent farmer', Caird went on, 'ought to keep this steadily in view. Let him produce as much as he can of the articles which have shown a gradual tendency to increase in value.'[6] The watchword for farmers living in the new era of free trade was flexibility. They had to be flexible in shifting their production, so far as was possible, in favour of those foodstuffs most in demand and less subject to foreign competition. The 'agricultural improver cannot stand still', Caird emphasised; otherwise he would 'soon fall into the list of obsolete men'.[7]

Under-drainage of wet soils, together with heavier applications of manures, machinery, and the introduction of improved breeds of stock, helped make farms more flexible. The system of 'high farming', as Caird argued, involved a greater reliance on green crops, grass and forage, as against corn. It was much more productive than old systems, and through it Caird himself had been able on his own farm to increase his yield of wheat from 20 to 36 bushels, double the yield of oats, and greatly increase his yields of turnips and potatoes.[8] Leading farmers took Caird's advice, and on their arable farms the improved yields made it possible to earn higher profits and pay increased rents despite the failure of wheat prices to rise. And, increasingly, the more far-sighted arable men were shifting the patterns of their cropping, using more green crops and roots to

feed their dairy cows and fatten bullocks and sheep, and occasionally taking up horse-breeding in addition. Further, it has also been argued that they went in for stall-feeding with grain when corn prices were exceptionally low.[9]

Not all was plain sailing in the high farming era. High farming improved yields initially, but eventually they reached a plateau and levelled out, while competition for farms was forcing rents up. After 1860, imports of live animals increased substantially, and with them came outbreaks of rinderpest, pleuro-pneumonia, and foot-and-mouth disease. In 1865–66 outbreaks of the first two diseases forced the government into the compulsory slaughter and quarantine of infected animals. In 1869 a new Contagious Diseases (Animals) Act controlled the movements of livestock within infected areas, and the measures proved effective in combating the rinderpest outbreak of 1877.[10] However, apart from losses of livestock, there were many farmers who were too ignorant or conservative to change their farming systems; or they were saddled with soils of heavy clay, still undrained, which greatly restricted their room for manoeuvre. The contrast between the progressive farmer, employing the latest ideas and techniques, and the backward man, bound up in the meshes of the past, was very noticeable in 1850, as Caird observed. He saw crops still being sown broadcast, and wooden ploughs drawn by six oxen turning over a mere three-quarters of an acre a day – a medieval rate of ploughing. Cattle were kept hungry in primitive conditions, and there was great waste of labour when crops were still threshed by hand, and where excessive numbers of hands were employed in old-fashioned methods of tillage and dairying.[11] The contrast was still observable a generation later, if perhaps not quite so widely, when the sharp and prolonged fall in corn prices forced on arable farmers a more radical and painful process of adaptation.

MARKETS, METEOROLOGY AND MECHANISATION

The changed conditions of the last quarter of the nineteenth century have gone down in history as the 'great depression'. For those farmers in eastern England who still depended heavily on the corn crops to pay their rents and return a profit, the term was not inappropriate. For the pasture farmers of the western half of the country it was not so fitting, partly because they suffered less from the increased foreign competition, and partly because market trends were still moving in their favour. Nevertheless, pasture farmers still experienced a fall in

prices, if less severe and for a shorter period than did the arable farmers. Between 1883 and 1895 the prices of fatstock fell by about 20 per cent for the best quality meat, and by considerably more for the middling qualities. By 1896 mutton had fallen to 8.5 per cent below its 1871 level.[12] The situation of pasture farmers was considerably relieved by the long-standing division of the meat market into two separate ones, that of the more well-to-do consumers, and that of the poorer ones. Better-off customers preferred to pay a higher price for the superior qualities of home-produced beef and mutton, while poorer ones bought the lower qualities of home-produced meat and increasingly took advantage of the cheaper imported chilled or frozen beef coming in from the United States and Argentina, and of the mutton shipped from Australia and New Zealand.

These imports supplemented, rather than replaced, the flow of live animals from Europe, which indeed continued to expand. The large-scale imports of chilled or frozen carcasses from much further afield became feasible as steamships were fitted with refrigerated holds and cold stores were installed at the docks. Now meat from across the world could be brought in, as well as the old cargoes of hides and wool – the meat carried cheaply over thousands of miles of ocean to supply the dinner-tables of the British working classes. In the seventeen years between 1867-68 and 1893–95, total imports of meat more than doubled, from 336,000 tons to 689,000 tons: of the increased total the bulk of the growth – 286,000 tons – was carcasses, while only an additional 67,000 tons consisted of live animals. The quantities of home-produced meat, beef and veal, mutton and lamb, and pigmeat, rose slightly to reach 1,374,000 tons, so that by the 1890s, the quantity of imported meat had come to be about half as large as the home supply, and represented a third of the total meat supplies.[13]

Changes in means of transport wrought their effects also on the carriage of grain. Between 1861 and 1916 the railroad route mileage in the United States rose from 31,286 to 254,251 – more than a seven-fold increase. Railways were spreading in other parts of the world, too, helping to bring larger quantities of cheap wheat on to the world market as interior territories suitable for grain production were opened up for farming. Meanwhile, as a result of the development of more efficient engines and the growth of steamships on the ocean routes, together with competition between steamships and sailing ships, freight rates plummeted. The cost of bringing a quarter of wheat (eight bushels) from Chicago to Liverpool fell from 11s in 1868–79 to as little as 2s 10½d by 1902, a fall of nearly 75 per cent.

In consequence, wheat in Britain fell in price by 37 per cent: in 1868–77 it had averaged 53s 6d the quarter; in 1878–1900 only 33s 8d. Barley also fell by 11s a quarter in the same period, from 39s to 28s, or 23 per cent. The imports of wheat, which had averaged some 47m cwt in 1868–77 increased to an average of over 78m cwt in 1878–1900, a rise of two-thirds. Imports of barley rose proportionately much more, for an average of only 1m cwt a year had entered the country in 1868–77, while an average of over 32m cwt came in during the depression years, 1878–1900. Wool also was affected, its price falling by 26 per cent between 1877–86 and 1887–96.[14]

In the years after 1877, therefore, arable farmers found that three of their main cash products – wheat, barley and wool – all fell heavily in price, with wheat falling the most. Since also after 1883 other important elements of their produce, fat bullocks and sheep, brought in lower returns, their whole integrated system of cash crops of grain, green crops and the feeding of bullocks and sheep proved to be uneconomic. In response to their complaints, their landlords were forced to reduce rents; but even so those who carried on, hoping for better times, were either forced to retire, give up farming or emigrate. They were not helped, further, by a series of markedly unfavourable seasons, which indeed were so inclement that the first Royal Commission to enquire into the depressed condition of agriculture in 1882 came to the conclusion that it was the weather that was primarily to blame for the farmers' complaints.

The almost unending rain and cold of the summer of 1879 brought the worst harvest of the whole of the nineteenth century. In Suffolk, for instance, towns, villages and fields were flooded, stock lost, and hay washed away by swollen streams. The wheat had to be carried in sopping wet. In earlier times such a bad harvest would have been at least partially compensated by a rise in price. But in 1879 and 1880 wheat, and barley too, were substantially lower than in the preceding two years. Continued general wetness over the three years after 1879 gave rise to widespread outbreaks of pleuro-pneumonia among cattle, and liver-rot in the sheep. It was estimated that more than 5m sheep perished in the first half of 1880, and further losses were suffered in the blizzards of January 1881. The summer of 1882 was wet and was followed by a very wet autumn, while the summers of 1885 and 1887, by contrast, were droughty, with farmers short of roots for their stock. The great blizzard of 8–13 March 1891 brought 20–foot snowdrifts to parts of the West Country, and again severe losses of stock. The harvest was wet yet again in 1891, while 1892, 1893 and 1894 saw severe droughts. Witnesses before the second

Royal Commission into agricultural conditions in 1896 complained almost as much of the drought of 1894 as their predecessors had of the rain of 1879.[15] Then the long, hard winter of 1894–95 caused further losses, while prolonged droughts ravaged large parts of the country when Rider Haggard was making his journeys for his book on *Rural England*, published in 1902.

The succession of calamitous weather conditions combined with the upsurge of foreign competition and low prices to create a sense of unending disaster among the farmers. Even the small dairy farms, which had little interest in cereals or sheep, were hit by the mounting imports of butter, cheese and bacon, the fruit farmers of Kent and the Vale of Evesham by the competition of foreign fruit, and potato-growers by the French and Dutch potatoes brought across the Channel and the North Sea. When Rider Haggard was touring the countryside he found that the food in his hotels was mainly of foreign origin, and even the village shops stocked French and Danish butter, American bacon and canned meat, Canadian cheese, and Dutch eggs and margarine.[16] Liquid milk – rapidly becoming the most important single product of British farming – together with hay, were the only major items in which foreign competition was lacking, or in the case of hay, slight.

In consequence, there were major shifts in British farming towards those products whose prices were maintained, or where demand was rising as living standards improved. Dairy produce, fruit, vegetables and poultry were all influenced by improvements in real incomes – which indeed owed much to the fall in the prices of bread and meat. Between 1878 and 1894 the wheat acreage fell by nearly 1.3m acres or 40 per cent. However, because of the relatively small fall in the acreage of barley – one of 15 per cent – and the rise of 20.5 per cent in the acreage of oats, together with the reduced but still large acreages of roots and green crops, the fall in the total arable acreage was much less than the decline in wheat-growing might suggest: between 1878 and 1894 it fell by only a little over 13 per cent.[17] Moreover, although many run-down farms in Essex and elsewhere in eastern England were converted to dairying, often by Scots or West Country men, these new dairy farms still continued to have some arable, particularly for roots and potatoes to be used as fodder or as cash crops. It was wheat which was the main casualty of the depression, and dairying, especially for liquid milk sent to urban markets by railways, which was the main beneficiary.

As a result of the continued importance of oats, roots and green crops, the expansion of the area of permanent pasture was not as

great as the problems of the traditional mixed farming systems might indicate: permanent pasture rose by over 2.5m acres, or 18 per cent, while rotational grasses rose proportionately more, by 2.4m acres, or about 30 per cent. The demand for horse-fodder arising from a swelling horse population in the country gave rise to the large increase in the oats acreage mentioned above; and the area sown to potatoes remained steady at about half a million acres. There were substantial percentage increases in the areas of orchards, 30 per cent, and of small fruit, 84 per cent, in the six years from 1888 – the earliest year for which separate records for small fruit exist. But in terms of the total acreage for both orchards and small fruit, 306,000 acres in 1900, the rise of commercial fruit-growing represented only a small proportion of the total cultivated area. The same might be said also of hops, which in 1900 occupied only 51,000 acres, and indeed had fallen by a substantial 21,000 acres since 1878.[18]

The effects of the depression were thus complex. There were major shifts away from wheat, and to a lesser extent from barley, but only a relatively small reduction in the arable area taken as a whole. The area of permanent pasture expanded, while between 1880 and 1900 cattle numbers rose by 16 per cent, and sheep numbers fell by 17 per cent, the fall in sheep resulting mainly from the decline of the old mixed arable farming in which sheep were integrated into the system to provide manure and feed off the green crops. There was a significant increase in fruit-growing, but this affected a relatively small acreage in only a few parts of the country. The yields of cereals rose over the period between 1884 and the end of the century, perhaps as a result of the retreat of wheat and barley from the least suitable soils, and despite an increase in the practice of 'land-skinning' or farming with a very low level of inputs. Yields of wheat averaged 29.7 bushels over 1884–89, and 31.2 bushels over 1894–99, an increase of 5 per cent. Yields of oats rose by nearly as much, and barley by a rather lower proportion.[19]

The rise of milk production as a major branch of farming resulted partly from the expansion of urban demand and the fast means of transport to urban markets offered by the railways – by 1891 some 40m gallons of milk were being carried by rail each year to London. In the West Country and Midlands farmers turned from making cheese to catering for the more lucrative milk trade. By 1880 three-quarters of the milk sold in Derbyshire – about the limit for profitable transport – was destined for London, while the Vale of Pewsey, 80 miles distant, emerged as the capital's largest source of supply. Milk displaced 'king wheat' as the most valuable product of farming. In

1867–71 wheat accounted for 22 per cent of the gross agricultural product; by 1894–98 it was down to only 7 per cent. Milk, in the same period, rose from 12 per cent (comparable to beef and mutton, each at 11 per cent) to reach 18 per cent (with beef at 14 per cent and mutton at 18 per cent). The importance of milk continued to grow in the new century: in the 1908 census of production milk represented a fifth of the total value of agricultural production.

The national dairy herd rose by nearly a quarter between 1866–70 (when annual agricultural statistics were first collected by the government) and 1896–1900, and had gone up by a further 28 per cent by 1926–30. Corresponding to the rise in liquid milk production was the decline in the making of butter and cheese. It is estimated that in 1860 butter and cheese together accounted for some 70 or 75 per cent of total dairy output; by 1914 these had fallen to only 25 per cent, displaced by liquid milk at 70 per cent.[20] Part of this change can be attributed to the greater ease for dairy farmers of producing and marketing milk than of making butter and cheese, but much may be put at the door of foreign competition; imported butter and cheese gained a reputation for consistent quality that British dairy farmers were largely unable to match.

The main burden of change fell on the old-style arable farmers, for wheat was the mainstay of their system. Numbers struggled on, even after it became clear that the flood of imports would not abate, and that there was little prospect of a return to protection. These were the men who just after the end of the century told Rider Haggard that they should have gone years before, when they still had some money in the bank. They had many complaints – about the high charges of the railway companies, the lack of good hands, indeed the shortage of men of any kind, for which the schools were widely blamed – but the central issue was the unprofitability of arable farming, especially in the drought conditions of the turn of the century. But although the farmers certainly had their difficulties, Haggard saw that it was the landlords who were the ultimate losers. Land tumbled in value, and owners in the hard-hit arable districts, more particularly those with the poor soils and wet clays that had not been under-drained, were faced with huge falls in rent and a lack of new tenants when old farmers gave up. Even on the famous Holkham estate in Norfolk, where would-be tenants once waited patiently for the chance of a vacant farm, rents fell drastically and new men were hard to find. In 1896 it was reported that landlords in Hertfordshire had a fifth of their farms in hand; Essex had eight estates where the rentals had fallen by over a half and much land had gone down to 'coarse, weedy pasture';

eleven great proprietors in Lincolnshire were faced by rentals which showed an average fall of 48 per cent, while in Suffolk six similar proprietors were confronted by one of 55 per cent.[21]

Hardest hit, perhaps, were those smaller owners who had bought land at what proved to be excessively high prices in the halcyon years of the 1860s, and now had to meet the certainty of heavy losses if they were obliged to sell by an insupportable burden of mortgage debt. On the worst soils, as in the clays of Essex, net receipts of rent fell to zero, and landlords were obliged to advertise in the Scottish newspapers in the hope of attracting new tenants. It was these and similar farms, obtainable at knock-down rents, which attracted the thrifty Scottish dairy farmers who fled the high rents in their part of Scotland and came south with their herds of Ayrshires to produce milk for the London market. By reducing the arable and converting the remainder to grass, these new men were able to succeed where the former tenants had foundered. They economised severely in labour, making the maximum use of their own families, and by thrift and hard work they survived on a combination of cheaply produced milk and potatoes.

Even many pasture farms in the Midlands and West Country did not escape the effects of greater competition in meat, butter and cheese, which was particularly marked towards the end of the century. The effects were often not felt until the later 1880s and 1890s, but then falls in rents became widespread, although unlike in eastern arable districts, bankruptcies and unlet farms were few. Further north, in Cumberland, farmers and their landlords had come through well by making economies, while Lancashire was helped by moving away from corn and from cheese towards milk. Like Lancashire, Cheshire found its numerous nearby large towns provided good markets for its dairies, cattle, market gardens and potatoes. But over the Pennines a different story was told wherever arable predominated. By the end of the century the East Riding wolds farmers were said to have suffered 'huge losses'. In the North Riding and in Durham there was less corn and so less depression, while Northumberland had been hit by the fall in the prices of stock which had followed on the earlier fall in corn.[22]

In 1901 Rider Haggard made his journeys through twenty-seven of the counties of England and the Channel Isles, and described what he saw, and was told, in the *Daily Express*, as well as subsequently in his two large volumes entitled *Rural England*. His enquiries were met by some farmers with suspicion and reserve, one believing that his motive was not to gather rural information but free drinks! One

farmer remarked that he was not interested in 'what folk were doing in *other* places; I want to know what they are doing *here*'. Yet another argued that Haggard's evidence of depression must be mistaken since his own farm was prosperous.[23] But there was certainly widespread depression where corn-growing was concerned, and especially on poor soils.

Kent, for example, had its pastures, dairies, fruit and hops, which were generally profitable, but many Thanet arable farmers had been bankrupted and had vanished. Around Canterbury rents had fallen by a third, and land values there, and even on the Romney Marsh sheep pastures, had fallen by a half.[24] In Wiltshire Haggard was told that a farm of 700 acres on the Downland was sold in 1812, when the land had been ploughed up for highly profitable corn, for the figure of £27,000; in 1892 it was sold again for only £7,000. In 1901 its tenant was paying £250 a year in rent, a mere 7s an acre. Hill farms in the county could be made to pay only if they contained good pasture suitable for dairying. And in Herefordshire some farmers were doing well with their fruit and hops, but sheep-and-corn land could not be made to pay and was being laid down to grass.[25]

Haggard believed that in Essex, one of the worst-hit of the eastern counties, landlords were receiving 'but an infinitesimal return from their estates'. Net rents, after allowing for tithes, repairs and other outgoings, were perhaps down to 5s per acre. But those farmers well-placed for marketing seeds and vegetables in London had survived reasonably well. Younger farmers had adapted themselves better to the conditions; it was the older men who could not shake off their traditional practices and suffered accordingly. Farmers who had bought their land before or about the beginning of the depression had lost heavily, with an acre bought for £60 now not worth more than £20. Around Maldon thousands of acres of land, said to be once the finest wheat-growing country in England, were now derelict, few of the fields producing grass 'high enough to hide a lark': the tithes of such land were worth more than the rent.[26] Haggard himself farmed not very far away on the Norfolk-Suffolk border. His conclusion, after some years of farming 'with economy and not without intelligence', was that in his part of the country, unless the land were in good condition, it could not be made to pay at the prices which had prevailed in the recent past. There was no margin for error: 'one bit of bad luck, such as a disease among the stock, or a drought or a flood, will swallow all the profit'.[27]

On the arable lands of East Anglia the high-input methods of high farming were found not to answer in depression conditions. 'Light

farming' proved more suitable, though the economies made might result in neglected buildings and unkempt hedges, poverty-stricken pastures and deterioration in the quality of the soils. Where local farmers were unable to adapt and tenants were lacking, Scottish farmers began to appear from 1880, notably in Essex, Hertfordshire and Suffolk. They were attracted by the low rents and easy conditions of tenure, both of which contrasted strongly with the terms available in their native counties, particularly in Ayrshire, whence the majority of them came. In eastern England they were able to make good by a drastic excision of the wasteful methods and inappropriate implements of their predecessors. Root crops were often abandoned in favour of temporary pastures of rye-grass, and wheat in favour of oats. For fertiliser they mostly used London gas-lime, and finding that the Essex clays would not make permanent pastures, they adopted rotations of seven or eight years, of which three to five years consisted of the ley or temporary pasture. It was noted in Suffolk, where wives and daughters of native farmworkers had for some years 'withdrawn from farm work', that Scots women were not above 'mucking out a pigsty'. The Scots also ate their frugal porridge and brown bread which the Suffolk men would not touch.[28]

But it was the emphasis on dairying that most distinguished the Scots. They were considered poor farmers by local people, who believed a fine crop of wheat the hallmark of a good cultivator, and despised the dairy. To some they were 'mere adventurers', who rarely stayed more than five years and so ran down the land that no Scot, it was said, would follow a Scot. They were occupying the land, but not farming it. Similarly, working farmers from Cornwall and Devon moved into east Somerset, Gloucestershire and Worcestershire, holding their own by dairying for the industrial cities that lay within easy reach.[29] However, not all the old East Anglian farmers lacked adaptability. Dr Collins in his study of Essex farming found that most of the leading vegetable-growers there were men who had already moved out of corn-growing in or around the middle decades of the nineteenth century. Some of these vegetable specialists sought to bypass the middlemen by setting up their own stalls in the London markets, while others joined a wholesale cooperative, the East Anglian Farmers Corporation. Their peas and potatoes might be 'home picked' and sent to London by road or rail, while other crops were sold standing to a dealer. Vegetables could yield high returns per acre, but the expenses were great and the risks considerable: in some years of glut farmers were forced to plough in their crops or feed them to the livestock.[30]

Gluts were also present in milk production, and there was the persistent difficulty of low prices in spring and summer and shortages of production in winter. Consequently farmers joined the Eastern Counties Dairy Farmers Association, which made contracts with dealers and established cooling and butter-making plants to utilise the surplus milk. An initial problem facing both native Essex men and Scottish newcomers was the adaptation of buildings on former arable farms to dairying purposes, until landlords were obliged to undertake conversions or provide new buildings. The construction of a dairy might well be a condition on which the tenant would accept the farm, and further, the landlord might have to agree to meet the tithes, rates and taxes. In the course of the depression years certain districts, such as the clays of south Essex, became dominated by Scots and West Countrymen. They did not establish themselves without encountering some degree of hostility, being accused of causing unemployment among the farmworkers – which was at least partially true – and being called 'earth robbers' and 'dog and stick farmers'.[31] Nevertheless, with their rigid economy and willingness to work, they showed how the depression could be overcome on unfavourable soils, not least by taking advantage of geography and profitable access to the huge London market.

REDUCED IMPORTANCE OF AGRICULTURE

Some contemporaries believed that the opening of the twentieth century brought some lifting of the agricultural gloom.[32] It is true that the years immediately preceding the outbreak of the First World War, 1908–13 did show some improvement in the prices of cereals, but when the whole period 1900–13 is compared with the last decade of the nineteenth century the improvement is seen to be very small. On average, wheat prices rose by some 6 per cent between 1900 and 1913, and oats by under 5 per cent; barley did not rise at all. Imports of barley stabilised, but those of wheat rose substantially. The acreage of wheat, perhaps the best measure, continued to decline, and that of permanent pasture to increase. Imports of meat pursued their rapid upward rise, though the price of wool took a turn for the better. However, farmers had by now adapted to the conditions of large imports and persistent low prices. They had moved more towards dairying and fattening, and to fruit and other specialities, and crops of cereals were now of much less importance to them. Indeed, in 1909–13 wheat and barley put together had only about the same

importance in English farm production as hay and straw, and only about a third of that of milk.[33] Farmers still complained of hard times, of foreign competition, of the poor service offered by the railways, and the shortage of good hands. But their real incomes were now on the mend, they were showing greater confidence, no longer spoke of crises, and accepted new tenancies more readily.

In meeting the great price-fall farmers economised by relying more on family labour and economising in labour costs by working and cleaning the land less thoroughly, by neglecting hedges and ditches, and also by saving on fertilisers. Landlords, for their part, ceased to drain or build, except where such improvements were essential to obtain new tenants. The depression had some effects, too, in slowing down, but not stopping, the pace of mechanisation. In the years before the First World War many of the old implements of former times were still in use. A wide variety of ploughs was employed, with some antiquated designs surviving, notably the wooden turnwrest plough of Kent and the Sussex weald. This huge plough was sometimes still hauled by teams of oxen, a practice which persisted down to the 1930s. In some remote counties, like Pembrokeshire, corn and hay were still mown with the scythe, at a period when the reaping machine had been available for half a century.

However, in more enterprising areas the reaper, improved since 1880 by the addition of the binder, had made large inroads into the demand for harvest labour, and by the new century most farmers had a wide array of labour-saving machinery at their command. Cultivation by means of pairs of steam engines, utilising wire ropes to haul ploughs, had never caught on because of technical difficulties and the cost, and at the height of steam cultivation during the First World War only about 450 twin-engine hauling sets were in use in England. However, in 1910 the steam tractor was being tried out, and it was correctly prophesied that it would be the tractor powered by an oil-engine that would come to meet the farmers' needs best. Lastly, the dairy, which had assumed such increased importance on British farms, remained unmechanised. The cream separator was never much more than a specialist's tool, and milking machines of varying degrees of practicability were little known or tried before the Royal Agricultural Society's Show of 1913.[34]

The great price-fall marked the decline of British agriculture as a major force in the national economy. By 1901 employment on the land had fallen since 1851 by 449,000 men and 143,000 women. In percentage terms, farm employment for men had been reduced from 27.3 per cent of the labour force to 11.6 per cent; for women

the fall was proportionately much greater, from 7 per cent to only 1.2 per cent. In respect of its contribution to the National Income, agriculture, together with horticulture and forestry, had declined from 20 per cent to under 7 per cent.[35] Agriculture was still a major industry, comparable with any of the other great industries of the time, but it could no longer claim to be the largest single occupation in the country and essential to the nation's welfare, and therefore of special concern to the legislature. More important now than the well-being of landowners, farmers and farmworkers was the availability of cheap food. The imports of cereals, meat, dairy produce, vegetables and fruit – so damaging to thousands of British farmers – were the basis of the rising living standards in town and country. And as the franchise was extended to embrace more and more households, so the prospect of returning to agricultural protection became more and more remote.

As we have seen, the much reduced political strength of the squire was accompanied by his slowly shrinking role in local government. Through a variety of reforms the old administrative powers of the justices were whittled away, leaving only those more strictly concerned with law and order. His wide-ranging influence on the local community was diminished in a variety of areas, by the creation of elected authorities to supervise the maintenance of roads and bridges, to deal with housing and sanitary matters, provide schools, and by the arrival of the new police which came to be established under the Rural Police Act of 1839. In 1888 many of these functions were brought together under the control of the newly established County Councils, and at a more local level under the Urban and Rural District Councils created in 1894. In that year even the smallest unit of government, the parish, which in many instances had been dominated by landowning families for generations, was given its own elected Council, although its powers, and hence its role, were miniscule. True, the squire might very well be elected to one or more of these bodies and his voice yet be heard, but his voice was now only one among many, if still an authoritative one.

In central government, however, the landed aristocracy maintained a very considerable influence for a remarkably long time after the forces of democracy were first unleashed in 1867. The cabinets of the era down to the First World War, even the Liberal ones, were well-seasoned with a rich sprinkling of notable peers, and post-war cabinets continued the same tradition, if on a diminished scale. The House of Lords even felt strong enough to reject proposals for reform, and contested – unwisely, as it proved – the imposition of novel taxes in Lloyd George's Budget of 1909. Peers headed or sat on important

Royal Commissions and Parliamentary Committees which enquired into subjects ranging far beyond those concerning agriculture and the land, such as education, housing, labour and the Poor Law. And so land continued to exert a major influence in national affairs long after the main factor in its economic significance – agriculture – was evidently in decline.

However, it was in the social sphere that the landowners' role proved more lasting. In London the 'season' – with its dinners, receptions and balls, its 'coming outs', flirtations, engagements and weddings, and its scandals too, as the works of Oscar Wilde remind us – remained the summit of high society. True, some members of that society whose assets were still largely in land were already feeling the pinch of reduced rentals, as again Oscar Wilde reminds us. Some of the aristocracy were being obliged to make economies, to sell off or close secondary mansions or dispose of libraries. They sold outlying pieces of land, even closed the main mansion or let it off with the shooting rights to wealthy sportsmen. Nevertheless, the period when large numbers of London houses were sold for conversion into offices, apartments and night clubs was to come only with and after the First World War.

In the nineteenth century relatively few of the new or re-modelled country houses were being built for established landowners. Most of them were commissioned by newcomers, and by the beginning of the twentieth century they were usually modest affairs compared with the Gothic magnificence of the aristocratic edifices such as Bryanston, Stoke Rochford Hall, Thoresby Hall, Worsley Hall, Westonbirt, and the expensively rebuilt Eaton Hall and remodelled Alnwick Castle. But the arrival of new wealth was signalled by the numerous houses built for *nouveaux-riches* who had made, or inherited, fortunes from banking, overseas trade, textiles, commerce, railway contracting, shipbuilding, engineering, iron and coal. Cragside in Northumberland was transformed from a small shooting lodge for Armstrong, the engineering and armaments magnate; Dobroyd Castle in Yorkshire for John Fielden, the cotton manufacturer; Normanhurst in Sussex for Thomas Brassey, son of the great railway contractor; Bracebridge Hall in Lincolnshire for F. J. Clarke, wholesale druggist and manufacturing chemist; and Bearwood, Berkshire, for John Walter, chief proprietor of *The Times*; Didsbury Towers, near Manchester, for J. E. Taylor, proprietor of the *Manchester Guardian*; and Lindisfarne Castle on Holy Island for Edward Hudson, owner of *Country Life*.[36]

The new houses and their estates marked the richness and vitality of new sources of wealth beyond those of land; though it took

211

some considerable time for the newcomers to be accepted among the old aristocracy, who often regarded them with resentment and sarcasm – as no doubt had always been the case with parvenus. The opulence of the newcomers might be impressive, but it was in the great houses of the established aristocracy that the highest concentrations of social influence and political power were still to be found. In a period when, for long, political parties were ill-defined, and even their names sometimes in doubt, and when party loyalty was uncertain – in mid-century it was impossible after a general election for the exact state of the parties to be known until the first division was taken – political power rested with leading figures who could carry large numbers of supporters with them.[37]

In this situation it was inevitable that many political decisions were taken when party notables gathered at a country house weekend, during after-dinner discussions or between paying calls, playing cards, and hunting and shooting. The houses of certain great landowners were the favourite venues, Belvoir, Chatsworth, Cliveden, Hatfield or Raby; or during the London season the town houses of the magnates. The parliamentary session over, Benjamin Disraeli left London to entertain extensively at his country home, Hughenden, situated on a spur of the Chilterns, and remodelled for him in 1862. As leader of the party he was also obliged to confer with eminent members of the aristocracy and gentry, and being no sportsman, endured the discomfort and tedium of the great country house with as good a grace as possible.

In the last decades before 1914 the expansion of the electorate, the tightening of party discipline, and the rise of middle-class politicians such as Asquith led to a decline in country-house influence, although, as we have seen, cabinets of the period continued to include substantial numbers of peers: Balfour's cabinet, formed in 1902, had as many as ten out of twenty, and Asquith's first cabinet of 1908 still had six out of the same number; even as late as 1937 Neville Chamberlain's cabinet of that year contained six peers out of twenty-one. But since 1911 the chief political power was seen to reside in the Commons, and no peer headed a British Government after Lord Salisbury in 1895–1902.

NEW RULES FOR LANDLORD AND TENANT

The slow decline of landowners' role in government and society was paralleled by their reduced influence with their own tenantry. In part

this was due to their political decline, which made it no longer possible to command farmers' votes at will, and correspondingly, the inability of landowners to reward the farmers by securing legislation which might keep farming prosperous. The Corn Laws had gone in 1846, and just when they were most needed – in the price-fall of the late nineteenth century – the landowners were powerless to restore them. The little favours which a landowner had been able to grant his tenants in the past, such as those concerning parish offices, the holding of funds on their behalf, and providing protection from arsonists and animal-maimers, became fewer. The later nineteenth century was a more sophisticated era of elected local authorities, widespread access to banks and stock markets, and a professional police force. The squire no longer represented the sole source of patronage, while local services, such as poor relief, sanitary improvement and schools, were provided by more impersonal organisations.

Again, the squire's not infrequent absenteeism – when he preferred to travel, or even to live permanently away from his estate – greatly reduced the old personal ties that formerly existed between him and his tenantry. The tenants, too, had often changed, both in character and in personnel. They might very well be strangers from another part of the country, men with a highly commercial attitude to the land, and who accepted their farms only after some protracted and hard bargaining; and as a result they had little of the traditional respect for the squire and the length of his lineage. As the landowners' power to control and help their tenants diminished, so the farmers' own independence grew. Moreover, the legislation of the later nineteenth century enhanced the position of the tenant *vis-à-vis* that of the landowner. The Agricultural Holdings Act of 1883 made it compulsory, rather than optional as previously, for landlords to compensate tenants for improvements made during a tenancy, and the Market Gardeners' Compensation Act of 1895 gave tenants of market gardens the right to claim for the value of fruit trees and bushes when leaving the holding. Further, the Agricultural Holdings Acts of 1906, 1910 and 1914 gave the tenant the right to farm entirely as he saw fit, ignoring any covenants in his lease (except that the landlord could still prescribe the rotation in which the farm was to be left in the last year of the tenancy), and enforced on the landlord payment of compensation for disturbance costs when a tenancy was terminated by a sale of the holding.[38] And earlier, in 1881, the Ground Game Act allowed occupiers to destroy rabbits and hares on their farms despite any clauses to the contrary in their leases.

But the farmers' concerns were much wider than leases and compensation for improvements. They wanted to harness the collective force of the farmers – and in 1891 there were more than 200,000 of them – to further their interests by bringing pressure to bear on government in order to secure greater prosperity for the land. Since the 1850s there had been a few farmer Members in Parliament, but they had been gentlemen-farmers and not really representative of farmers in general. The Chambers of Agriculture had been dominated by men of title and had achieved little, while the Farmers' Alliance founded in the fatal year of 1879, did not succeed in its object of getting farmers elected to Parliament, and after a short period of influence with the Liberal government that won the election of 1880, faded away. Lord Winchelsea's National Agricultural Union, which attempted to combine the diverse interests of landlords, farmers and farmworkers, and showed strong Unionist leanings, grew to be of some consequence in the villages after 1892 but failed to survive the death of its founder in 1898.[39]

The Chambers and the National Agricultural Union had tried to work through landowners and farmers acting together, while the Farmers' Alliance sought to exert influence through association with the Liberals. By the turn of the century some farmers had come to believe that they must depend entirely on themselves and rely on nationwide strength to bring force to their views. The National Farmers' Union, founded in 1908 on small beginnings in Lincolnshire, sought to realise these principles. It was largely the work of Colin Campbell, one of those Scotsmen who had moved into English farming, and who capitalised on the idea then current of forming a 'Country Party' to express the farmers' dissatisfaction with Parliament's neglect of their problems, and particularly their disappointment with the limited provisions of the Agricultural Holdings Act of 1908. The NFU saw its membership grow to reach 10,000 in 1910, and as many as 80,000 by the end of the First World War, though even then the union represented only a third of all farmers in England and Wales, and those the larger ones.[40] Quite unlike the earlier bodies, it was solely a farmers' organisation, with landlords and their agents, and middlemen such as factors and dealers barred from membership. Despite its limited representation, it soon became the most powerful voice in agriculture, and its influence was soon shown by its role in advising government in framing measures to deal with the food shortages of the First World War.

Cooperation was a possible answer to some of the other problems faced by farmers. It was associated with farmers' movements in the

United States in the second half of the nineteenth century, and in Denmark it had given rise to cooperative cheese and bacon factories, achieving such consistently high standards of products as to enable a nation of small farmers to capture much of the British market. In this country cooperation offered the possibility of raising the quality of the output, securing better contracts with wholesalers and dealers, and achieving lower input costs through bulk purchasing. However, it failed to catch on except where there were large numbers of farmers involved in the same type of production, such as in dairying or market gardening. Market gardeners round London joined in an association as early as 1867, and by 1914 there were some 200 such organisations, with about 24,000 members, concerned with bulk purchasing of seeds, fertilisers and feeding stuffs.[41] Marketing cooperatives grew in dairying and horticultural areas, and some cooperative cheese and butter factories were established in the Midlands. Generally, however, the majority of farmers preferred to remain independent and deal directly with individual middlemen or retailers; and many clung to the traditional weekly visit to the nearby market town, an occasion which had its social as well as business purposes. Cooperation flourished best where farming was highly specialised, where large groups of producers faced the same problems, and where they valued force of numbers to increase their bargaining power with the middlemen. It is significant that after 1931, when producers could secure a statutory Marketing Board if a two-thirds majority voted for it, Boards appeared only in specialised sectors of farming plagued by annual or seasonal gluts, as well as by low standards of produce and low prices – in milk, pigs, bacon, potatoes and hops.

Looking back to 1870 from the standpoint of 1914, an observer could see that a great deal had changed in the relationship between the landlord and his tenants in the course of less than half a century. In 1870 the landlord had been able pretty much to determine the terms of the tenancy, except where the holding had been badly run down by the previous tenant. He might also, if he wished, choose his tenant by reference to his political and religious affiliation. He would usually rely entirely on the local practice of 'tenant right' for compensation to be made by the incoming tenant for improvements made by the outgoing one. And, in general, he still expected a high degree of deference to his position as a member of the ruling class.

In 1914 the landlord's bargaining power with prospective tenants was greatly reduced, especially for farms on inferior soils. Legislation had very greatly limited his authority over the way the land was farmed, had compelled him to compensate outgoing tenants for

unexhausted improvements, and had also made any choice of tenant on political grounds rather pointless. In areas badly affected by the price fall, indeed, he was obliged to accept whatever tenants offered themselves and the quite revolutionary styles of farming they were willing to undertake. As his authority as landlord had diminished, so the independence of his tenants had increased. They were now beginning to look to their own organisation to assist them politically, and in some districts to cooperation among themselves in order to overcome the weaknesses of their specialised forms of farming. The mutual dependence of the old landlord-tenant system, which had developed over the two centuries before 1870, had been replaced in a far shorter space of time by a more strictly commercial nexus. Landlords had become more largely mere investors, rather than partners, in the land, while their tenants had emerged as more largely independent men of business. Both of these trends were to become further accentuated in the long period of change and turmoil which began in 1914.

NOTES

1. See **G. E. Mingay** (ed.), *The Agricultural Revolution: Changes in Agriculture 1650–1880*, A. & C. Black, 1977, pp. 38–40.
2. *Journal of the Royal Agricultural Society of England*, **X**, 1849, 535–6.
3. **E. J. T. Collins**, 'The diffusion of the threshing machine in Britain, 1790–1880', *Tools and Tillage*, II (1) 1972, pp. 19–21, 25.
4. *Journal of the Royal Agricultural Society of England*, **XII**, 1851, pp. 642–3.
5. Calculated from **B. R. Mitchell** and **P. Deane**, *Abstract of British Historical Statistics*, Cambridge University Press, 1962, pp. 488–9.
6. **James Caird**, *English Agriculture in 1850–51*, 1852, 1968 edn, Frank Cass, pp. 484–5.
7. *Ibid.*, p. 503.
8. **James Caird**, *High Farming under Liberal Covenants, the Best Substitute for Protection*, 1849, pp. 6, 24–7, 29, 31–2.
9. **E. L. Jones**, 'The changing basis of English agricultural prosperity, 1853–73', *Agricultural History Review.*, **X**, 1962, pp. 112–13.
10. **C. S. Orwin** and **E. H. Whetham**, *History of British Agriculture 1846–1914*, Longman, 1964, p. 138.
11. Caird, *English Agriculture*, pp. 42–3, 498–9.
12. Orwin and Whetham, *History*, p. 259; **J. H. Clapham**, *An Economic History of Modern Britain*, III, Cambridge University Press 1938, p. 74.
13. Orwin and Whetham, *History*, p. 260.
14. Mitchell and Deane, *Abstract*, p. 98–9, 489; Clapham, *Economic History*, p. 72.
15. Clapham, *Economic History*, p. 78.
16. **H. Rider Haggard**, *Rural England*, II, London 1902, p. 266.

17. Mitchell and Deane, *Abstract*, pp. 78–9.
18. *Ibid.*, p. 78.
19. *Ibid.*, p. 90.
20. **G. E. Mingay**, *British Friesians*, British Friesian Cattle Society, 1982, pp. 22–3.
21. Clapham, *Economic History*, pp. 78–9.
22. *Ibid*, pp. 79–81.
23. Haggard, *Rural England*, I, pp. xxxii–xxxiii.
24. *Ibid.*, pp. 141, 148, 151.
25. *Ibid.*, pp. 6, 30, 302.
26. *Ibid.*, pp. 437–8, 452, 467, 470.
27. **H. Rider Haggard**, *A Farmer's Year, being his Commonplace Book for 1898*, Longmans, Green, 1906, p. 41.
28. Clapham, *Economic History*, pp. 84–5.
29. *Ibid.*, p. 85.
30. **E. J. T. Collins**, *A History of the Orsett Estate 1743–1914*, Thurrock Borough Council, Grays, Essex, 1978, pp. 68–9.
31. *Ibid.*, pp. 70–1.
32. Clapham, *Economic History*, p. 83.
33. **Michael Turner**, 'Output and prices in UK agriculture 1867–1914, and the Great Agricultural Depression reconsidered'. *Agricultural History Review*, **XL**, 1, 1992, p. 46.
34. Clapham, *Economic History*, pp. 89–90; **G. E. Mingay,** *The Agricultural Revolution: Changes in Agriculture 1650–1880*, Black, 1977, pp. 42–3.
35. Mitchell and Deane, *Abstract*, p. 60, 366.
36. See **Jill Franklin**, *The Gentleman's Country House and its Plan 1835–1914*, Routledge & Kegan Paul, 1981, pp. 255–69.
37. **E. L. Woodward**, *The Age of Reform 1815–1870*, Clarendon Press, 1938, p. 154.
38. Orwin and Whetham, *History* pp. 298, 301, 315.
39. **Nicholas Goddard**, 'Agricultural Societies' in **G. E. Mingay** (ed.), *The Victorian Countryside*, I, Routledge & Kegan Paul, 1981, p. 254.
40. **Lord Ernle**, *English Farming Past and Present*, 6th edn, Heinemann, 1961, pp. 409–10; and **Pamela Hurn**, *Rural Life in England in the First World War*, Gill and Macmillan, 1984, p. 3.
41. **Edith H. Whetham**, *The Agrarian History of England and Wales VIII 1914–39*, Cambridge University Press, 1978, p. 27.

CHAPTER TEN

War and Peace

THE PLOUGH CAMPAIGN

It has always been said that a bloody war is good for farming – and certainly English agriculture had not done very well through much of the long *Pax Britannica* which had persisted between 1815 and 1914. There had been wars, of course – the Crimean, the American Civil War, the Franco-Prussian, the Boer War – but these had either not involved Britain directly or had been far away in other lands. Their influence on our farming had been slight. But then in 1914 there broke out the terrible four-year conflict which brought to battle the greater part of Europe and affected also Australasia, North America and large parts of the Middle East, Africa and the Far East. Huge fleets and armies were mobilised, and the losses were correspondingly enormous: a million British and Dominions combatants did not live to see the Armistice, and more than two and a quarter million more were wounded. In dead and wounded Russia lost more than nine millions, Germany and France more than six millions, Italy more than two millions, and other countries sustained losses running into the hundreds of thousands. A high proportion of a whole generation of active and intelligent young men was wiped out.[1]

At first the War was expected to be shortlived. Indeed, Germany's 'Schlieffen plan' for driving through Belgium and north-west France very nearly succeeded in its objective of destroying the French army within a month. But then the war in France settled down into the costly stalemate of trench warfare, and so superior were the weapons of defence over those of offence that massed attacks on prepared positions resulted only in colossal casualties and never, until the very end, in the breakthrough that Allied commanders looked for. At sea

the stalemate extended only to surface fleets. The German High Seas Fleet ventured out of its harbours only twice in four years, with results that were indecisive. And once the Pacific squadron of Von Spee had been destroyed at the Battle of the Falklands in December 1914, and isolated German cruisers in various parts of the world had been hunted down, the raiding of the commerce of Britain and its allies was left to the German submarine fleet. Slow, unarmed merchant ships were easy prey, first to surface raiders and mines, and then mainly to the U-boats. It was not until the Admiralty belatedly resumed the sailing of merchant vessels in convoys protected by warships – a measure used with success against French privateers in the Napoleonic Wars – that shipping losses, although still heavy, dropped from crisis levels. Convoys, it must be said, involved some wastage of merchant tonnage while ships waited in port for the convoy to gather, and the speed of the convoy itself was reduced to that which the slowest ship in it could maintain, but nevertheless the convoy proved to be the main method of defeating the U-boats.

In the early years of the war food shortages in Britain were gradually intensified by the increasingly heavy shipping losses. Before the war Britain had imported as much as 80 per cent of its cereals, 40 per cent of its meat (with the remainder fed partly on imported feeding stuffs), and 75 per cent of its fruit, as well as substantial proportions of other foodstuffs, especially butter and cheese, and the whole of its sugar and colonial produce. However, it was not until the spring of 1915 that the government took alarm at the deteriorating supply position. In both May and June of that year British Empire merchant shipping losses totalled over 90,000 gross tons. A committee under Lord Milner was appointed which recommended radical measures to increase the output of the land. For the time being most of the Milner recommendations were left in abeyance; but the rate of shipping losses accelerated, and in 1916 British Empire vessels to a total of over 1.2m tons were sunk, with nearly a half of this loss occurring in the last three months of the year. The following year, 1917, saw the crisis at its height: the one month of April recorded the peak loss of over half a million tons, and the loss for the whole year was over 3.6m tons (and over 6m tons for the total world losses). The German attempt to defeat the Allies by starving them of food and other essentials looked very likely to succeed. Even in the eleven months of the last year of the war, to November 1918, British Empire ships totalling 1.6m tons, and over 2.5m tons for the whole world, were lost, although from July 1918 newly built tonnage was balancing the tonnage destroyed.[2]

From December 1916 the new Coalition government under Lloyd George at last grasped the necessity of acting on the Milner recommendations. But the problems of increasing home-produced food supplies had become far from simple. There was a shortage of skilled farmworkers as many had been recruited into the army, and even those who remained were subject to the paramount requirements of military service. One of the sorest grievances in the countryside was the ability of farmers to keep their sons out of the trenches by swearing that they were essential to running the farm. Indeed, the 'Plough Campaign' was hampered from the start by a shortage of skilled ploughmen. Besides skilled hands the conversion of grassland into arable also needed horses and their gear and implements. But horses, too, had been commandeered for army use, and blacksmiths and harness-makers were scarce, as were also wheelwrights and saddlers. Manufacturers of farm machinery and implements had turned over to producing weapons of war, and fertilisers were in short supply since sulphate of ammonia was diverted to the making of munitions, and imports of phosphatic rock and iron pyrites for making superphosphates were restricted. The 1916 harvests of corn and potatoes were poor, and the severity of the following winter actually saw a reduction in the area of winter-sown wheat.[3]

The need to restrict food consumption, by means of higher prices and by rationing, was compromised by the contrary objective of meeting the interests of consumers long used to cheap and plentiful food. The 4 lb loaf was stabilised at 9d, partly at the expense of the farmer, whose home-grown wheat was artificially cheapened; similarly, the best and worst qualities of home-grown beef and mutton were sold at the same price to suit low-income consumers. It was evident that in bringing about a rapid extension of the arable acreage the voluntary cooperation of many patriotic farmers would not be enough: compulsion would have to be used to force the ploughing-up policy on the reluctant minority. Farmers used only to dairying or fattening had to see their treasured pastures broken up for corn and potatoes. There was no alternative: an acre of arable could feed many more people than one of pasture, and in view of the shortage of fertilisers only the release of the stored-up fertility of old grasslands could meet the situation. At the same time, with reductions in imported feeding stuffs, additional fodder had to be produced from arable land to ensure sufficient supplies of home-produced meat and winter milk.[4]

Already County War Agricultural Committees had been set up on the recommendation of the Milner Committee. Smaller Executive

Committees – many of the members farmers – were now established to operate the new powers given them in January 1917. This was too late, however, to have much effect on the area available for cropping in 1917, and only some small additions were achieved by the ploughing up of pastures during the spring of that year. It was not until the last year of the war that vigorous application of the ploughing-up policy showed major results.[5] In 1918 the wheat area was expanded by 645,000 acres over that of 1916, and oats by 695,000 acres, increases of about a third and a quarter respectively, while the potato acreage grew by nearly a half. These changes were obtained at the cost of about 9 per cent of the 1916 acreage of permanent grass, and nearly 20 per cent of that of temporary grass. There were reductions also in the acreages of hops, mustard seed, and bulbs and flowers, while a big expansion in the numbers of allotments enabled many part-time cultivators to add substantially to domestic food supplies.[6]

On the face of it these appear to be modest results in view of the drastic nature of the powers given to the County Executive Committees. Farmers were obliged to plough up grass lands specified by the Committees, on pain of a fine or imprisonment, and without right of appeal. The occupiers of badly farmed lands could be forced to quit, and the Committees themselves could take over badly cultivated farms. There was opposition from some farmers who protested that the land to be ploughed up was unsuitable for arable cultivation, or that they lacked the labour, horses, equipment and money for the work. But there was also a large measure of cooperation, and at the end of 1918 it is remarkable that, despite the supposed inefficiency of many of Britain's farmers, only 125 farms of over 50 acres had been taken over by the Committee, a total of a mere 24,000 acres.[7]

The reality was that too many difficulties stood in the way of achieving a more rapid conversion of grass to arable. In particular, skilled labour was scarce, and was made scarcer by the continuing demands of the army for fresh drafts of men. The farmers were helped over this problem by the deployment of a wide variety of other kinds of labour, some skilled, but many unskilled or only partially skilled – men released from the army to help on the land, prisoners of war, the Women's Land Army, village women, and schoolchildren. By November 1918, 84,000 soldiers and 30,000 prisoners of war were working on the farms, together with the 16,000-strong Women's Land Army and some 30,000 village women – though many of the last were part-time. Farmers took a rather jaundiced view of the

efforts of many of these new hands, especially the poorly paid and inadequately motivated prisoners of war, as also those of the village women, many of whom, somewhat surprisingly perhaps, had long ceased to work on the land and had lost any traditional skills they once possessed. In regard to power and equipment the farmers were assisted by the release of horses from the army, and by rather belated supplies of tractors and steam ploughing sets, as well as numbers of reapers and binders, and thousands of ploughs, carts and lorries, cultivators, harrows and rollers.[8]

To give farmers a financial inducement to cooperate in the ploughing up of their pastures, the Corn Production Act of 1917 introduced guaranteed minimum prices for wheat and oats. (Barley was excluded because of objections from the temperance movement.) In the event, market prices, controlled by the Ministry of Food, proved to be substantially higher than the minima. In 1917 the prices for wheat paid by the government buyer were over 25 per cent above the minimum price (and as much as 116 per cent above the 1914 price). Part II of the Corn Production Act established minimum rates of wages for farmworkers, to be set by local Agricultural Wages Boards. As a result, minimum wages rose from 25s for a week of fifty-two hours in 1917 to 30s 6d in 1918–19. *Average* wages rose from 16s 10d in July 1914 (for a week of approximately fifty-eight hours) to 31s 9d in August 1918, an increase of 89 per cent. However, the apparent large improvement was illusory since the cost of living rose even more steeply in the years between 1914 and 1918–19, so that in real terms farmworkers experienced a fall in wages.[9]

While farmworkers' living standards came under pressure, their employers generally did well. The prices of farm products were higher than had been known for many years, indeed since before most of that generation of farmers had been born, with potatoes and dairy prices showing exceptionally great rises. Their costs, of course, were higher too, but did not rise so steeply as prices. One of the major outgoings, rent, rose hardly at all, because some rents were fixed by leases, and because landlords shrank from driving up the rents of existing occupiers who had no leases and thus taking financial advantage of a national crisis. Labour costs, a second major outgoing, rose by some two-thirds – substantially less than the rise in agricultural prices – and although the costs of feed and fertilisers rose very steeply, difficulties in obtaining supplies of these inputs kept down farmers' expenditure on them.[10]

Dr Peter Dewey has calculated that farmers' net incomes (not the same thing as profits) had risen by 1918 more than three-fold over

the pre-war level, and that the average return on their capital rose from under 1 per cent before the war to as high as 7 per cent, or even more, depending on the basis of the calculation. Certainly the liability to pay income tax was increased. Before the war farmers' tax assessments were based on a third of the rental, which meant in practice that few farmers paid any income tax at all. The assessment was increased during the war to take account of the rise in profits, and by 1918 it had been increased to double the rental. However, since rents had increased very little and profits had soared, they still came out of the change very well indeed.[11] Moreover, farmers were in a position to divert scarce produce to their own tables and lived relatively well when the remainder of the community had to accept reduced living standards; and when many families had to grieve over the loss of their loved ones, farmers and their sons were often able to avoid conscription.

The fall in imported food supplies was severe. Imports of wheat and wheatmeal, for instance, had by 1918 fallen to little more than a quarter of the 1914 figure. By way of partial compensation home produce in 1918 rose by 43 per cent, still leaving a very large gap in total supplies. The reduced quantity available for consumption was eked out by adding barley to bread flour, and by using a higher extraction rate of flour from the grain – though this device left a reduced supply of wheat offals for farmers to use as feed. In the middle of the war the situation had been made worse by the poor harvest of 1916, which obliged livestock farmers to rely more heavily on hay and roots, supplies of which had not increased. Indeed, the harvests of 1916 were poor around the world, adding at that time to the problems of importing foodstuffs just as the German submarines were making increasing inroads into the availability of shipping. In the last two years of the war meat production, especially of mutton and pork, fell away, and there was also a slight fall in milk output because of shortages of feeding stuffs. The broad effect was that by 1918, despite the efforts made in 1917–18 to expand the arable acreage, the total food value of UK agricultural production was still slightly below that of 1914. What kept the nation fed at the height of the submarine warfare was not the government's Plough Campaign but the stringent control of food, notably the rationing of livestock products, the higher extraction rates in flour-milling, and the diversion of barley and oats into baking flour. In the course of what was really only one farming season, and in the face of shortages of skilled hands, farming equipment and fertilisers, it proved impossible to revolutionise the structure of farm production which had developed over more than

forty years of rising imports and the resulting long-term major shift from corn to grass.[12]

POST-WAR DEPRESSION

At the end of the war the three main elements of the landed interest found themselves in contrasting and somewhat novel situations. The landowners, whose rents had either fallen substantially since the 1870s, or at best risen but little, were now even worse off. Few were able to advance their rentals during the wartime prosperity of farming, and indeed many had not wished to do so. With taxes and the expenses of maintaining country mansions much higher than before the war, they had been obliged to cut back on both houses and estates. They had reduced the numbers of their staffs and servants, and not a few country houses had been converted into hospitals, convalescent homes for the wounded or training centres for the army. Some landowners had taken advantage of the improved value of farmland brought about by the war and disposed of parts of their estates: and there were instances where reduced rental incomes and a higher burden of taxation – not overlooking death duties – had made sales of land inevitable.

The farmers, generally speaking, were far better off by the end of 1918 than they had been before the war. Certainly they had experienced many problems over supplies of labour, fertilisers and equipment, and numbers of them had had to adapt to sudden and drastic changes in their accustomed mode of farming. But they had been well compensated by large improvements in their profits – how large depending on the type of farming in which they were involved. Undoubtedly they had been through a troublesome and uncertain time, but for the most part they had done very well out of it.

The farmworkers, by contrast, had not done so well out of the war. Their weakness in organisation – the National Agricultural Workers' Union is estimated to have lost a quarter of its members by 1916 – meant that they could not prevent the dilution of the farm labour force by soldiers, prisoners of war, women and even schoolchildren. Their wages, assisted by the minimum wage provisions of the Corn Production Act, had risen by some 90 per cent, but this figure should be compared with the 103 per cent rise for wages in general, and a 112 per cent rise in the cost of living. Of course, the experience of individual farmworkers' families depended on circumstances, whether there were young children, for example, or whether the wife was able to spare time for work on the farm. Looking at the share of each

group in the net return from agriculture, it appears that the share of labour had fallen by 1918–19 by 2 per cent, and that of landowners by 13 per cent; the farmers' share had risen by 15 per cent.[13]

When in 1920 the government, acting on the interim report of the post-war Royal Commission, passed the Agriculture Act which extended indefinitely the price supports for wheat and oats, and the setting of minimum wages for farmworkers, the farmers were taken aback. Having put up with compulsory ploughing of pastures during the war and the controlled prices set by the Ministry of Food, the farmers looked for an early return to free market conditions. Indeed, in anticipation of the removal of price supports and a return to pre-war patterns of production, some farmers had already begun to re-seed their ploughed-up grasslands. They were opposed to both price and wage controls, and tended to confuse price supports, ineffective in wartime but of potential value in peacetime, with a continuation of the setting of maximum prices which had cheated them of making the most of wartime shortages. Strong attacks on the new Act were launched in the belief that farming would do best in a free market; and when the government realised that the imminence of bumper crops around the world meant that the price guarantees would prove expensive they took the farmers at their word, and in 1921 repealed the Agriculture Act. Later, farmers forgot how bitterly they had opposed the Act, and there developed among them a myth of a government breach of faith, a betrayal of the farming industry.[14]

The myth grew more deep-rooted as the price fall of 1921–22 plunged into the depths of post-war depression. The average price for wheat in 1920 was 80s 10d, and in 1921 71s 6d. Then came the big fall: in 1922 it was 47s 10d, and the following year 42s 2d. There was some small improvement in the years 1924–27, but then came another decline. The nadir was reached in 1934 at 20s 9d – a figure even below the 22s 10d reached in the worst year of the Great Depression, 1894, when of course money was worth far more. Barley and oats fell also, but not so heavily – indeed in certain years both fetched more than wheat, though barley was affected by a long-term decline in the demand for beer. However, with the return to the dominance of grass, it was pasture products that were again of much greater significance than cereals.

Numbers of the farmers who formerly grew cereals turned to dairying, as many had done before the war. Or they concentrated on potatoes, vegetables and sugar-beet, encouraged by the sugar-beet subsidy which the government introduced in 1925. Others grew only enough cereals to feed their pigs and poultry, and to meet their

need for straw. The acreage under cereals fell back from the nearly 2m acres of 1918 to only just over 1m acres at the lowest ebb of 1932 – 200,000 acres fewer than in 1914. Where land could be readily turned down to pasture the advantage of conversion seemed unquestionable. However, during the 1920s livestock prices were also depressed, and it was only from 1928 onwards that the price advantage over wheat lay clearly with stock. Then the difference was very marked, and livestock, furthermore, had other attractions: capital was turned over more rapidly, home-grown feed and purchased feeding stuffs were cheap, and less labour was required when all, or a large part, of the farm was in grass.[15]

But it was milk, as before the war, that was the most important single product of British farming. Its price had already begun to fall when the wartime price control was finally removed early in 1920. The average price for the winter season subsequently dropped from 20d per gallon in 1922–23 to 16½d in 1926–28. The summer price levelled out at 12d per gallon. These were the prices agreed between representatives of farmers and distributors, and locally prices varied considerably. Liquid milk now accounted for about three-quarters of total sales off farms, the other quarter being made up mainly of butter, with small quantities of cheese and cream. Most dairy farmers had given up making butter and cheese before or during the war, and now lacked the skilled labour and equipment to resume production had they wished to do so. In any event, they faced a market that, so far as liquid milk was concerned, was more or less stationary, while the butter and cheese markets were increasingly dominated by imports and were also subject to falling prices. Yet dairy farmers continued to expand their output with a substantial rise in average yields. The gloomy outlook for dairy farmers continued in the 1930s when the renewal of milk contracts was uncertain, and distributors and butter and cheese manufacturers were able to force prices down to very low levels. In 1931–32 milk used in manufacturing was below 5d per gallon. In these circumstances it was hardly surprising that in 1933 the 100,000 dairy farmers voted in overwhelming numbers for the establishment of the new Milk Marketing Board scheme.[16]

This departure had been made possible by the Agricultural Marketing Act of 1931, which allowed a majority of the producers of an agricultural commodity to set up a statutory Marketing Board – really a producers' cartel – with powers to regulate sales, dispose of surpluses, and enforce grading and packaging schemes. The Hops Marketing Board which, exceptionally, had the authority to negotiate over imports with the sole buyers, the brewers, had already been

established in 1932. What made the subsequent Boards – in milk, potatoes, pigs and bacon – attractive to producers was the control of imports which developed from the general return to protection in Britain in 1932. Where Marketing Boards were not established, other forms of assistance were introduced, including duties on imports, the renewal of the subsidy for sugar-beet, and new subsidies for wheat, barley and oats, and for fat cattle.

These government initiatives hardly amounted to a comprehensive or consistent policy for agriculture; but piecemeal as they were, they were a recognition of the need for intervention on a scale that would have been thought quite unacceptable before 1914. The new measures arose from the changed environment of farming in the 1930s: first, agricultural prices and incomes had fallen to unprecedentedly low levels; second, when the supposed advantages of protection and schemes of reorganisation and regulation were being introduced into depressed industries such as iron and steel, coal, cotton and shipbuilding, it was illogical and politically impossible to exclude agriculture from access to similar measures; and third, there was in the 1930s a world-wide trend towards higher levels of protection in attempts to maintain employment and incomes, and farmers in other countries, in continental Europe and the United States, were also receiving assistance from their governments. Against these considerations were the damage to consumers' interests through engineering a rise in food prices, though the period remained one of very cheap food generally; there was the cost of subsidies to the taxpayers; and there was also the harm done to trading relationships with traditional suppliers, for example, with Denmark, whose farmers had enjoyed free access to the British market for many years. Further, it could be argued that the subsidies (in so far as they were effective) were keeping inefficient British farmers on the land at unwarranted economic and social costs. However, against this argument could be cited the low value of the total subsidies – only £14m for England and Wales at the peak of 1938–39, as compared with the £219m value of the gross output of farming in that year.[17] The effect on farmers' incomes was therefore small, and probably had only a marginal influence in keeping small producers in being, the more especially as it was the bigger farmers who gained most from the subsidies.

The Milk Marketing Board for England and Wales (separate ones were instituted for Scotland and Northern Ireland) had only moderate success in raising milk prices for producers. The problem it faced was that there were two separate milk markets with very different prices obtaining: that for liquid milk, in which there was no foreign

competition; and that for manufacturing, which was dominated by imports of butter and cheese. Between 24 and 35 per cent of the average annual total of almost 1,000m gallons of milk sold by the Board in the first five years of its operation went for manufacturing, and the low price received for this, despite a subsidy, considerably reduced the 'pooled' price for both liquid and manufacturing sales that was paid to the producers. As a result, the average pooled price rose by only just over a penny a gallon, from 11.8d in 1933–34 to 12.9d in 1937–38. Regionally, the pooled price varied according to the proportion sent for manufacturing: between 1933 and 1938 it averaged 12.8d in the South-east, where very little went to the factories, and 11.6d in western areas, where the amount used for manufacturing was nearly a half. The effect was probably to even out prices somewhat between regions. [18]

Concern soon arose over the protected margins which the Board provided for distributors. These had the effect of yielding good returns to large firms but only barely adequate ones for small producer-retailers. Moreover, as wages tended to rise from the depths of the depression, the better-organised milkman who merely brought the milk to the urban doorstep came to earn nearly twice as much as the man who milked the cows. Further, the rise in retail prices, from 24.8d per gallon in 1933–34 to 27.5d in 1937–38, worked against the producers' long-term interest, which was to expand the market for liquid milk. [19] On the other hand, the Milk Board, like the Bacon and Potato Boards, did take steps to improve both farm production methods and the quality of the products. Funds from the government helped to provide incentives for farmers to increase the proportion of higher-grade milk, and also that from tuberculosis-free herds. The Board supported schemes to spread the drinking of milk in schools (where bottles containing one-third of a pint were sold for ½d each), while milk at 2d a pint was delivered to nursing and expectant mothers in towns with high rates of unemployment. Funds were also found for research, and for the subsidising of milk-recording schemes. And the Marketing Boards, generally, opened up new career prospects for farmers' sons who had little chance of having a farm of their own, or indeed any job on the land itself. [20]

FURTHER GOVERNMENT INTERVENTION

The Marketing Boards and subsidies of the 1930s were the most striking of the government interventions in agriculture in the whole

of the inter-war period, but there were a number of other measures, mostly of a similar kind to the palliatives which had been applied during the pre-1914 depression. There were new Acts affecting smallholdings in 1919 and 1926, and under the second Act the losses arising from purchasing land and establishing new smallholdings, as against the rents which could be charged, were met by public subsidies. Losses were incurred also on the 17,000 new holdings provided under the 1919 Act and which were intended for ex-servicemen: bad seasons, the fall in prices, and the difficulty of earning an adequate living from a smallholding without some supplementary employment meant that many of the holdings became uneconomic and were neglected by the occupiers. By 1932, including holdings provided before the war, the county councils owned some 468,000 acres of agricultural land, occupied by about 32,000 tenants. It is difficult to assess how many of these tenants were genuine small-holders able to obtain an independent livelihood from their land.[21] Many holdings were part-time only, or were taken over by farmers for additional land, or became under-used. As was the case before 1914, relatively few farmworkers found an independent livelihood on them, and the number of holdings was still small when compared with the total full-time farm labour force in England and Wales, which in 1932 still stood at nearly 600,000.

The year 1919 saw another measure influenced by the war: the establishment of the Forestry Commission. This body (which is still in being) was provided with Treasury funds for purchasing land on poor soils for the purposes of afforestation against the needs of another war. In addition, it could lease forest lands from private landowners and it was also given the management of some forested Crown lands, such as the New Forest and the Forest of Dean. By 1929 the Commission owned over 104,000 acres and managed a further 223,000 acres. It was criticised for planting great belts of quick-growing conifers, introducing species that were not native to the district, and inflicting a monotonous uniformity on the landscape. Moreover, because of the risk of fire, its forests were closed to walkers and riders, a restriction of former open spaces that was particularly felt at a time when country walking was growing as a leisure activity. On the other hand, it bought up very cheaply some of the poor land abandoned by farmers, such as the 'blowing sands' of the East Anglian breck country, and it also established a number of small livestock farms to provide summer employment for its men employed in the forests in the winter.[22] By 1939 it owned and managed a total of 1m acres.

In 1923 a new Agricultural Holdings Act provided tenant farmers with greater security of tenure. Compensation of up to two years' rent had to be paid by a landowner to a tenant given notice to quit, unless the owner could obtain a certificate of bad husbandry from the county agricultural committee. The committees were, however, notoriously lenient towards farmers, and indeed only a few hundred certificates were issued between 1921 and 1929. Tenants knew that, no matter how impoverished and inefficient was their farming, there was but a small chance that they could be obliged to quit. In these circumstances there was little support from them for the suggestion of a scheme for radical land reform, with the object of consolidating small farms and changing farm boundaries so as to create efficient 1,000-acre units with modern buildings and improved drainage and fences. Few farmers would have been able to stock and manage so large a unit without greater experience and substantial financial help. Nor, in a period of financial stringency, was there any likelihood that the government would involve itself in proposals that would cost the nation £1,000m merely for the purchase of land, and produce a very modest return of under 3 per cent. Nor yet were existing landowners willing to part with estates at prices based only on the current income produced, leaving aside all other factors such as sentimental value and social and sporting amenities.[23]

A more practical way of helping agriculture was the decision in 1929 to de-rate all agricultural land in England and Wales totally. Already, in 1923, agricultural land had been made liable to only one-quarter of the local authority rates, reducing the total of local taxes paid by farmers by about £2.75m a year; and in 1925 agricultural buildings were relieved of paying rates entirely. From 1929 only the farmhouses and cottages themselves were liable to pay rates. How far these changes helped landlords to maintain their rents and keep up the value of their land, rather than help farmers to stay in business, was a question which was argued in Parliament at the time. Another burden on farming, the tithe, was still levied on a considerable proportion of the land. In the early 1920s more than £3m a year was being paid to owners of tithe, and subsequently anti-tithe agitation, involving refusals to pay and the seizing of farmers' goods by bailiffs, broke out in some of the worst-hit farming areas. Here, again, legislation was passed to stabilise the tithe charge on occupiers of land and to compensate the tithe-owners with fixed amounts of government stock.[24]

Lastly, there was the introduction of a government subsidy for the support of a sugar-beet industry, which brought some badly needed

money and employment into parts of the country most severely affected by the decline in cereal growing. The major obstacle to the growth of a tiny sugar-beet industry, which had been struggling to survive since 1912, was the excise duty levied on home-produced sugar – a counter-balance to the duty levied on imported sugar. In 1925, however, despite the opposition from the refiners of imported sugar, the government provided a ten-year subsidy for the production of sugar-beet, and by the end of the 1920s eighteen factories were in operation. The acreage under sugar-beet in Britain rose ten-fold in five years, from only 22,600 acres in 1924–25 to as much as 230,500 acres in 1929–30, with the bulk of the acreage concentrated in various parts of East Anglia. By 1938–39 the total acreage had grown to 336,000, and in the areas concerned it had become an important crop. Research revealed how the sugar-beet could be grown most productively, and how the residues returned to the farms from the factories and fed to stock could raise the yields of subsequent crops. Consequently, farmers readily took it up as an alternative to growing roots in the normal rotation, and an average of 8.6 tons per acre was achieved in the years 1929–38.[25]

THE LAND BETWEEN THE WARS

In 1938–39, on the eve of the Second World War, the value of the gross output of farming in England and Wales totalled £233.4m, of which £14m represented the subsidies paid on fat cattle, wheat, barley and oats. Omitting the subsidies, the value was then £219.4m, a little above the average of the years 1933–34 to 1938–39, which was £212.7m, but was still below the figure for 1927–28, £220.6m. It is clear that government subsidies played a very minor part in the total value of farm output, and that the major factor was prices. Taking the average price level of 1911–13 as 100, prices rose rapidly during the war, peaked in 1920 at 292, and fell to the lowest point of 107 in 1933 (if subsidies are removed, the last figure would fall to about 103). A recovery followed, raising the index to 133 (including subsidies) in both 1937 and 1938.[26]

What do these figures imply for farmers' incomes? In general, with the price index averaging only about 121 in the 1930s, and with some costs, particularly the large item of labour, much higher than before the war, it is apparent that farmers were often as badly off as, and frequently worse off than, before 1914 – in real terms, allowing

for the fall in the value of money, even more so. However, it is very difficult, if not impossible, to generalise about farmers' incomes. Much depended on the size of the unit – in the major branches of farming it was impossible to obtain a large income from a small unit – and for the individual farmer, much depended also on the extent of his capital, the quality of his stock and equipment, and his skill and management. The type of farming he was engaged in was also fundamental. He might be better off in expanding sectors such as dairying and poultry and eggs, or fruit and vegetables, than in a declining one like grain production; while others like livestock and wool, and potatoes, more or less held their own.[27]

One might expect the economic blizzard of the period to have resulted in a high rate of failure among farmers, but the record of bankruptcies hardly bears this out. Between 1922 and 1936 bankruptcies among farmers ran at an average of just under 400 a year, a figure not so greatly higher than the average of 322 in 1911–13. Bankruptcies were probably most common among the larger arable farmers of eastern England, who faced very low prices and large wage bills, and had few means of reducing their costs. However, when compared with the total number of 200,000 holdings of over 20 acres, the failure rate was really very low, only a fifth of 1 per cent a year. Small farmers could struggle on by farming very economically, using little or no labour outside the family, and enduring a meagre standard of living. Larger businesses went on year after year by running down capital and piling up debts, while creditors, such as the banks and the feed suppliers, were often prepared to stay their hand, hoping for an improvement in conditions, and knowing that to force a run-down farm business into bankruptcy might produce very little towards satisfying their claims. In fact, the average liability of those who failed was only about £2,000 or less.[28]

So far as they can be estimated, it seems that farmers' incomes (like the incomes of their farmworkers) fell well behind those of other comparable occupations, averaging perhaps only about half their level. In 1937 and 1938 investigation showed that a large minority of farmers made either a loss or earned no more than did a skilled farmworker, who unlike them, had no worries about prices, weather and burdensome borrowings. Only a small proportion earned more than £480 a year, about the bottom level of the earnings of professional men. The volatility of prices and uncertainties of government policy made many farmers cautious, and together with limitations of capital resources and accumulation of debts caused them to operate the farms at low levels of production.[29]

As before the war, many farmers lacked education, and kept only the most rudimentary kind of accounts. Despite the urging of farming experts over many generations past, they often had no accurate records of yields in relation to the different fields which made up the farm, or of their stock, or of different feeds, rotations and manures. In the growing dairying industry, for example, the great majority of farmers did not keep any records of the yields of different cows, which would have served to show them the ones which were 'freeloaders' and needed to be rooted out. The first milk recording society in England was not in being until 1914 – the thrifty Scots had begun one in 1903 – and although milk recording expanded rapidly in the inter-war years to involve some 5,300–5,800 herds, these figures represented only about 4 or 5 per cent of all milk producers.[30] The majority of dairy farmers went blithely on feeding their cows with only a hazy notion of which cows, and which feeds, were the most productive and economical.

It is evident that better-educated and more enlightened farmers could have made more of their land, but what concerned them most was how to reduce their costs. Thus their attitude towards the purchase of new machinery or acquisition of improved livestock was a negative one: 'do not spend'. In any case, after the losses of capital suffered in the early 1920s, not many had money to spend. Rents were already so low that it was unrealistic to think they could be driven down any further. The average, as Edith Whetham states, was probably less than £1 per acre in the early 1930s, varying from £2 on the rich fenland soils and market gardens near to towns, to only a few shillings on less attractive soils and hill land. In East Anglia farms were even offered rent-free, merely to keep them from deterioration. Hence few landlords were doing well, especially as the net rent received was often very much lower than the rent paid by the tenant. When maintenance and improvements to the farms were deducted, and where tithe, land tax and a drainage rate had also to be allowed for, then the net rent was only about 30 per cent of the gross; that is, on average the landlord might receive only about 6s per acre or less.[31]

On farms where full-time farmworkers were employed, the wage-bill formed a major item in the total outgoings, usually 25–30 per cent. The basic number of hours worked for the minimum wage fell from fifty-two soon after the war, levelling out at about fifty to fifty-one hours in the years between 1921 and 1939, and this was substantially less than before the war. The minimum wage fell steeply from just under 47s a week in 1920–21 to 28s in 1923–24 when the

Corn Production Act had been repealed; then, when the regulation of wages was restored in 1924, there was a slight recovery to something over 30s between 1924–25 and 1933–34, followed by a further gradual rise, so that by 1938–39 the minimum wage was 34s 8d. From the point of view of the farmer's costs, therefore, after 1922 there was only one short period, between 1923 and 1924, when the minimum wage fell appreciably, while from 1924–25 to the outbreak of the Second World War farmers faced stable or slowly rising labour costs. It has to be noted also that often a majority of the farmer's men, especially the more specialised hands, were paid at above – frequently significantly above – the minimum wage. In the same period the index of agricultural prices fluctuated wildly, falling from 321 in 1920 to as low as 123 in 1933, and recovering only to 144–145 in 1937–39 (average 1906–08 = 100).[32] Consequently, farmers faced volatile, and between 1930 and 1936 especially, very low prices, at a time when their wage-bills were generally inflexible.

Not entirely inflexible, however; for as Miss Whetham points out, it was possible to substitute purchased cattle feed as winter feed and reduce the quantity of labour-intensive fodder crops, hay, and silage produced on the farm. But the money spent on purchased feeds was also a major outgoing, and if he were obliged to reduce this expense, the farmer was forced back on growing more fodder and hay himself at the cost of more calls on family labour or a higher wage-bill.[33] Increasingly, as farmers turned away from arable and towards livestock, they economised in labour by keeping their sheep and cattle on grass, permanent pasture or temporary leys, rather than on the more costly roots. There was also considerable cutting back on manures, and some of the least profitable land was not farmed at all but allowed to revert to scrub in the worst years of the slump.[34]

Another way of reducing costs might lie through the acquisition of up-to-date machinery. By the 1930s the tractor had become a proved and standard item of farm equipment, though it was still rarely seen in Wales and the North and West of England. A tractor made it possible to keep fewer horses, but not to dispense with them entirely, and even in 1938 only some 38,500 wheeled tractors were in use as compared with the 45,000 holdings that were of over 300 acres. Horses were still highly valued because tractors were not as yet very versatile and showed little reduction in costs over horses, and also because the larger farmers needed more than one source of power, while gates and yard entries often had to be adapted to take the tractor.

In the later 1930s some 563,000 horses were still employed on farms. Certainly this was only about two-thirds of the number used

before the war, and they were soon to be completely superseded during the Second World War and the remarkable development of mechanised farming in the post-war era. But, after all, in the 1930s a new tractor cost about as much as a pair of good horses, and lasted only half as long. Many of the farmers who had a tractor used it mainly for the hard and urgent work, keeping the horses for lighter tasks and for carting. Investigations showed that tractors did not generally result in lower costs than those of farms worked entirely with horses, but they managed to achieve a higher output.[35]

On some of the larger farms in the South and East the hay baler was coming into use, and a variety of other machines were being tried, with even old cars being used for haulage purposes. But many labour-intensive tasks remained unmechanised; in particular, the work of hay-making in the North and West, the planting, lifting and collecting of potatoes, the hoeing, singling and harvesting of root crops, and the moving and forking in of dung. The milking machine, after a long history of innovation and unsuccessful trials, had become a practical device by the middle 1930s, and was adopted rapidly in the larger herds as good hand-milkers became more costly and rather difficult to find. Nevertheless, the great majority of dairy farmers persisted with hand-milking, especially as the machine required electrical power which was not always available, and either the adaptation of existing buildings or the construction of a separate milking parlour.[36]

Farmers' experience of the depression years necessarily varied with their personal circumstances, the area in which they farmed, and the type of farming in which they were engaged. Nearness to a town or good railway communications were prime factors for market gardeners, fruit-growers and producers of eggs and flowers, and also for dairy farmers who sought to sell their own milk on a milk round. Small farmers could help matters out by taking on supplementary jobs, and those with spare horses and wagons could help out other farmers and engage in local transport, as they had always done. In some areas of the country seed-growing was important, some of it long-established, as in north Kent, where mustard, radish, canary and other seeds had featured in rotations for well over a century past. Numbers of farmers went in for breeding horses to meet the demand for hacks, hunters and children's ponies, as well as agricultural horses, while it should not be forgotten that in the 1930s, despite the coming of the lorry, there was still a large demand from the towns for horses to haul milk floats, bakers' vans, coal merchants' wagons and brewers' drays. The breeding of pedigree stock might also be made

to pay, if the breeder's herd acquired a high reputation for producing stock of quality and high production.[37]

Living standards among farmers had always varied greatly, from the relatively comfortable life of the large-scale gentleman-farmer, who had leisure for hunting, shooting and a diversity of political and social activities, down to the small man who undertook much of the farmwork himself, and laboured long and hard the year round with but little time for himself. The depression often brought the gentleman-farmer's life-style somewhat nearer to that of his humbler neighbour. When prices and profits fell drastically, some of the old pleasures had to be foregone, economies made, and a much closer eye kept on the outgoings. It was a period when some breeders of pedigree cattle ceased to register their stock because they could no longer afford the fees, and long-planned improvements to the farm buildings and equipment were postponed indefinitely. Many of even the better farmhouses were rather modest in size and furnishings, and were considerably removed from those of the gentleman-farmers who had lived in the style of country squires in the halcyon days of the 1850s and 1860s. Among the small farmers it was the young men with young families, and the old ones whose families had grown up and left home, who were at a disadvantage compared with those who had sons and daughters, and a wife too, able and willing to help with the poultry, the milking, the sowing, planting and harvesting, and all the other multifarious jobs on the land.

Farmers were generally able to eat well since much of the food on their tables came, uncosted, from the farm itself, just as most of the labour on a family farm was uncosted. The great majority of farmers still kept little or nothing in the way of financial accounts, the more especially as the assessments for income tax were based on the farm rental rather than the profits. Consequently they had little idea of their financial position beyond what was shown by their bank book, which for many was their Bible and only guide. Farmers' incomes were erratic and uncertain, and they relied heavily on credit to tide them over periods when little or nothing was coming in. The receipts from the harvest or from sales of stock were earmarked for paying the rent or settling the accounts of the corn merchant, seedsman, blacksmith and suppliers of equipment – though many farmers bought only second-hand machines acquired cheaply at farm sales. One of the advantages for dairy farmers of contracting with the Milk Marketing Board was the regularity of the monthly milk cheque. Socially, many farmers lived a more isolated existence when financial stringency limited their outgoings and hospitality had to be

curtailed. The motor-car, certainly, gave them a more convenient means of getting about, though at the same time it brought into the countryside the careless day-trippers who left gates open and trampled on growing crops, while thefts of stock, poultry, Christmas trees and even holly were increased. One of the effects of the great financial improvement in the farmers' situation brought about by the Second World War and the subsidised post-war era was an improved ability to get about, to attend shows and meetings, often driving new and handsome cars which were the envy of other country-dwellers.

When farmers did badly, landlords often did worse. Those whose incomes depended entirely or mainly on agricultural rents fared very badly indeed in the inter-war years, for the net rents they received were seldom more than a pound an acre and, as we have seen, might very well be only a third of that figure. In eastern England, indeed, rents of arable farms had never recovered from the late nineteenth-century depression, and in 1939 were often below what they had been in 1880.[38] In the meanwhile the expenses of maintaining country estates had mounted, and many of the day-to-day expenditures of the upper classes, such as those, for instance, on clothing, hotel dinners, taxi fares and whisky, had risen in price between two- and four-fold. Those burdened with maintaining a large country house found staff difficult to engage, and much more expensive as wages doubled, while the outgoings on repairs and grounds all became much more costly. The larger mansions, especially those built or remodelled in the nineteenth century, had been designed on a lavish scale. No consideration was given to economy of labour, and they required a small army of domestics to service them. Only the greatest plutocrats – such, for instance, as the Duke of Westminster or the Duke of Bedford – could afford to support the kind of magnificence which really belonged to a past age.

What enabled aristocrats such as these to regard the fall in agricultural rents with some degree of complacency was the size of their incomes from other sources, notably in these two instances, urban, specifically central London, property. It was diversity of resources, whether urban land, government stocks or industrial and commercial investments, which helped many of the biggest landowners to survive. From some time back in the nineteenth century numbers of them had been gradually moving out of land and taking advantage of the possibilities for greater profit offered by both the expanding British and world economies. It was those who had failed to take this road, or failed to take it early enough, who found the fall in farm rents calamitous. Fortunately for owners of estates, many had been able to dispose of

agricultural land at what proved to be exceptionally favourable prices in the brief period of farming prosperity between 1914 and 1921. In those years, and particularly between 1918 and 1921, vast landholdings were put on the market: over a million acres were sold in 1919 alone, when the *Estates Gazette* spoke of a 'revolution in landholding'. In 1918 and the following three years some 6 or 8m acres changed hands. The great majority of the purchasers were sitting tenants who were usually offered first refusal by their landlords. One consequence was that the proportion of land that was owner-occupied rose from a little over 10 per cent in the period before 1914 to as high as 36 per cent by 1927 – perhaps the greatest and most rapid revolution in landholding in English history.[39]

Another consequence was that many landowners were able to restore their finances, exchanging a rent which in net terms was only about 3 per cent or less of the land's capital value – and moreover was surrounded by uncertainty and various difficulties and annoyances – for a higher, more certain and less troublesome return of 5 per cent, as many former tenants became mortgagees of their old landlords. For the new owner-occupiers, however, the effect was soon to be less than happy, because in the depression years after 1921 they had to cope with a burden of fixed mortgage payments that was heavier and less flexible than their former rents. Such farmers were among the most adversely affected when prices collapsed and remained unprofitable in the eighteen years after 1921.

Landowners chose to sell for a wide variety of reasons. Some had been hard-pressed financially for a long time and had anxiously awaited an upturn in the land market. They had temporised by cutting back on expenses and parting with hounds, pictures, even the long-accumulated family library. In other instances the need to resort to sales of land was made urgent by the toll of death duties. These taxes, for long slight in their effect, had been reformed in 1894, and by 1913–14 the yield they produced for the Exchequer had more than trebled to reach £27.4m. A part of this rise was due to an increase in the amount of wealth passing at death, but much of it was the direct result of the stiffening of the duties themselves. The premature deaths of owners and their heirs in the war meant that estate changed hands more rapidly than in normal times, and accordingly the higher incidence of the duties enforced some considerable sales of land and other property. In the 1919 Budget land was valued for the purposes of death duties at its market value, which was considerably higher than the capitalised value of the rental income it produced. Consequently, it paid owners to sell land rather than other assets;

and more generally, since there was no capital gains tax, it paid all landowners who needed liquid capital to sell land and take the untaxed capital gain rather than to raise rents which were liable to both income tax and super-tax.

But underlying individual and fiscal motives was the decline in the non-monetary value of land. Land had always given its owners a social cachet and political influence, but the first was considerably weakened by the rise of rival wealth among industrialists and commercial magnates, and the second by the reforms of the franchise and of local government which had severely clipped the wings of politically orientated landowners. True, a few of the greatest could still command places in the Cabinet and an audience in the House of Lords, though the Lords itself had had its wings clipped, almost to the extent of total impotence, by the Parliament Act of 1911. However, relatively few peers were regular attenders of the Lords, and the great majority of owners, titled and untitled, set more store by their local influence; but this, in turn, had been whittled away by the transfer of the justices' powers to elected bodies, and by the creation in 1888 of County Councils and in 1894 of District Councils.

Nevertheless, landowners still retained great local prestige, even after the revolution in local government, and even after the consequences for their incomes of the decline in farm rentals and the sharp rise in prices and taxes that followed 1914. Those who remained in residence and contrived to maintain in some degree the traditional country-house life-style were still prominent on important county occasions, at royal visits, the opening of new hospitals and schools, at sporting and all kinds of charitable events and the like. Their houses featured in *Country Life*, and their photographs taken at balls and dinners filled the pages of *The Tatler*, along with those of the *nouveaux-riches* businessmen, financiers, industrialists and war contractors. But increasingly the aristocracy was a rural upper class in retreat, not a few having to seek paid work, or take other extraordinary measures, to balance the books. The trends were being set which were to become more marked during and after the Second World War. Some landowners took up city directorates, and more farmed; some let off the larger part of the house and lived on in a small section converted to a private flat; others gave the house and estate to the National Trust or turned the grounds into amusement parks to draw in the money of gaping townspeople. What had often been built up through several generations of inheritance and acquisition, and kept intact by carefully designed legal devices, was lost or transformed in a matter of a few years. Such were the long-term

consequences of democracy, political and fiscal reform, agricultural depression and war.

In the country towns and villages many of the old craftsmen and tradesmen – still very numerous in 1900 – had disappeared or sharply declined in numbers. Some, like the wheelwrights, went with the arrival of the motor car and lorry, while the millers began to depart earlier when milling was concentrated in large plants at ports or major route centres. The blacksmiths experienced a more lingering decline as the numbers of horses fell gradually from their pre-1914 peak numbers. Some surviving smiths could still be seen at work shoeing, even in urban forges, as late as the 1930s, and in the countryside considerably later. On the other hand, builders and their allied craftsmen, carpenters, joiners, plasterers, glaziers and the like, found a new lease of life where their districts became dormitories for town workers or sites of light industry. And a number of professions and trades remained well-entrenched where the country town retained its importance as a centre of business: doctors, solicitors, estate agents, auctioneers and dealers in livestock, corn and feed merchants, nursery-men and seedsmen, and hop factors too. In such towns the shopkeepers also thrived, perhaps because of their convenient situation, perhaps because they specialised in the types of goods not easily found in the ordinary towns. In the lesser country towns and villages, however, the shops disappeared one by one until there was only a mere 'general store' and newsagent remaining of the former ironmongers, drapers, grocers, butchers, bakers and confectioners of former times.

A major declining element in village populations was that of the farmworkers. In some heavily industrialised villages they had always been in a minority, at least until the old rural crafts faded away. But everywhere they were continuing to move off the land, as they had been doing over the previous hundred years. Between 1921 and 1938 the number of full-time farmworkers in England and Wales fell from 685,000 to 513,000, a drop of 172,000, or a quarter. Very likely this fall would have been even greater had it been easier to find other work, but the old industrial areas had high rates of unemployment, and the newer types of industry that were growing often demanded female, rather than unskilled male, labour. Part-time and seasonal workers in farming, many of them the families of the full-time hands, also fell: from 184,000 in the prosperous year of 1921 to only 80,000 in 1938, a fall of well over a half.[40] Their numbers were affected by the decline in arable farming, the need of farmers to cut costs and use more of their own family labour and, not least perhaps, mechanisation.

The reasons why the full-time men were departing were much the

same as before 1914: the lowness of farm wages, the relatively long hours and lack of holidays as compared with those of other labouring occupations, the shortage of decent housing, the lack of prospects for promotion, the dullness of village life (only slightly alleviated by rural bus services) and the absence of the amenities found in towns, such as a wide range of shops and pubs, cinemas and variety theatres – and, not least, the low regard in which the farmworker was held. This last was shown most clearly by the wide gap between the farmworker's earnings and those of alternative occupations: in 1930 the milk roundsmen in Lancashire were paid a whole pound a week more – an enormous differential – over the figure prescribed by the County Wages Committee for the cowmen who produced the milk. Farm wages had fallen much more abruptly when the wages boards were abolished in 1921 than had wages in comparable occupations, so much so that in 1923 there was much discontent and strikes, the most serious occurring that year in Norfolk before wage regulation was restored.

More generally, when in 1937 the average wage for ordinary male farmworkers was 33s 7$\frac{1}{2}$d, railway goods porters and permanent way labourers were paid 47s, building labourers 53s 3d, and labourers employed by local authorities 54s 4d – the last figure representing a 38 per cent margin over the farmworker's wage. It is not surprising then that rural workers' families could not buy as much meat, bacon, ham, fruit, butter, eggs and vegetables as industrial workers' families, and that they also spent less on travelling, entertainment and medical care. Moreover, it was only in 1936 that, belatedly, farmworkers were included in the National Insurance scheme, and even then at a low rate of benefit, 14s for an adult male, and a ceiling of 30s for the family, rising to 35s in 1939. Again, when in 1938 the Holidays with Pay Act was introduced the farmworkers were singled out for discriminatory treatment: so that farmers should not be inconvenienced, their employees, where the Wages Committee decided, could not take more than three days off consecutively.[41]

The housing occupied by farmworkers' families was still, in the inter-war period, usually the worst in point of size, age, state of repair and sanitary condition. Other country-dwellers who were better paid could afford to pay higher rents and so got the better houses, while the farmworkers necessarily occupied the cheapest, many of which (estimated at two out of every five) were tied cottages provided by the employer. Although legislation of the time provided for the building of new council houses, the rents were such that relatively few farmworkers could afford them. Further, the tied cottage offered the advantage, beyond its cheapness, that it was usually very close to

the farm, avoiding long walks to work in every kind of weather. From the farmer's point of view the tied cottage was essential in order to enable him to be sure of getting men, and particularly stockmen, who needed to be available at all hours every day of the week. The disadvantages of the tied cottage for the farmworker were that when he retired, or changed his job for one that offered no housing, he was without a home; and also that he was often afraid that he might be told to go if he asked for repairs or improvements to be made.[42]

In 1937, when 51,080 rural houses were classified as unfit, there was already a programme of demolishing condemned houses and of reconditioning others with the aid of government grants. The results of that policy, however, were meagre in relation to the large number of old, defective and insanitary houses in the countryside. Rural electrification, it is true, was bringing improved living to numbers of farms and cottages, but in 1939 there were still more than 3,000 parishes which had no piped water supply, and not a few homes that did not even have the substitute of a usable well and so were forced to rely on rainwater or a nearby stream, having to purchase water by the bucket from a water-cart in times of shortage. Many parishes, too, lacked main drainage, and despite outbreaks of typhoid, the slump of the early 1930s brought a severe reduction in sewerage schemes. The earth closet and midden remained familiar features of old cottages, as did the outside standpipe and rainwater tub.[43]

In these circumstances, it is remarkable that farmworkers as a whole enjoyed an unusual measure of longevity, though considerable variations existed among different types of farm labour. Generally, farmworkers were likely to live almost as long as, if not longer than, their employers, the farmers, and significantly longer than other kinds of labour. Long life did not necessarily mean enjoyment of a high quality of life, however. Farmworkers suffered from complaints associated with poor nutrition and bad housing conditions: tuberculosis, rheumatism and bronchitis. Nor was farmwork without its own peculiar hazards, such as diseases that could be contracted from animals, and the non-respiratory form of tuberculosis which resulted from the drinking of raw milk, while the use of dangerous chemicals in seed-dressings, sheep-dips, fruit sprays and insecticides presented special dangers. Accidents were also very common, arising from unsafe ladders, slipping on ice-bound yards and roads, and attacks by vicious animals – all very old causes of injuries. And the increasing use of machinery, particularly tractors, caused numbers of fatalities as well as serious injuries.[44]

Not many farmworkers, perhaps, expected to rise above the level

of foreman, if that far, and fewer still succeeded in becoming farmers. Lack of capital, but also of education and ambition, were major obstacles.[45] Other obstacles, shortage of free time and of money, prevented the majority of them and their families from taking part in sport and social clubs, while a limited schooling and narrow interests inhibited them from joining evening classes or amateur dramatic societies. The combination of long hours, exhausting work, low wages, and not least, low social status, meant that for them the village was an even duller place than for country-dwellers in general. The village pub, and perhaps the garden or allotment, were for most their sole outlets for relaxation.

And so the farmworkers voted with their feet. Their union, the National Union of Agricultural Workers, had lost support with the collapse of agricultural prosperity in 1921–22, and between 1922 and 1938 never commanded the support of more than 36,000 members – indeed, between 1924 and 1935 fewer than 26,000 members – at best a mere 4.5 per cent of full-time workers on farms. The fragmented nature of farm employment and close contact with the employer were major factors in this very limited level of membership, and the union, with small funds and a highly scattered membership to organise, could do little for them. Moreover, the radical policies espoused by the union were by no means those held by many farmworkers.[46] On the contrary, many of them believed that the answer to their situation would not be found in changes unlikely to be realised, such as a major advance in wages or nationalisation of the land. Rather, the solution lay off the land altogether, in a move to other occupations that offered immediate gains to those bold enough to take the step.

NOTES

1. **Alan Lloyd**, *The War in the Trenches*, Granada, 1976, p. 194.
2. **Lord Ernle,** *English Farming Past and Present*, 6th edn, Heinemann, 1961, pp. 394–7.
3. *Ibid.*, pp. 398–9.
4. *Ibid.*, pp. 400–1.
5. *Ibid.*, pp. 401–5.
6. **Jonathan Brown,** *Agriculture in England: a Survey of Farming, 1870–1947*, Manchester University Press, 1987, p. 72; Ernle, *English Farming*, p. 405.
7. Ernle, *English Farming*, p. 403; Brown, *Agriculture*, p. 72.
8. Ernle, *English Farming*, p. 404; **P. E. Dewey,** 'Government provision of farm labour in England and Wales 1914–18', *Agricultural History Review*, **XXVII**, 1979, pp. 111–20.
9. Brown, *Agriculture*, pp. 71–2; Ministry of Agriculture, Fisheries and Food, *A Century of Agricultural Statistics*, Great Britain 1866–1966,

HMSO, 1968, p. 65; **Alan Armstrong,** *Farmworkers: a Social and Economic History 1770–1980*, Batsford, 1988, p. 167.

10. Brown, *Agriculture*, pp. 61–2.
11. **P. E. Dewey,** *British Agriculture in the First World War*, Routledge, 1989, pp. 231–6.
12. Brown, *Agriculture*, pp. 63, 68, 73–4.
13. Armstrong, *Farmworkers*, pp. 167–9.
14. Brown, *Agriculture*, pp. 77–9.
15. *Ibid.*, pp. 87–8.
16. **Edith H. Whetham,** *The Agrarian History of England and Wales*, VIII, *1914–1939*, Cambridge University Press, 1978, pp. 143, 146–8, 249–51; Brown, *Agriculture*, pp. 92–3.
17. Whetham, *Agrarian History*, p. 260.
18. *Ibid.*, pp. 251–3.
19. *Ibid.*, pp. 254–5.
20. *Ibid.*, pp. 256–7.
21. *Ibid.*, pp. 137–9, 217.
22. *Ibid.*, pp. 170–1.
23. *Ibid.*, pp. 219–20.
24. *Ibid.*, pp. 162–3.
25. *Ibid.*, pp. 166–8, 221, 326.
26. *Ibid.*, pp. 213, 260.
27. *Ibid.*, pp. 230, 260.
28. *Ibid.*, p. 238.
29. *Ibid.*, pp. 216, 220, 315.
30. **G. E. Mingay,** *British Friesians*, Rickmansworth, British Friesian Cattle Society, 1982, pp. 158–9.
31. Whetham, *Agrarian History*, pp. 263–4.
32. *Century of Agricultural Statistics*, pp. 64, 85.
33. Whetham, *Agrarian History*, p. 264.
34. Brown, *Agriculture*, pp. 86–7.
35. Whetham, *Agrarian History*, pp. 205–10, 266–7.
36. *Ibid.*, pp. 268–9.
37. *Ibid.*, pp. 270–1.
38. Whetham, *Agrarian History*, p. 317; **Robert J. Thompson**, 'An Inquiry into the rent of agricultural land in England and Wales during the nineteenth century', in **W. E. Minchurton**, (ed.), **Essays in Agrarian History**, II, David and Charles, 1968, p. 65.
39. **F. M. L. Thompson,** *English Landed Society in the Nineteenth Century*, Routledge & Kegan Paul, 1963, pp. 329–31.
40. *Century of Agricultural Statistics*, p. 62.
41. Armstrong, *Farmworkers*, pp. 195–7.
42. **W. H. Pedley,** *Labour on the Land*, King & Staples, 1942, pp. 72–3.
43. *Ibid.*, pp. 80–3, 85–8, 94–100.
44. Armstrong, *Farmworkers*, pp. 198–9, 233.
45. *Ibid.*, p. 200.
46. *Ibid.*, pp. 185–93.

CHAPTER ELEVEN

The Second World War and After

THE LAND IN THE SECOND WORLD WAR

It took a second enormous world conflict to put the sickly British agricultural industry back on its feet again. This time the need to increase home production of foodstuffs was perceived even before the beginning of the conflict. Indeed, growing alarm at the deteriorating international situation, the re-arming and belligerence of Hitler's Germany, the seizure of Austria and part of Czechoslovakia – all combined to urge on planning for war in Britain. The Ministry of Agriculture set in train the drawing up of plans for the expansion of agricultural production from as early as the spring of 1935. The Agriculture Act of 1937, in fact, although a logical further step in the process of reinvigorating farming by government intervention as developed in the inter-war period, was designed to bring the arable branch of the industry up to a state of better preparedness for war.

To achieve this the Act extended the existing wheat subsidy, introduced deficiency payments to encourage the growing of barley and oats, and gave the farmers financial inducements to employ more lime and basic slag as fertilisers. In addition, grants were provided for drainage, and a campaign was mounted to stamp out disease in farm livestock, especially tuberculosis in dairy cows, which still remained a serious problem. Further measures were announced, somewhat belatedly, in the Agricultural Development Act of May 1939, although the necessary administrative machinery for wartime expansion and control had been established with the formation of War Agricultural Executive Committees as early as 1936, and of a dormant Ministry of Food in 1937. But steps to stockpile tractors,

machinery and fertilisers had made little progress by September 1939, when the outbreak of war overtook the plans.[1]

There was much else to be done. Large areas of land had deteriorated in condition and had lost fertility in the poverty-stricken inter-war years. Among the first tasks of the County War Agricultural Executive Committees was the urgent pressing forward of land reclamation schemes. Moreover, the measures of the 1930s had done little to revive arable farming, and British farming as a whole had become ever more dominated by livestock, especially dairying. Accordingly, wartime intervention had to be directed towards a rapid advance in the weak arable sector and a reining back of the too predominant livestock farming. Targets for the ploughing-up of pasture land were set county by county, and by 1943 the area of permanent grass had been reduced by nearly 5.5m acres, or just over a third. However, problems of declining fertility meant that considerable acreages had to be put into temporary pasture as grass leys in order to recover. The shift towards arable farming was thus circumscribed by conditions, but was nevertheless impressive. The production of cereals rose by an average of over 85 per cent in the three years 1942–45, while milk production fell marginally, and the output of beef and veal declined by over 12 per cent, mutton and lamb by nearly 23 per cent, pigmeat by a huge 65 per cent, and eggs by nearly 44 per cent.[2]

Food rationing was introduced from the beginning of the war, and included meat, butter, cheese, eggs, tea and sugar. The rations per person were small, but the items concerned were price-controlled and subsidised so as to enable the poorest persons to afford at least those quantities of basic foodstuffs. Along with having to wait in queues to purchase other unrationed, but scarce, goods, the food rations were a constant source of irritation and frustration. To some extent the rigidities of the rationing system were overcome by individual consumers swapping coupons: families who liked a lot of sugar, for instance, exchanged their butter coupons for the sugar ones of friends and neighbours who happened to like butter better than sugar. Nevertheless, consumers remained dissatisfied, not only because of the limited amounts they could buy, but also because the selection of food available was not that which they would have purchased in a fully stocked free market.

The shortages were intensified by the severe reduction of imports, as ships were lost to German submarines and scarce shipping space was allocated to cargoes more essential for the prosecution of the war. Further, home output of food was affected by the need to expand production of some non-food crops, such as flax, which was

in demand for the manufacture of parachutes. The shortage of feeding stuffs for livestock made it necessary to cut back in that large sector, although steps were taken to maintain milk supplies – for instance, by urging dairy farmers to cull low-producing cows from their herds. Imported feeds had fallen by as much as 85 per cent by 1943–44, and of course farmers also lost the pasture and hay formerly provided by the newly ploughed-up grasslands. Moreover, the extraction rate for milling wheat was raised from 76 to 85 per cent in 1942, thus diverting into bread the brans which normally went to animals, while for most of 1942 barley and oats were diverted from other uses to be mixed in with the bread flour.[3]

As in the First World War, farmers faced many problems in meeting calls to expand or curtail production in highly abnormal conditions. Many of the older farmers, indeed, were coping with an almost identical situation for the second time in little more than twenty years. They were obliged to accept unwelcome orders to plough up treasured pastures, cultivate crops with which they were not familiar, and drastically cull their carefully built up herds and flocks. Painful years spent in achieving some degree of financial stability through livestock farming were set at naught. Inevitably, there was much grumbling and some resistance. But the Agricultural Executive Committees' powers were extensive and they were not afraid of using them, though in the event only some 1,500 farmers suffered the extreme penalty for non-cooperation – dispossession.[4] The government helped in the transition by purchasing and making available large quantities of tractors and farm machinery, although many pasture farmers had little or no experience of tractors, nor of such machines as combine harvesters, potato spinners and diggers, and milking machines. Mechanisation, which had proceeded at only a slow pace before the war, now went ahead rapidly. Over the war period the number of tractors increased more than three-fold, while horse numbers declined, and combine harvesters – seldom-seen curiosities before the war – had come to total 3,460 by 1946. Mechanisation would have spread even more if agricultural engineering works had not been turned over to making military equipment, and if finding shipping space for tractors imported from America had not been so difficult. Nevertheless, the change was a dramatic one, and presaged the highly mechanised farming of post-war Britain and the final displacement of horse power on farms.[5]

Again, as in the First World War, labour was a major problem in the wartime changes in agricultural production. To some extent machinery could be substituted for labour, but skilled manpower

was short as numbers of young farmworkers were mobilised in the Territorial Army at the outbreak of war, and more of them were called up subsequently as the needs of the Forces became pressing. Some farmworkers were mistakenly allowed to move away to other occupations before direction of labour was imposed, and farmers were perforce obliged to rely, reluctantly, on other kinds of labour. The Women's Land Army played a much bigger role than in the First World War, with its numbers rising from 19,000 in 1941 to a peak of 87,000 in 1943; subsequently possible recruits were directed to munitions factories. Among the more common farm tasks Land Army women carried out were milking, working in the fields on the labour-intensive sugar-beet crop, and clearing derelict land. For the latter tasks the women were organised in gangs to be sent where required, an operation reminiscent of the notorious 'gang system' which had been the subject of government regulation in the 1860s.[6]

Prisoners of war – more than 50,000 of them in 1944 – were used for heavy work such as drainage, lifting beet and threshing. For the grain, potato and fruit harvests the farmers had to rely in part on casual workers and part-timers, village women, schoolchildren, and adult volunteers from the towns. Schools even arranged their half-term breaks to accommodate the employment of children in the lifting of potatoes. In 1942, 50,000 troops helped gather in the grain harvest, along with 250,000 schoolchildren and 100,000 adult volunteers who lived in specially organised harvest camps. In total, these various sources of labour more than made up for the loss of permanent farmworkers. Moreover, somewhat surprisingly perhaps, labour productivity rose substantially as shift working was introduced to get more done in the hours of daylight, and the farmers themselves put in longer hours; while the greater use of machinery, of course, was an important factor in raising output per man-hour. Yields were increased by more intensive use of fertilisers, especially a greater resort to the benefits of 'artificials'. Urged on by the Ministry's propaganda, and encouraged too by subsidised prices, farmers who had never used chemical fertilisers before the war came to change their ideas. By 1943–44 three times as much nitrogen was being used, and twice as much phosphate, as in pre-war days.[7]

The farmers' willingness to work harder, radically change their farming and accept new ways of doing things was not entirely due to patriotic fervour. The prices of farm products rose very substantially from the low pre-war levels, especially for cereals, and farmers saw an opportunity of making a good income for the first time since 1921. A hundredweight of wheat, for example, which fetched only

6s 9d in 1938, and had averaged under 6s 3d in the previous seven years, soared to 14s 8d in 1941, and to 16s 3d in 1943. By 1943–44 cereals as a whole (excluding barley) had almost doubled in price, while fat cattle, although rising by over 50 per cent, had become less profitable. Price adjustments made by the government ensured that cereals were more attractive than fatstock in order to encourage farmers to follow willingly the changes in production patterns set out by the County Executive Committees. Nevertheless, farming as a whole was more prosperous, as over the war period agricultural prices in general nearly doubled over the levels of 1936–38, while wholesale prices rose by two-thirds, and the cost of living by only a third.

Farming costs also rose of course, though by less than prices, especially as rents remained stable (as had been the case in the First World War).[8] The introduction of a national minimum wage for agricultural workers resulted in the weekly minimum for an adult male more than doubling, from the 34s 8d average of 1938–39 to 72s 2d in 1945–46. It should be stressed that these were *minimum wages*, paid for a reduced number of basic hours (which over the period fell from 50.2 to 48.4 hours). *Actual earnings* were substantially higher, although diluted by the rise in the cost of living. Nationally, the cost of living index (1937–38 = 100) rose from 103 in 1938–39 to 154 in 1945–46. The farmworkers thus shared in considerable degree in the prosperity of wartime farming.[9]

THE FARMING REVOLUTION

By the end of the war the farming structure of England and Wales had changed considerably from the pre-war situation. The cultivated acreage (excluding rough grazings), at 24,316,000 acres, had shrunk by 547,000 acres, or 2.5 per cent. The area of tilled land had risen by over 12 per cent as the result of the wartime ploughing-up policy, while that of permanent grass had fallen by 18 per cent. Temporary grass had risen substantially, by nearly 6 per cent. The permanent grass area (excluding rough grazings), which had accounted for 61.4 per cent of the total area of crops and grass in 1926–35, fell in the post-war era to under 45 per cent.[10]

In post-war years the long-term trend towards larger holdings, which had been in evidence since the First World War, continued steadily, influenced by changes in technology and the agricultural

policies adopted after the Second World War. Holdings of 20 to 50 acres fell from 68,762 in 1944 to 52,713 in 1966, and those of 50–100 acres from 60,320 to 51,757. Even those holdings of 100–300 acres, considered good-sized farms down to the time of the First World War, fell back from 65,415 in 1944 to 58,418 in 1966. For the growing number of big farms the largest proportionate rise was in those of over 1,000 acres: these more than doubled, from 432 to 933, while there was a rise of 54 per cent in farms of between 500 and 1,000 acres, from 2,905 to 4,460. Farms of between 300 and 500 acres showed only a more modest rise of 17 per cent. The figures show clearly how market and technical forces worked strongly in favour of the very large holdings, relatively rare before the First World War, where the economies of scale of machinery, and specialisation of management, could be employed most profitably.

The number of holdings owned, or mainly owned, by the occupier, which had been 62,680 in 1922, tripled by 1960 to reach 188,871, while rented, or mainly rented, holdings declined sharply, by well over a half, from 352,035 to 144,305.[11] The remarkable growth of farmer-owned holdings reflected the landowners' disillusionment with farmland as a long-term investment, an attitude which had its origins in the great depression of the late nineteenth century, but was reinforced by the failure of rents to rise very greatly thereafter, and indeed to fall in real terms. Periods of farming prosperity, as in 1914–21, and from 1939 onwards, gave landowners opportunities for disposal of their farms in a favourable environment, and many took advantage of them. The consequences were to put farmers at the mercy of mortgagors and the banks, and to make it increasingly difficult for a young man who did not inherit a farming property to enter on a career in the industry. The farmer-owner gained complete security of occupation (so long as he could service his loan), but whether it was a sensible investment for farmers to make, in view of the low level of rents, is arguable. In such generally prosperous times they might well have made a higher return by extending their farming operations as tenants.

Mechanisation, stimulated by the war, proceeded apace thereafter. The numbers of tractors in use in England and Wales, estimated at nearly 180,000 in 1946, had more than doubled to 418,000 twenty years later. Combine harvesters increased enormously, from the 3,253 of 1946 to almost 58,000 in 1966, while milking machines rose from something over 40,000 to more than 100,000. The numbers of agricultural horses fell correspondingly, from the 436,000 employed on farmland in England and Wales in 1946 to only 19,000 in 1965.[12]

With the help of more machinery and much heavier use of fertilisers, the yields of cereal crops rose dramatically: those of wheat, for instance, rising from about 19 cwt per acre in 1946 to over 32 cwt twenty years later; barley rose from 18 cwt to 29 cwt and oats from 16 cwt to 24 cwt. Potatoes, sugar-beet, and turnips and swedes also showed sharply rising yields, while cattle numbers in Great Britain rose by over 15 per cent, and the numbers of sheep by some 40 per cent. With more attention paid to breeding, nutrition and treatment of disease, and with the high-yielding Friesian gradually displacing other dairy breeds, the UK average yield of milk per cow rose by over 25 per cent, from 503 gallons in 1945–46 to 632 gallons in 1962–63. The home production of beef and veal in the United Kingdom expanded from 62 per cent of total supplies to over 72 per cent, and that of mutton and lamb from 26 per cent to 44 per cent. Pork, down to under 22 per cent of total pork supplies at the end of the war, compared with a pre-war average of nearly 78 per cent, rapidly recovered to reach some 97 per cent by 1965–66. Only in bacon and ham, and particularly in butter, did UK suppliers fail to capture a significantly larger share of the home market than before the war.[13]

During the war years crops had expanded to reach nearly 30 per cent of the gross output of UK agriculture, as compared with 16 per cent in 1938–39. This growth was mainly at the expense of the share of fatstock and eggs, which fell from 20 per cent to 16.2 per cent, and 10.5 per cent to 6.0 per cent, respectively. After the war, however, and despite a far different economic climate and greater government intervention, the pre-war pattern rapidly re-asserted itself. Already by 1956–57 fatstock had revived to claim 31.4 per cent of gross output, and eggs to 10.7 per cent, while crops had slipped back to 17.7 per cent. Milk and milk products did not change greatly, though their 1956–57 share of 25.1 per cent was substantially below the pre-war 28.8 per cent. The net income of farming in the United Kingdom rose dramatically in money terms, from £53m in 1938–39 to £447.5m in 1962–63.[14] In real terms, of course, this advance was much less impressive, as inflation eroded the value of money. Over the same period the index of retail prices, with 1958 = 100, rose from 38 to 110. Nevertheless, farmers in general became far better off in the post-war era, their real incomes having more than doubled in the quarter-century since the beginning of the war.

The farmers' post-war prosperity owed a good deal to the boom conditions which pervaded the national economy. Unlike the succession of short-lived boom and long-lived depression which followed the

end of the First World War, the post-1945 economy enjoyed con-
tinuous economic progress, albeit with ups and downs. The fluctuations, however, merely disturbed, and did not disrupt, the flow of
improved material well-being. One reason for the difference was that
the wartime shortages took much longer to be made good than after
1918. Food supplies remained restricted, with rationing continuing
for several years after the end of the war. Growing consumer demand
was fed by annual rises in money wages (though rather smaller
ones in real terms as prices tended to rise continuously); a state
of full employment existed – over-full employment in the opinion
of some – and pre-war levels of unemployment failed to return,
as had been widely expected; more women were working, and so
many households had more than one income coming in, while public
expenditure, with a much expanded system of social security, settled
at a substantially higher level than before the war.

Of more direct bearing for farmers were the much more positive
policies for agriculture adopted by intervention-minded governments
in the post-war era. Farming was not merely helped to survive
but was consciously encouraged to grow. The wartime expansion
made it possible for home production to provide almost a half
of the food formerly supplied by imports, and the policy now
was to reduce dependence on overseas farming even further. The
cooperation between the Ministry of Agriculture and the National
Farmers' Union during the war had shown what could be achieved
by the two working together, and the friendly relations between
them laid the basis for a new period of cooperation, with the object
of pushing farming output to higher levels.[15] The new policy was
bound to be expensive for the Treasury, completely dwarfing the
assistance provided in the 1930s. In 1955–56 the agricultural subsidies
cost the taxpayer as much as £206m, and the figure rose in 1964–65 to
£265m, and in 1970–71 to £273m. Since prices were rising, however,
the outlay was tending to diminish in real terms; and, indeed, from
1966 the Ministry's policy, with future membership of the Common
Market in mind, was to reduce reliance on imports further while
transferring more of the cost of supporting agriculture from the
Treasury to the consumer. Food prices rose by 44 per cent between
1965 and 1973, although the unpopularity of this development was
muted by a rise in personal incomes of as much as 70 per cent.[16]

The farming subsidies fell into two categories: payments in respect
of guaranteed prices, and grants and subsidies in aid of production.
The 1947 Agriculture Act formalised an annual review of the industry
which had begun during the war, and was used as an instrument

for the planning of agricultural production and adjusting its various elements in order to minimise shortages and avoid gluts. Guaranteed prices, set to cover a certain quantity of output, encouraged farmers to produce to at least that level, while any surplus was sold at whatever price was offered in the market, so limiting the liability of the taxpayer. The other leg of agricultural policy was the provision of grants and subsidies designed to improve soils, raise yields, encourage improved practices and speed up modernisation, such as the electrification of farms. Consequently, fertilisers were subsidised and grants were given for under-drainage, the application of lime, conversion of pasture to tillage and the provision of new buildings. Peacetime County Agricultural Committees took over from their wartime counterparts and continued their role of bringing unwilling farmers into line, while a National Agricultural Advisory Service was formed to help farmers with the introduction of improved methods and with technical assistance, and also served as a channel for the approval of farmers' applications for grants.[17]

The long-term effects of this comprehensive approach were seen in the rise of output, extensive technical progress, and improved returns to land, capital and labour. The value of gross output (at historic prices) rose from £625m in 1945–46 to £1,594m in 1960/61–1962/63, and to £8,911m in 1980–81. With heavier use of fertilisers and improved strains of seeds, yields rose sharply, the yield of wheat, for instance, continuing to increase from the 19 cwt per acre of 1944–46 to as much as 48 cwt by 1980–81, and that of barley from 19 cwt to 36 cwt. The production of milk was increased by a variety of advances, not least artificial insemination, with the average yield per lactation of dairy cows rising from 691 gallons in 1955 to 1,038 gallons in 1980.[18] In the thirty-five years after 1946 the numbers of tractors and combine harvesters in use considerably more than doubled, helping to make British agriculture probably the most highly mechanised in relation to its size in the world. The post-war era was thus undoubtedly the real age of the 'agricultural revolution'.

One consequence of this modern revolution was that the proportion of food consumption met by home production rose greatly, so that wheat, barley, beef, cheese and eggs from British farms all provided at least 70 per cent, or well over that figure, of home needs.[19] Farmworkers' wages rose, and although they continued to be at the bottom of the wage structure, farming offered a diminishing number of workers a substantially better condition of life. Farmworkers gradually became much better housed, and with the rest of the population they could afford such modern luxuries as cars, television

sets and refrigerators. Again, while hill farmers struggled to eke out a very poor living from the flocks grazed on their marginal lands, the big cereal producers, fatstock specialists and leading cattle breeders could speed through the lanes in their Jaguars, or even travel by helicopter, to supervise their scattered enterprises, attend business meetings and speak at conferences.

Farming policy shifted over time as the needs of the country changed and the economic situation varied. Changes of government brought fresh looks at farming and constant changes in the nature and levels of financial support. Politically, however, it was difficult to cut back very significantly on agricultural support, and certainly impossible to think of going back to the more *laissez-faire* attitudes of the 1920s and 1930s. The most important shift in policy came with Britain's entry into the European Economic Community in 1973. Adjustments were made necessary in order to adapt to a system which had been devised to help small-scale and often backward peasant farmers who, when the Community was formed, were still very numerous on the Continent. By 1973, UK agriculture was, by comparison, large in scale and highly mechanised, although small in relation to total employment and to the British economy as a whole, contributing only 2.9 per cent of the Gross Domestic Product in 1970, and occupying only about the same proportion of the working population. The situation of agriculture in Britain contrasted sharply with its counterpart in the countries which had devised the Common Agricultural Policy. The average proportion of the working population engaged in agriculture for the original six members of the EEC was at this date as high as 14 per cent, with Italy having a figure of 21 per cent, France 15 per cent and Germany 9 per cent.

Although these figures shrank subsequently, so that by 1985 the enlarged EEC average was down to 8 per cent, the importance of maintaining a policy of agricultural protection and subsidy in the EEC was underlined by the addition of new members such as Spain (with 18 per cent of its population engaged in agriculture) and Portugal (25 per cent).[20] Thus, for political reasons, the admitted flaws in the Common Agricultural Policy were difficult to eradicate: food prices remained above world levels for consumers, while costly surpluses accumulated, to be disposed of only at heavy losses. Moreover, since it was the larger farmers, with their high levels of output, who benefited most from the protection of the EEC market from outside competition and the support of artificially high prices, the CAP had the effect of making rich farmers even richer while doing little to help

small farmers. Indeed, many of the latter were encouraged to abandon farming, to retire or to move into other occupations.

In Britain, where farming was already on a relatively large scale, the gap continued to widen between those farmers who had extensive businesses and the small men who still scraped along on a meagre income – and who might be very poor indeed if their holdings were in upland areas where there was little or no alternative to stock rearing and grazing. The largest farmers sometimes joined together and amalgamated their separate holdings into one business, offering not only greater economies of scale but also the further advantage that each of the member farmers could specialise in a different aspect of the venture, in production, marketing, finance and so forth.

Not surprisingly, large farm units continued to get larger and to grow in number, so that within a decade of Britain's entering the CAP farms of over 500 hectares (1,235.5 acres) numbered in England and Wales as many as 1,546; and altogether farms of over 200 hectares (494.2 acres) had risen to a very substantial 9,995, covering 34.1 per cent of the total area. Over a tenth – 11.4 per cent – of the total area was occupied by the very large farms of over 500 hectares. Small farms declined correspondingly: those of between 20 and 50 hectares (49.4 and 123.6 acres) fell to 47,547, and accounted for only 14.5 per cent of the total area; in England by itself as little as 11.6 per cent. The category that contained the greatest number of farms in England alone, 27,528 of them – those of 50–100 hectares (123.6–247.1 acres) – covered less than a fifth of the total area, only 17.9 per cent.

In England and Wales the small farms of between 20 and 50 hectares decreased in number by nearly 2,500 over the five years 1978–82, or by an average of 1 per cent a year; the very small units of between 2 and 10 hectares (4.9 to 24.7 acres) fell even more sharply, by 7,556 or 10.7 per cent, rather over 2 per cent a year.[21] Of course, influences other than agricultural policy were responsible in part for these changes. Many small units were highly specialised and so were peculiarly liable to be affected by market changes and climatic influences, and some no doubt sold out profitably as sites for housing and industrial concerns. But the persistence of the decline, and the remarkable growth of very large units indicate the prime origin of the changes.

INCOMES AND SOCIAL RELATIONSHIPS

Farmers' incomes have always varied with the size and nature of the enterprise and its geographical location. It was possible, of course, to

make a good, if unreliable, income from small acreages devoted to such precarious crops as hops, fruit and early vegetables. Dairying, too, was often still on a small scale. In England and Wales in 1982 the average size of a dairy herd was fewer than fifty-nine cows, even though this figure was much higher than in the past. At that date there were still as many as 8,563 holdings with fewer than twenty cows, and 4,834 holdings with nine cows or fewer.[22] In other branches of farming, too, small men, many of them working their holdings only on a part-time basis, and often accepting a meagre return on their labour, skill and capital, could manage to survive, but in practice fewer of them were attempting to do so.

Indeed, the character of farmers as a whole was changing. The total of farmers in Great Britain remained fairly static at between 260,000 and 270,000 from the 1920s to the 1960s; and by 1982 they still totalled 258,869, if both full-time and part-time farmers, together with partners and directors of farms, are included. The figures show, however, that over the five years 1978–82 the numbers of part-timers were increasing while those of full-timers were falling. Part-time farmers (which included the so-called 'hobby farmers') could of course supplement their farm incomes from other sources, and no doubt many of them were very glad they could do so: they could not have stayed in farming otherwise. But if one takes medium-size units of 150–200 acres worked by full-time occupiers, their average income was rising substantially. Before the Second World War it was only some £250–300 a year (before deducting interest on capital). By 1955–56 the figure had risen to an average of £1,278 on a unit of 193 acres. Over a decade later, in 1966–68 the average income had gone up to about £2,000, and subsequently it climbed steeply to reach £6,000 in 1972–74, and £9,500 in 1980–81.[23] In real terms, of course, these figures are much less impressive, though they still show a very considerable rise.

Average figures, however, are of little meaning when the range of incomes was so wide. In 1956–57, for example, the largest arable farmers earned about £7,700 p.a., while the smallest stock farmers made only £315, less than many industrial workers and clerks.[24] At the top farming had become a very lucrative business, the more especially as farmers benefited from various tax concessions, and paid no local rates; at the bottom it remained as badly rewarded as it had been in the years between the wars, and perhaps relatively worse when the improving living standards of the nation as a whole are taken into account.

The structure of the labour force in farming is of considerable interest. In 1982, for instance, the 229,517 full-time and part-time

farmers of England and Wales were assisted by as many as 61,197 wives or husbands, while large units gave employment to nearly 7,000 salaried managers. The posts of farm managers (which were gradually declining in number, except in Scotland), together with jobs with the Marketing Boards or firms supplying farmers with equipment and specialist services, afforded avenues to employment in the industry for those farmers' sons and others who had no farm to inherit and who lacked the capital with which to start farming on their own account.

The regular labour force included members of the farmer's family who worked on the farm, either on a full-time or a part-time basis. These persons totalled 36,825 in England and Wales in 1982, of which number 8,796 – almost a quarter – were female. Full-time regular hired workers numbered 119,437 (of whom 10,126 were female), while the part-time hired hands amounted to 37,641 – in this case with the females, numbering 21,161, making up the larger part in England, though not in Wales.[25]

The situation was, therefore, that farmers and their families provided over a half – 52 per cent – of the labour force, excluding seasonal and casual workers. Even if the 88,099 seasonal and casual workers of 1982 are added to the regular hired labour force, the family workers still outnumbered hired hands by just over a quarter, and it has to be remembered that some of the seasonal and casual people were in fact members of farmers' families. This situation was not entirely new, of course, since family members had always played a significant role in the working of farms; but the size of the family commitment in 1982 partly reflects the scarcity of skilled farmworkers as well as the continued importance, if a diminished one, of the small family farm.

If regular full-time family workers are added to the full-time hired workers of 1982, it appears that the fall in the numbers of full-time workers since 1939 was one of over 368,000, and since 1962 one of over 225,000 – falls representing proportionate declines of 72 per cent and 44 per cent, respectively. In the meanwhile, the average minimum wages for adult male farmworkers had risen from 34s 8d in 1938–39 (for 50.2 basic hours) to 172s 7d in 1961–62 (for 46 hours) – a five-fold rise in money terms. By 1980 the basic minimum wage had risen to £70.00 for 40.5 hours. Although the increase is impressive in percentage terms, showing a rise of over seven-fold between 1961–62 and 1980, the longstanding gap between farmworkers' earnings and those of industrial workers – a gap which had been reduced over the war and immediate post-war years – remained wide. In 1980 it was as much as £40 a week, or 57 per cent.[26]

But it was earnings which mattered rather than the regulated minimum wage, for in practice a great deal of overtime was worked, the additional income helping to bring farmworkers' living standards up to a more acceptable level. There were other factors which helped also: the tied farm cottage, which though often still an antiquated one, was cheap, and often near to the farm so that no money or time was spent in getting to and from work; while in the villages there was often part-time or seasonal work available for the womenfolk in such tasks as pruning fruit trees, harvesting vegetables and lifting potatoes, as well as in processing factories and packing stations, together with house cleaning for wealthier residents. Against this there were the time and money spent in getting to towns for shopping, the more necessary as the village shop, more convenient but expensive, was fast disappearing.

The improved living standards enjoyed by farmworkers and their families as a result of better pay (and more of it at overtime rates), together with the part-time earnings of the wife and older children, exhibited themselves in a variety of ways. Diet improved, bicycles were replaced by small cars, the cinema by television, and family outings became more common. On the farms the work itself became more interesting with the mechanisation of many operations, and also less arduous physically, although the appeal of the job to mechanically minded men and boys was not sufficient to stem the flow from the land. Nor was the rise in wages enough to keep men on the farm, despite the fact that by 1980 the real earnings of farmworkers had increased by 58 per cent over those of 1960, the biggest improvement in real terms that had ever been experienced in the space of twenty years.[27]

Recognition of the skilled status of the farmworker by the general public was slow to appear: the gap between his wages and those of industrial workers was too widely known, while the extent of farm mechanisation and the improvement in the farmworker's life-style were less easily appreciated. It was also not appreciated that the publicised wages earned by farmworkers were in fact *minimum* wages, and that many of them earned considerably in excess of the standard rates, either because of overtime, or for special skills. This last was particularly true of the stockmen employed by wealthy breeders, whose experience in the management of valuable bloodstock, especially highly prized bulls, was well rewarded. For other kinds of farmworker the introduction in 1971 of a progressive wage structure, in which premiums were paid to supervisors and craftsmen, went some way towards providing a promotion ladder in farming.

Nevertheless, in 1980 as high a proportion as 59 per cent of all workers fell into the lowest 'ordinary' category. In consequence, the lack of good prospects of promotion, as well as low pay and other factors, continued to feature among the reasons given by farmworkers for leaving the job.[28]

It is important, therefore, not to exaggerate the farmworkers' advance in living standards. Cars became necessities when farmworkers lived at a distance from the farm, and as rural bus services, once needed for shopping, outings and visits to the doctor, declined to vanishing point. However, many farmworkers found the maintenance of a car, even when used sparingly, a strain on a tight budget (which was one reason why some preferred the much cheaper three-wheeled vehicle). The lack of transport also limited the ability of wives to find better-paid and permanent jobs in the towns: many farmworkers' families lived at some distance from a railway station, and furthermore the great majority of villages had no station at all. Large families relied in some degree on social security payments, and very often bought their clothing, furniture and household durables at second-hand. Holidays away from home were rare, and were largely confined to occasional visits to distant relations.[29]

Most serious was the situation when a farmworker was made redundant or when he retired. Then he and his family were obliged to move to a relatively high-rented council house, and elderly couples were dependent on income support to eke out the state retirement pension which was their only, and inadequate, source of income. Although the numbers of farmworkers living in tied cottages declined with the years, the proportion doing so actually rose considerably, so that more than 60 per cent were living in tied cottages in the early 1970s. The increase reflected not only the inability of most farmworkers to find the capital for buying a cottage of their own and the income for meeting mortgage payments, but also the shortage in many villages of alternative rented housing. With this inability to move, numbers of farmworkers who might otherwise have changed to better-paid work in other occupations were prevented from doing so.

The place of the farmworkers in village society had been on the decline for many years. There were many fewer of them, to begin with, and of course in semi-industrialised villages, and in those near to large towns, they had long been in a minority. Railway branch lines, and much more important, the motor-car, had brought increased numbers of middle-class residents who commuted to their work in the towns. This development, a relatively slow one down

to the 1950s, grew apace thereafter. Not all villages were equally affected, of course. Many of the more remote and smaller ones, and those deemed to be ugly or otherwise unattractive, were hardly affected by middle-class invasion. But in others the effects were often considerable. The farmworkers and their families, already a small minority, tended to be driven more in upon themselves, forming an 'encapsulated community within a community';[30] and they also tended to be drawn into a closer relationship with their employers, the farmers. Even the farmers' new signs of affluence – most obvious perhaps in their Land Rovers and Mercedes – apparently aroused little resentment among their men, most of whose animosity was directed against industrial workers whom they saw as getting more than their fair share of the cake.[31] Another consequence of the growing middle-class presence was to accentuate differences in living standards and life-styles. Further, newcomers who too peremptorily assumed the leadership of village societies and other social activities were resented, while the demand for old cottages, capable of conversion into comfortable residences and weekend retreats, drove up property prices and made it difficult or impossible for farmworkers and their children to acquire homes in the villages where they had always lived and grown up.

The country landowning class, meanwhile, continued in retreat. Landed incomes, unless amply supplemented from other sources, proved increasingly inadequate to meet the burgeoning outlays involved in maintaining great rambling mansions and extensive grounds, as also the expense of the leisured country life of the past. Prudent steps taken to avoid, as far as might be possible, the damaging effects of death duties limited financial losses arising from this cause, but more positive measures, such as marriage with wealthy heiresses, it has been found, were exceptional, and were of little general importance in helping major landed families to survive. Some owners survived by converting their grounds into 'safari' or amusement parks, and opening the house and its treasures to inspection by a car- or coach-borne public, who might also add to the revenue by consuming teas in the coach-house and buying souvenirs in the gift shop. Others took more drastic steps, converting most of the house into flats and living on in the remainder. The more attractive properties were passed over to the National Trust – which had the advantage that the former owner could continue to live in the ancestral mansions in at least some degree of state – or were sold for conversion to hotels, business conference centres and research establishments. The less attractive deteriorated while their owners failed to find buyers,

and were eventually allowed to moulder into decay, their stonework flaking, their windows boarded up, and their drives and grounds hopelessly overgrown.[32]

The extensive sales of farmland after the First World War had made great inroads into the former dominance of landed estates and tenant-farming in British agriculture; and tenant-farming continued to be eroded as, before the 1960s, farm rents failed to rise very substantially, and legislation placed further limits on the rights of landlords to do what they liked with their property. Even so, in 1950, such high proportions as 62 per cent of the agricultural area, and 60 per cent of holdings, were still in the hands of tenants. By 1982, however, the corresponding figures had fallen to only about one-third in each case. Some two-thirds of the country's farmland had by then passed out of the control of landowners. For the traditional landowners, as distinct from new kinds, such as various industrial and financial enterprises, pension funds and government departments, the proportion of all holdings still in their hands may only have been about a fifth (though another estimate suggests a less alarming third); in 1914 it had been between two-thirds and three-quarters.[33]

As previously, many of the new owners of farms were the former sitting tenants, for the rising land market gave them the incentive to buy in the expectation of making a capital gain, in addition to the attraction of having the security of being the owner. But to some considerable extent land passed into the hands of new institutional owners, who replaced or supplemented the older kinds of corporate landowners, such as hospitals and colleges, as well as the private landlords. Thus, on a truncated scale, the management of land occupied by tenant-farmers continued, as survived also some still substantial aristocratic estates. Numbers of the traditional landowners had taken over farms themselves, and benefited at first hand from the prosperity conferred by highly supportive agricultural policies. Farming and forestry became major resources for hard-pressed landowners seeking to survive in the later twentieth century, as well as, or instead of, managing their estates and following a career in business or, more probably, the City.[34]

The position of the landowner *vis-à-vis* his tenants has changed significantly since the end of the Second World War. In a post-war environment of highly protected and subsidised farming, rents began to rise, slowly at first, and then more steeply, reflecting not only an increased demand for land, but also more effective management of tenanted property. By the late 1950s the average rent was still only something in excess of £2 per acre – about the same as the better land

fetched in the 1870s, when of course money was worth far more. By 1970, however, the average had shot up to over £12 per acre, and by 1980 to as much as £30. This was certainly a great and long overdue rise from the landowner's point of view, although in net terms, when taxation, repairs and improvements, management costs, and other outgoings are deducted, the advance was considerably less impressive.[35]

Meanwhile, the landlord's relationship with his tenants had been further regulated by new legislation. The revolution which began with the Agricultural Holdings Act of 1875 and extended by subsequent laws was taken much further by the post-war Agricultural Holdings Act of 1948: this gave established tenants security of occupation and placed the fixing of rents in the hands of arbitrators. The Agricultural Tenure Act of 1977 made further changes, extending the security of tenants for up to three generations – which might encompass more than a century and was therefore not very far from a freehold interest – and restricting in other ways the landowner's choice of tenants. In consequence, as had occurred with private housing governed by the Rent Acts, a wide gap arose between the value of the property if sold with vacant possession and that put on the market occupied by a sitting tenant. Partly for this reason, landowners devised terms of letting which circumvented the provisions of the legislation protecting tenure, and so retained a degree of control over their property. But it has to be noted that the new forms of tenancy, co-partnership with the occupier, and other devices, could often be justified in terms of meeting the needs of modern methods of farming, while also going some way towards satisfying the increased demand for access to land.[36]

The old kind of landed estate, which had existed prior to the Great Depression, and persisted in a modified form down to the Second World War, passed away completely in the post-war era. The traditional, largely informal, relationship between landlord and tenant, based pretty much on mutual trust and respect, with leases used only for the larger farm units, came to be more and more subject to restrictive conditions imposed by legislation. After the Second World War some farmers came to see landlord-controlled farms as anachronistic, while the landlords' limited powers over their property and the levels of regulated rents discouraged them from undertaking new investment in their estates. However, it was the case that for a very long time past, landowners had expected their tenants to help meet the cost of expensive improvements, such as the investment in subsoil drainage which was in vogue between

the 1840s and the 1870s; and from the late 1950s the direction of government grants and subsidies encouraged landowners once more to interest themselves in new investment in farm buildings and, again, in drainage. To that extent, the traditional partnership basis of estate farming was revived, even though the tenant had now become a far more independent element in the system.[37]

The modern basis of farming in Britain is not without its problems, however. One of the more evident is that of the difficulty of entry to the industry. With a much greater extent of farmland in the hands of owner-occupiers, and with a very slow turnover of tenants on the remaining estate farms, it has become much less easy for the newcomer to find land to farm. Most young farmers are the sons of existing or former occupiers, who have inherited the property or a tenancy, and who have also inherited the farm stock. Even if land can be obtained, the high capital cost of farm stock in these days of advanced machinery and quality livestock means high indebtedness and dangerous exposure to variations in interest rates and in levels of subsidies. For all farmers, changes in the policies followed by the CAP can prove fatal to highly geared enterprises, and when their capital costs are deducted, some farmers find that they are earning only a low return for their effort and enterprise. It is true, on the other hand, that the risks associated with farming have been reduced by the statutory provision of high security of tenure and regulated rents, while the markets have been made more consistently profitable by highly protective trade policies and government purchases of surpluses. Nevertheless, the market for individual farm products, like milk or barley, is perhaps more subject to changing political influences than in the past, with unforeseen consequences for levels of production and profitability, thus requiring from both landlord and tenant as much as or more flexibility than ever.

THE NEW FACE OF THE LAND

With the national and international circumstances in which British farming has operated since 1945 have come many changes, not a few in the appearance of the land itself. As we have seen, the average size of farm units has increased very considerably, and at the same time the size of the individual fields, influenced by the needs of the large-scale machines now in use, has also grown greatly. The kind of fields which suited the farming of the past, and notably those which appeared in the wake of the parliamentary enclosures, became inconveniently small,

except perhaps for such uses as orchards, soft fruit, hops and potatoes. Hedges, costly to maintain in an age of increasingly scarce and more costly manpower, have often been grubbed up or allowed to decay into scattered clumps, the gaps filled in by wire fences. However, in those northern districts where field divisions have traditionally consisted of stone walls, there has been less change, for these have been predominantly pastoral areas where the old field sizes have not been found to be unworkable.

Farm buildings generally have often become more unsightly as the owners or occupiers, exempted from the planning controls which regulate more ordinary mortals, have been allowed to erect great barns and sheds of steel, concrete and corrugated iron in place of the old brick, timber and tile constructions which mellowed into harmony with their surroundings. And, as farms have become larger, some of the older farmhouses, and even their outbuildings, have been profitably converted into private residences, the same metamorphosis appearing among the oasthouses of former hop-growing districts. Not a few landowners and farmers have made substantial capital gains from conversions of this kind.

Many villages, too, have changed in appearance and in social structure as more middle-class and former town residents have taken root. The increasingly wide ownership of cars has sounded the death-knell of most shops and crafts, except where the population has grown sharply or the village is so picturesque and well-known as to attract a tourist trade. In the past, as we have noted, the larger communities boasted numerous shops and craftsmen who met the bulk of the needs of the population. Now, the great majority of these have long disappeared, and in smaller places even a single surviving shop is an unusual sight. The villagers who have suffered most from this change are the rural poor, particularly the elderly poor, who having no car, are obliged to walk a mile or two to catch a train from the nearest station or to avail themselves of a surviving bus service, which operates perhaps only one day a week – and neither rail nor bus fares are now cheap. The writer once heard some villagers remark that, contradictorily, only the better-off residents could afford to go into town by bus; the less well-off have to use their cars.

Some villages have been at least partially transformed in appearance by the building of considerable private estates and groups of council houses, largely occupied by people working in nearby towns. Others have been completely swallowed up and urbanised by the spread of the suburbs of towns, or have been selected as the sites of new towns or the homes of 'overspill' populations from distant conurbations.

The Home Counties, in particular, have changed substantially as more and more commuters have chosen to live in a more pleasant and cheaper environment in market or seaside towns and villages, accepting the expense of railway fares and the weekly waste of many hours in the train as the inevitable penalty exacted for exercising this preference. As a result, not only have country towns and villages changed in character but the distinction between 'town' and 'country' has become blurred or even indefinable. And in the process many acres of what was often high-quality farmland have disappeared for ever, overlaid by roads, houses, garages, back gardens and the other accoutrements of suburban living. Even where a rash of new houses has not erupted, the land has been made unsightly by factories and works, by warehouses, power stations, transport depots, shopping centres, recreational facilities, garages, old car dumps, and the derelict remains of a variety of outmoded or failed enterprises. When people who live in such surroundings travel further afield they are inclined to remark, with some surprise, that nevertheless 'there is still some real country left'.[38]

Those sufficiently fortunate to dwell in the 'real country' find that, even there, the destruction of trees and hedges and the spread of so-called 'prairie farming', together with the brash utilitarian farm buildings mentioned above, have created many eyesores. Pollution and other forms of damage to the environment have stirred up hostility towards the modern farmer and his methods. The fire hazard, smoke and far-travelling cinders of straw burning are now grievances of the past, but there remains the heavy use of chemicals and insecticides, damaging to wild life, and possibly also to humans as the residues enter into the food chain and leach into water supplies. The noisy clamour of modern farm machinery is also more than a minor nuisance to those who live within its considerable range. All of this has influenced the view of farmers and farming by a public which believes that such means of obtaining maximum production can hardly be justified when consumers and taxpayers are called on to meet the cost of buying up farm surpluses, storing them and, often enough, of destroying them.[39]

As the conurbations, the old towns, and the new ones, the suburbs and urbanised villages have spread, so necessarily the area of land available for farms, woods, nature reserves and recreational purposes has declined. Of the total land area (excluding inland water) of England and Wales the proportion taken up by agricultural uses (including commons and rough grazing) was 84 per cent in 1920; by 1966 it had fallen to 78.5 per cent. The area of crops and grass

was at its peak in 1891, at 28m acres, or 75.5 per cent of the agricultural land area; in 1966 the corresponding figure had fallen to 24.3m acres, 65.6 per cent of the agricultural land area. More recent official statistics indicate that in 1982 the situation had not changed very much, with the area of agricultural land making up 77.5 per cent of the whole, though with crops and grass, at 23.6 acres, constituting 82 per cent of the area of agricultural land.[40] Evidently, the huge increase in agricultural output achieved since the Second World War has been produced on a declining agricultural acreage, one that in 1982 was 16 per cent smaller than in 1891 – a remarkable witness to the enormous potential of the new technology, of new strains of seed, new fertilisers and pesticides, machinery, electrification, artificial insemination and the rest.

This present-day agricultural revolution has been achieved not only with a declining agricultural acreage but also with a much smaller labour force than in the past. A much increased capital expenditure has compensated for, and allowed, the reduction in manpower. In 1982 the regular workers engaged in farming in England and Wales, including farmers, salaried managers, and the wives and husbands of farmers, totalled 491,586 persons, an average of one person to each 48 acres of agricultural land. Seasonal workers added only another 88,099 persons, making a total labour force of 579,685. (This last figure had fallen by 38,477, or more than 6 per cent, over the previous five years.) However, the *full-time* regular workers engaged in farming were many fewer. These, including both family and hired workers, numbered only 142,651 in England and Wales in 1982, making an average of one regular full-time worker to every 165.4 acres of agricultural land. This is a very far cry indeed from the customary nineteenth-century standard, when 165 acres of arable would have been deemed to require the full-time work of five or six men and boys, and the same acreage of pasture that of at least two or three.[41] The old levels of labour requirements on the land, which persisted down to the Second World War where the farmers could afford them, were whittled away by the effects of depression and mechanisation. After 1945 the scarcity of labour, and its rising cost, obliged farmers to mechanise and economise in tasks that were not essential for production. Rates of ploughing rose to reach 50 acres a day, compared with the single acre or so that was not unknown in some areas a hundred years earlier, while the modern combine harvester, which can achieve an output of 28 tonnes an hour, made short work of harvesting. Some labour-intensive tasks, such as maintaining hedges by hand, which used to occupy the men for

much of the winter, were simply not done: hedges were bulldozed out of existence, and surviving ones crudely shorn by a mechanical flail.

For Britain as a whole the numbers of full-time regular workers had in 1980–81 fallen by as much as 26 per cent since the end of the Second World War. In terms of employment, agriculture had shrunk to the status of a minor industry, and its contribution to the Gross Domestic Product, similarly, had also been, for long, of minor significance. Nevertheless, agriculture remained, and remains, politically and socially an industry of outstanding importance. This paradox is explained partly by the fact that agriculture affects so large a proportion of the country's surface, and hence is more publicly evident than many other larger industries more severely confined in area. Necessarily, a growing concern with the environment, and with public health, must focus a large part of its attention on what is happening in farming. Furthermore, agriculture gives employment to many more than those who work directly on the land itself: to the many people engaged in making and supplying agricultural machinery, equipment and fertilisers; to those involved in the researching and teaching of agricultural science and practice, and in advising and regulating the industry through marketing boards, breed societies and in the Ministry of Agriculture itself; and to those many thousands who daily transport, process and pack the produce of farming and distribute it to home and overseas consumers.

Most important, however, perhaps, is the fact that agriculture produces that vital resource, food, and that food continues of prime importance in living standards, health and consumers' budgets. Working-class families may no longer spend 60 per cent of their incomes on food, as was estimated before the First World War; but the figure, though now much smaller, still usually constitutes the largest single item of family expenditure. For many people the price of food is a highly significant matter, as also is their liability as taxpayers: hence the publicity given to the costly price-regulating policies of the CAP and their complexities – even if few people have the time, opportunity or patience to try to understand them.

TRANSFORMATION

The land, as we have seen, once provided the bulk of the population with both its food and its employment. Now, near the end of the twentieth century, the land, with its highly regulated and protected farming, has returned to producing much the larger part of the

nation's requirements of food. This has been achieved, however, with the direct employment on the land of Britain of fewer than 600,000 people, only 2 per cent of the national labour force. In 1851, when the numbers working the land were at their peak, the corresponding figures were more than 2m and as much as 21.5 per cent of the labour force. Until surprisingly recent times the land exerted also powerful political and social influences, even if they were declining ones. The peculiar social structure which the land supported became outmoded and has now very largely passed away; but nevertheless, the complex of activities which the land supports remains of great importance. These activities, it is true, have changed greatly in character, even though they have continued to be widespread and significant. The land, the farm, the village, the country town, have all been deeply modified by the influences of urbanisation, new forms of transport, mechanisation, the progress of science and, not least, by the extension of government intervention. Only the shell, the unchanging contours of the land, the ancient woodlands, the churches and some old surviving mansions, farmhouses and cottages, remains to give an element of continuity stretching back into the past. Thus transformed, the land yet remains of economic importance, even though much of the farming, and the society now supported by the land, would be largely unrecognisable to the squire, farmer and common villager of a hundred years ago. The story of this transformation, outlined here, is worth studying not merely for its own intrinsic interest, but also because it is a key element in understanding the rise of our modern industrialised and urbanised nation.

NOTES

1. **Jonathan Brown,** *Agriculture in England: a Survey of Farming 1870–1947,* Manchester University Press, 1987, pp. 125–7.
2. *Ibid.,* pp. 128–32.
3. *Ibid.,* p. 134.
4. *Ibid.,* p. 141.
5. *Ibid.,* pp. 136–7.
6. *Ibid.,* pp. 136–7.
7. *Ibid.,* pp. 138–9.
8. **B. R. Mitchell** and **Phyllis Deane,** *Abstract of British Historical Statistics,* Cambridge University Press, 1962, p. 489; Brown, *Agriculture,* pp. 133, 142–3.
9. Ministry of Agriculture, Fisheries and Food, *A Century of Agricultural Statistics,* HMSO, 1968, p. 65.
10. *Ibid.,* pp. 6, 13.

11. *Ibid.*, pp. 19, 24.
12. *Ibid.*, pp. 71, 129.
13. *Ibid.*, pp. 37–42, 50, 56, 58.
14. *Ibid.*, p. 78.
15. **B. A. Holderness,** *British Agriculture since 1945*, Manchester University Press, 1985, pp. 7, 10–11.
16. *Ibid.*, p. 24.
17. *Ibid.*, pp. 14–15.
18. *Ibid.*, pp. 172–3; *Agricultural Statistics of the United Kingdom 1982*, HMSO, 1983, table 2.1.
19. *Ibid.*, pp. 172–4.
20. **European Community Information Service**, *Green Europe*, March, 1978, p. 32.
21. *Agricultural Statistics of the United Kingdom 1982*, HMSO, 1983, tables 6.1, 6.2.
22. *Ibid.*, table 8.6.
23. *Agricultural Statistics of the United Kingdom 1982*, tables 4.1, 4.2; Holderness, *British Agriculture*, p. 126.
24. *Ibid.*, table 4.1; Holderness, *British Agriculture*, pp. 123, 126.
25. *Agricultural Statistics*, tables 4.1, 4.2.
26. MAFF, *Century of Agricultural Statistics*, p. 66; Holderness, *British Agriculture*, pp. 136, 175.
27. **W. A. Armstrong,** *Farmworkers: a Social and Economic History 1770–1980*, Batsford, 1988, p. 230.
28. *Ibid.*, pp. 228–9, 231.
29. *Ibid.*, pp. 230, 236–7.
30. Armstrong, *Farmworkers*, p. 239.
31. *Ibid.*, pp. 237–9.
32. **F. M. L. Thompson,** 'English landed society in the twentieth century: III, Self-help and outdoor relief', *Transactions of the Royal Historical Society*, 6th ser., **II**, 1992, pp. 2, 12.
33. Holderness, *British Agriculture*, p. 139; Thompson, 'English landed society', p. 1.
34. Holderness, *British Agriculture*, pp. 139–40; Thompson, 'English landed society', pp. 15–19, 20–1.
35. Holderness, *British Agriculture*, p. 144.
36. *Ibid.*, pp. 141–3.
37. *Ibid.*, pp. 143–5.
38. *Ibid.*, pp. 148, 150–1, 153.
39. *Ibid.*, pp. 157–8, 162, 165.
40. MAFF, *Century of Agricultural Statistics*, pp. 90–1; *Agricultural Statistics*, tables 1.2, 1.3.
41. *Agricultural Statistics*, tables 4.1, 4.2.

Bibliographical Note

There is a very extensive literature touching on the subjects dealt with in this book, and this note can indicate only a few of the more generally useful works for further reading. Some of the literature is primarily or entirely concerned with agriculture – with the nature, technology and vicissitudes of farming itself. Another large body consists of discussions of the elements making up the rural population; and particular attention has been paid to the landowners, as key figures in shaping the character of that population and influencing its well-being.

Two now quite elderly but still useful works are the companion volumes by F. M. L. Thompson, *English Landed Society in the Nineteenth Century*, and G. E. Mingay, *English Landed Society in the Eighteenth Century* (both published by Routledge & Kegan Paul, 1963). An understanding of the role of landowners in these centuries might well have these volumes as a starting point. The subject may be followed further with the two chapters by F. M. L. Thompson in G. E. Mingay, ed, *The Victorian Countryside* (two volumes, Routledge & Kegan Paul, 1981). Volume II of this work contains an extensive bibliography, and many of the other chapters in the collection bear on the subject of land and society, most notably perhaps those by W. A. Armstrong, Alan D. Gilbert, Louis James, W. J. Keith and R. J. Olney. A much briefer and more general treatment will be found in G. E. Mingay, *Rural Life in Victorian England* (new edition, Alan Sutton, 1990).

Among the basic works on the history of farming, J. D. Chambers and G. E. Mingay, *The Agricultural Revolution 1750–1880* (Batsford, 1966), and Christabel S. Orwin and Edith H. Whetham, *History of British Agriculture 1846–1914* (Longmans, 1964) are still useful.

The subject is taken forward in time, and in varying degrees of detail in Edith H. Whetham, *The Agrarian History of England and Wales, Vol. VIII 1914–1939,* (Cambridge University Press, 1978), Jonathan Brown, *Agriculture in England: a Survey of Farming 1870–1947* (Manchester University Press, 1987), and B. A. Holderness, *British Agriculture since 1945* (Manchester University Press, 1985). The century before 1850 is dealt with on a large scale in G. E. Mingay, (ed.), *The Agrarian History of England and Wales, Vol. VI, 1750–1850,* (Cambridge University Press, 1989), which contains important chapters on landownership by J. V. Beckett, rural population and poverty by W. A. Armstrong, and the development of rural society by J. H. Porter. A statistical appendix in this volume supplements the figures in the *Abstract of British Historical Statistics* by B. R. Mitchell and Phyllis Deane (Cambridge University Press, 1962), while other series of figures are available in *A Century of Agricultural Statistics: Great Britain 1866–1966* (HMSO, 1968), and in the books by Brown and Holderness mentioned above.

The most comprehensive and up-to-date treatment of the farm labour force – much the largest element of the people directly concerned with the land – is W. A. Armstrong's *Farmworkers: a Social and Economic History 1770–1980* (Batsford, 1988). Further discussions of a specialised nature will be found in B. A. Holderness and Michael Turner, (eds), *Land, Labour and Agriculture 1700–1920 Essays for Gordon Mingay* (Hambledon, 1991): particularly relevant are those by J. V. Beckett on the disappearance of cottagers and squatters, F. M. L. Thompson on the great depression period, and W. A. Armstrong on Kentish rural society during the First World War. A wider social tapestry of this last period is woven by Pamela Horn in *Rural Life in England in the First World War* (Gill & Macmillan, 1984), while the short sections on the countryside in C. L. Mowat's *Britain between the Wars 1918–1940* (Methuen, 1955) are still of interest. For the period following the Second World War there are valuable chapters by Alan Rogers, Philip Lowe, B. A. Holderness, W. A. Armstrong, C. W. Chalklin and Michael Winstanley in G. E. Mingay, (ed.), *The Rural Idyll* and *The Vanishing Countryman* (both Routledge, 1989). A recent collection of essays, edited by Brian Short, *The English Rural Community: Image and Analysis* (Cambridge University Press, 1992) offers new insights, especially in the chapters by Alun Howkins and John Lowerson. Alun Howkins' *Reshaping Rural England: a Social History 1850–1925* (HarperCollins, 1991), and Neil Philip's *Victorian Village Life* (Albion, 1993) are both excellent in evoking the nature of a lost rural life,

drawing heavily as they do on the contemporary local press, and forgotten poems, songs and reminiscences.

Such material would have delighted Thomas Hardy, whose celebrated novels provide truly authentic pictures of past country life; and indeed many other nineteenth-century novels offer realistic insights. Even Emily Bronte's romantic *Wuthering Heights* may be interpreted as a conflict between rival families over rights to landed property. Finally, the well-known works by William Cobbett (especially *Rural Rides*), Richard Jefferies (*Hodge and his Masters*), and Rider Haggard's more factual report on *Rural England* (1902), throw much light on contemporary problems on the land, as do the two contentious works published by rival political interests about the time of the First World War: *The Land: the Report of the Land Enquiry Committee* (1913), and *Facts about Land* (Land Agents' Society, 1916).

Index